Praise for MAESTRO: Greenspan's Fed and the American Boom

"A fascinating...new book by Bob Woodward, veteran Washington Post reporter, sheds light on the 'real' Alan Greenspan and his stewardship of the Fed."

-The Times

"Woodward finds a way to make monetary-policy gossip interesting...entertaining and compelling...Maestro admirably accomplishes what it sets out to do: demystify a Washington institution that is dimly understood by most Americans."

- Dina Temple-Raston, USA Today

"Reads like a good newspaper article...skilful..."

- Daniel Gross, The Washington Post

"this is a must-read for anyone concerned with the management of business today."

- The Director

"For those of us who were not awake enough in 1987 to realise that real world power would lie in the hands of central bankers, this book is a good starting point. Bob Woodward...gives to this somewhat dry material a twist and clarity that makes it riveting in a way similar to a detective novel."

- The Scotsman

Shadow: Five Presidents and the Legacy of Watergate
The Choice
The Agenda: Inside the Clinton White House
The Commanders
Veil: The Secret Wars of the CIA 1981–1987
Wired: The Short Life and Fast Times of John Belushi
The Brethren
(with Scott Armstrong)
The Final Days
(with Carl Bernstein)
All the President's Men
(with Carl Bernstein)

MAESTRO

GREENSPAN'S FED
AND THE
AMERICAN BOOM

BOB WOODWARD

POCKET BOOKS
New York   London   Toronto   Sydney   Singapore

This paperback edition first published by Pocket Books, 2001
An imprint of Simon & Schuster UK Ltd
A Viacom Company

1 3 5 7 9 10 8 6 4 2

Simon & Schuster UK Ltd
Africa House
64-78 Kingsway
London WC2B 6AH

www.simonsays.co.uk

Simon & Schuster Australia
Sydney

A CIP catalogue record for this book is available from the British
Library

ISBN 0-7434-3004-2

Printed and bound in Great Britain by
Omnia Books Ltd, Glasgow

AUTHOR'S NOTE

Jeff Himmelman, a Phi Beta Kappa graduate of Yale University in 1998, was my full-time collaborator at every step of this book—reporting, writing and editing. He was able to develop an extensive understanding of the Federal Reserve, the American economy and Alan Greenspan in less than a year. A truly remarkable man of unusual maturity, brainpower and charm, Jeff is an original thinker who retains a deep sense of idealism. He is also a natural, graceful writer who improved each section and chapter and expanded my thinking each day. Having to endure months in the so-called factory on the third floor of the home I share with my wife, Elsa, and young daughter, Jeff never lost his good cheer. He was great company each day, night or working weekend. He has the energy and staying power of a team of reporters and editors. Pressure only made him work harder and more imaginatively. His standards of accuracy and fairness are the absolute highest. One of the very best of his generation, he took the time and care to learn from the people we were studying. He always worked with tact, generosity and forbearance. No one ever did more or better in the crucible of book writing. This book would never have been completed without him, and it is his as much as mine. I consider him a friend for life.

CONTENTS

PREFACE

On January 20, 2001, a new president takes the oath of office. He assumes the presidency in a Greenspan era. Just as the 1992 presidential election was about fixing the economy and cutting the federal budget deficit, the 2000 election was about how to use a projected surplus of at least several *trillion* dollars. The expectations, even the very definition, of the new administration—protecting Social Security, expanding health care, improving education, revitalizing the military and cutting taxes—will be contingent on that surplus. Whether it materializes is yet to be seen, but the inherited economic conditions for everyone—from the next president to any citizen—are in many respects the Greenspan dividend.

Greenspan is slated to remain chairman of the Federal Reserve until 2004. Not only is he a major figure in the world's economic past, he is central to its future. He has been frank enough to stand before the new and amazing economic circumstances that he helped create and in the end declare them a mystery. It is impossible to account fully for the continuing high growth, record employment, low inflation and high stock market. This is my effort, only a beginning, to write the story of how and why we got there.

PROLOGUE

Look, this is a good time to have a meeting with the president. Why don't you come over?

That was the message James A. Baker III, White House chief of staff and Ronald Reagan's main political strategist, sent in the summer of 1984 to Paul Volcker, chairman of the Federal Reserve.

Baker arranged the visit in the East Wing residence, often the setting for delicate matters away from the official hubbub of the West Wing and the eyes of others. Volcker, a somewhat theatrical figure who towered at six feet seven inches, was hard to hide. In his five years as Fed chairman he had become the public face of a grueling war against runaway inflation.

Volcker's tough medicine of jacking up interest rates to an unprecedented 19 percent to cool the American economy had triggered recession and thrown millions out of work, making him a demon to many on Main Street. But now inflation was down and the Fed had achieved a semblance of stability in prices, making him a hero elsewhere, especially on Wall Street.

The chairman met every six months or so with the president. It wasn't unusual for him to hear carefully worded suggestions for lower interest rates to help the economy grow.

Volcker found only Reagan and Baker in the downstairs library in the East Wing.

Volcker and Baker had a cordial personal relationship. Both had gone to Princeton in the same clubby era—Volcker class of 1949 (summa cum laude), Baker class of 1952—and their alma mater was a subject of occasional, even fond, conversation between them. On a professional level, particularly on the matter of interest rates, their relationship was tense.

Volcker had first been appointed chairman by Democratic President Jimmy Carter in 1979. When the chairman's four-year term expired in 1983, Reagan, who saw virtue in Volcker's anti-inflation campaign, had reappointed him to a second term. In the aftermath of recession, with a jittery Wall Street, it was considered too risky to dump him.

Baker thought that Reagan should have his own Fed chairman—someone from his party, someone in tune with his values. As Baker frequently remarked, Volcker was a "known Democrat," as if the Fed chairman were a subversive. Baker had no illusions that a Fed chairman could be ordered about or subjected to political control. But he found Volcker needlessly aloof and prickly, unreceptive to the sorts of consensus solutions Baker preferred.

After polite preliminaries, Baker began by mentioning the fall election. Reagan was seeking his second term, and Baker was in charge of the campaign.

They didn't want any tightening, Baker said, referring to interest rate increases. He sounded tough and spoke of the upcoming election with some pride. The theme was "Morning in America," and Reagan was projecting the image of the caring, optimistic father. Higher interest rates would be off message.

Volcker was a little stunned that Baker would talk about interest rates in such an overt political context. Baker could as easily have signaled their desires in a subtle, less offensive way. The chairman stiffened. The setting, the bald language and the swagger made it certainly inappropriate, even improper. Baker was doing all of the talking. The president wasn't saying a damn thing. Nothing. Blank. Not nodding, not un-nodding, Volcker noticed grimly. How brilliant. Reagan never said anything, his deniability preserved: *I* never pressured Volcker. But the president's presence, sitting there calmly—detached or engaged, no one would ever know for sure, including Baker—gave Baker's words all the weight in the world.

Privately, Volcker was a bit worried about the economy. He didn't think there would be another recession very soon, but growth was slowing and the outlook wasn't good. His next action at the Fed was probably going to be exactly what Baker and Reagan wanted him to do, to ease up and lower interest rates. But he didn't tell them that because he didn't trust them. If he said anything, they would leak it to the press. Interest rates are going down, they'd say. Or worse, the Federal Reserve caved to their pressure, undermining Volcker's credibility.

The chairman left the White House sour and uneasy. Sometimes the best thing to do, he had learned, was to absorb the pressure, take it all into himself, do nothing. When he had been confirmed as chairman by the Senate Banking Committee, he had promised that he would report any attempt by the White House to influence him. He was unsure whether the pressure had reached the point where he was obliged to report it. He decided to say nothing.

For Baker, it was more a routine discussion. He didn't want to be seen as pressuring Volcker. Of course the administration wanted lower rates. The White House always did. But the Fed chairman was independent, and if Volcker didn't like meeting with the president, he didn't have to show up, or he could walk out or complain. He never did.

Volcker soon lowered interest rates in response to the economy's overall weakness, as he had expected to. Reagan was reelected in a landslide in November.

In early 1985, Reagan appointed James Baker as treasury secretary, the position that traditionally has primary liaison responsibility with the Fed. Baker saw another opportunity to gain some political input into the Fed's interest rate policies. Though the chairman dominated the Fed, he couldn't act unilaterally.

The Fed sets two short-term interest rates. The less important rate is the discount rate, the interest rate the Fed charges other banks for overnight loans. Although it has only a small actual effect on the economy, at that time the discount rate was the Fed's only publicly announced rate. As a result, changes to it had considerable psychological impact on the financial markets and the economy.

In order to change the discount rate, the chairman has to have a majority of the votes of the seven members of the Fed's Board of Governors. His vote is only one of those seven.

Under the law and the Constitution, the president makes the appointments to the board and the Senate confirms them. Board members are appointed to 14-year terms, partial life appointments designed to raise the board above politics, but many members wearied of serving in an institution so controlled by its chairman and had resigned after a few years. As a result, the administration had put a number of Republicans on the seven-member board. Baker, who had primary responsibility for finding board members, preferred "Reaganauts," those who shared the president's philosophy and had been part of his team. He particularly liked those who favored lower interest rates. The talk around Baker's Treasury Department had a theme: Times are changing. The message to Volcker was: Lead or be led.

One of Baker's early picks for the Fed board was Manuel H. Johnson Jr., his 36-year-old assistant treasury secretary, a former Green Beret intelligence specialist. Johnson had told his boss that he believed interest rates should be lowered, and that the Fed's interest rate policy should be coordinated with the White House and Treasury.

Soon after Johnson joined the board in 1986, he told Volcker he was expected to vote for an interest rate cut the first chance he got. "I feel compelled to vote for one. It's needed," Johnson said. Volcker was appalled, concluding that Johnson had made a deal.

Johnson informed Volcker that there were now four votes, a majority, to reduce interest rates. "I'll defer to how you want to do it," he told the chairman. "I'll defer to your leadership."

At this time, Volcker was opposed to a cut because he was worried about new inflation. "Is Baker pressuring you to do this?" Volcker asked, putting his feet on his desk and lighting a cigar.

"I'm sure Jim Baker supports this," Johnson replied. "He knows how I'll vote."

On February 24, 1986, Johnson and three other board members took charge and voted 4 to 3 to lower the discount rate. Volcker found himself in the minority for the first time.

"Good-bye," he announced to the board after the vote was taken. "You're going to have to do it on your own." He got up and walked out, slamming the door. Hard. He didn't type, so when he got back to his office he wrote out his resignation letter by hand. Voting down the chairman was an outright rebellion as far as he was concerned, an un–Federal Reserve thing to do. It was a staggering breach of club etiquette. Federal Reserve tradition virtually compelled the board to deal with disagreements and division by working toward consensus. Meet Tuesday. Meet Wednesday. Meet Thursday. If it was the chairman who disagreed, by God, they should meet endlessly.

Volcker told Baker what had happened. They could get a new Federal Reserve chairman, he said.

"It's not that important," Baker said soothingly. He expressed surprise at the vote and at Volcker's distress. "You're overreacting."

Volcker couldn't have disagreed more. What was the use of

being chairman of an organization if you couldn't run it? What was leadership if someone else decided the direction?

Baker wanted to remind Volcker, "Look, that's why we have seven governors—why we don't let the chairman decide these things by fiat. It's why it is a democratic vote on the board." But he refrained from making this obvious point. Baker, a patrician lawyer from Texas, poured on his charm and urged patience, saying in effect, Be realistic, Paul. No one—the Fed, the White House, Wall Street—wanted or needed the convulsion that would result if Volcker resigned.

But Volcker had concluded that the vote that morning had been a cabal, a blow to the heart of the independence of the Federal Reserve System. He also thought that Jim Baker saw it as a big political victory.

Baker called to reassure Johnson.

"You did everything you could," Baker said. "I support you completely."

Johnson knew that he and the other rebellious governors were playing into Baker's hands.

Later that afternoon, however, Johnson and the other three board members backed down. They agreed to reconsider, effectively rescinding the interest rate cut before it was announced. A Volcker resignation would be too unsettling. It would send a shock through Wall Street and out to the world.

And Volcker agreed to stay, though it was never the same. The Reagan administration wanted a puppet, he concluded.

"I did not trust them," Volcker said later. "It was impossible. There was no way you could restore the sense of trust."

Jim Baker didn't necessarily want a puppet. He just wanted a Republican. It was not a matter of trust, it was a matter of good politics. He also wanted a Fed chairman with a more agreeable temperament. Volcker's crankiness and his I'm-above-politics air were hard to take.

Baker had an ability to establish nearly instantaneous, automatic trust with most people. With a confiding, even impish smile he could find common ground effortlessly, most often by adapting to the other person initially. To someone from the political left, he would refer to the "fucking right wing," even in the first moments of conversation. Someone Baker associated with the political right might soon hear him refer to "the fucking left wing." At large meetings, Baker sometimes shared a knowing wink with those around him to underscore a personal bond.

Baker had failed to win Volcker over, so his campaign continued. In the fall of 1986, Baker was visiting his native Houston and ran into Edward W. Kelley Jr., a prominent Texas businessman he had known since childhood. Baker and Kelley had grown up three blocks from each other in Houston. They had both attended the private Kinkaid School, played ball together and stayed in touch since then.

Hey, you want to be on the Fed? Baker asked.

Yeah, I'd be glad to do that, said Kelley. He had never taken a formal economics course in his life, though he did have an MBA from Harvard.

Soon Kelley was appointed and confirmed by the Senate.

In 1987, Volcker's second term was about to expire, and Baker was arguing forcefully to the president. "It's time to have your own Fed chairman," he said. "To my mind there is only one person we can turn to."

That was Alan Greenspan, 61, a high-profile, low-key New York economist who had served as chairman of the Council of Economic Advisers (CEA) in the Ford White House. Greenspan was perfect, Baker felt. He had seen the man up close for a dozen years. Baker had been undersecretary of commerce in 1975 in the Ford administration and had attended White House economic policy meetings where Greenspan was the key, sensible voice. When Baker was running Ford's presidential campaign in 1976, he had brought Greenspan on Ford's campaign plane as the economic spokesman. And in 1980, Greenspan had provided critical help in crafting a key economic speech for candidate Reagan.

One of Greenspan's finest moments had come as head of the bipartisan National Commission on Social Security Reform that had restored the Social Security system to temporary financial solvency in 1983. It had been a masterstroke of consensus building, Baker thought, as both Democrats and Republicans signed on. Baker himself had led some of the secret bipartisan negotiations at his own home.

When Baker left the White House in 1985 to become treasury secretary, he had asked Greenspan to help him on his Senate confirmation hearings. Again, he found Greenspan's advice informed and politically astute.

Baker prided himself on being able to anticipate the second, third, even the tenth bounce of a decision. He was not unmindful of the importance of the next year's presidential election, when his longtime Texas friend Vice President George Bush would be seeking the presidency. Having a Republican Fed chairman serving in 1988 and in a future Bush presidency could make all the difference in the world.

Baker was convinced that Greenspan was the person they needed at the Fed—a team player.

In 1987, Reagan had brought in former Senate Republican Majority Leader Howard H. Baker Jr. as chief of staff to salvage the presidency during the Iran-contra scandal. Howard Baker, a courtly, Washington-wise pol, had represented Tennessee in the Senate for 18 years. He had served as vice chairman of the Senate Watergate Committee in 1973–74 and watched the Nixon presidency dissolve in lies and self-deceptions. When he accepted Reagan's offer to become White House chief of staff, he insisted that he be in on all important decisions and secrets.

The Tennessee Baker sat in while the president and the Texas Baker talked several times about the coming Fed chairmanship decision. Jim Baker wanted to dump Volcker, and he was pushing hard for Greenspan. Howard Baker knew Greenspan pretty well. The two had associated in Republican circles in the 1970s, and they had played tennis a number of times at Greenspan's private club in the Virginia suburbs.

One day in the spring the Bakers invited Greenspan, who headed a private business consulting firm in New York City, to fly to Washington to meet with them at Jim Baker's house in Northwest Washington.

They had one question. Would Greenspan be available?

If it's not going to be Paul, Greenspan replied, I would accept.

The president was weighing his options, Jim Baker said. They wanted just to make sure that if they needed him, he was there.

"If you need me, I will be there," Greenspan said. He wanted assurances that the very existence of the meeting, and certainly the topic, would not be revealed. It would be devastating if it got out that they were thinking of replacing Volcker. Very damaging, he said. The financial markets were really quite unstable.

Howard Baker said that discussion of the Fed chairmanship was on the president's agenda during the next several days, but that it might take time to sort it all out. They pledged secrecy.

• • •

Now that was interesting, Greenspan said to himself as he headed home on the shuttle. He was aware of some of the friction between the administration and Volcker, but not that it had reached this point. The circumstance of the meeting with the Bakers was in certain respects almost more important than the content, he thought. They could have picked up the phone and asked, In the remote case Paul leaves, would you be willing to come down? Instead, they had arranged a fairly elaborate get-together—chief of staff in the middle of the day, treasury secretary in the middle of the day at the same place, their visitor flying in from New York. That's not the way things were done around Washington, Greenspan knew. The White House and Treasury were next to each other, and convenience normally drove such matters. Something unusual was up. He was a math whiz and was always calculating probabilities. The chance that he would get the appointment was not in the low range, 1 out of 10. It was high probability, Greenspan figured, maybe 3 out of 4.

Back in his Washington days in Ford's White House, Greenspan frequently visited his mentor, Arthur F. Burns, who was Fed chairman from 1970 to 1978. He had studied under Burns as a graduate student at Columbia in the 1950s. As Greenspan learned about the job of Fed chairman, he concluded that it was amorphous, not something he would enjoy doing. It seemed to be an arcane exercise, and there were large elements he frankly didn't get. Greenspan liked the mechanical, analytical work of basic business economics—inventories, arithmetic, physical reality. Monetary policy, the setting of interest rates, was far more complex. It entailed trying to figure out what the business conditions and inflation were going to be *in the future*. Interest rates had their impact months or a year or more down the road. Seeing the future was about the most impossible task imaginable.

In monetary policy, Greenspan believed, it was very easy to be wrong even if you had virtually full knowledge. Someone who was right about 60 percent of the time would be very fortunate, he believed.

But now he wanted the job. He had watched what Volcker had done to transform the chairmanship and perhaps save the American economy. It was anything but amorphous.

And it was obvious to him that Baker wanted him in the job. Could Baker deliver Reagan? He had done it once before. In working out the compromise on the Social Security Commission, they had faced one seemingly insurmountable obstacle: Reagan himself.

The Democrats were demanding a payroll tax increase as part of the compromise. One of Reagan's core convictions—it was almost rule one—was opposition to more taxes. But Reagan had supported the plan. Greenspan had been astonished that the most ideological of presidents could be so pragmatic. Baker had been able to deliver the president.

The next morning, Howard Baker reported to President Reagan. Had the president decided what he wanted to do?

No, Reagan said, he hadn't really decided yet.

Baker pressed. Have you made up your mind that you want to replace Volcker, that you're not going to reappoint him?

Reagan waffled and seemed uncomfortable. Baker saw that the president seemed to be of two minds.

"I will set up an appointment to go speak to Paul," Baker recommended, "and I'm going to try to find out if he wants to be reappointed because, you know, there's a fair chance, Mr. President, that he doesn't." That would take the administration off the hook. "I would not be at all surprised if he read the handwriting on the wall just by the fact that I had asked for the appointment and was over there."

Reagan agreed.

Over the years, Howard Baker had found that Fed chairmen acted as if they had taken the Orders and were serving as priests—independent to a fault and just a little short of arrogant. Perhaps that's the way it was supposed to be. His job was to decipher the intentions of both Reagan and Volcker.

In Volcker's office the next day, Baker said he was there at the president's request. The president had to make a decision about the Fed chairmanship and wanted to know whether Volcker was interested in being appointed to a third term.

Volcker paused. "If I were," he said finally, "would the president reappoint me?"

I don't know, Baker said. Of course, he added, that's up to the president. If you are interested, you should tell me, and I'll pass it on to him.

On one level, Volcker realized they might not care about his desire unless they were seriously considering offering him reappointment. On its face, Baker's inquiry suggested that Reagan might be ready to reappoint him.

Let me think about it, Volcker finally replied. He was going fishing, he said, and he would call when he returned.

Baker left unsure. Part of him thought that if Volcker had said he would be honored to have a third term, the chances were that Reagan would reappoint him. At the same time, Baker knew that Volcker didn't want to beg. Perhaps the proud Volcker didn't want to be seen as not having been asked. Perhaps he wanted to know in advance if he had the option to stay. Or, more darkly, it was possible that Volcker wanted to be asked just to turn it down.

After his fishing trip, Volcker called Howard Baker and asked to see Reagan. Baker set up a meeting the next day. He figured it could go either way. The chairman came to the White House living quarters to see them. After brief greetings, Volcker pulled out a letter and gave it to the president. It said that he chose not to be reappointed, and he was there because he wanted to tell the president personally.

For the next 10 minutes, Reagan and Volcker had a pleasant conversation. The president was cordial and solicitous. Volcker's wife, Barbara, was ill and had remained in New York. Volcker said he wanted to get back to her.

For Volcker, it had been a difficult decision. His wife was living in an apartment the size of a student's. It did not have air-conditioning. After a life almost exclusively of government service, he had little money. In addition, neither the president, nor the secretary of the treasury nor the chief of staff would offer him reappointment on terms that would ensure his independence and dignity as he defined them. He told colleagues that he had never asked for a job in his life, and he wasn't going to start now.

He was going to be 60 in several months. When had a person done his job? When was it over? When was it time to leave? High inflation had been driven out, but in some respects, so had Big Paul. The Volcker era was over.

Howard Baker called Jim Baker to report that Volcker didn't want to stay. Jim Baker was delighted. "We got the son of a bitch," he told a New York friend.

It had been about two months since Greenspan had heard anything more about the Fed chairmanship.

Then Jim Baker was on the phone. Volcker had decided to leave. Was Greenspan still interested?

Yes, he said in milliseconds.

Greenspan and Baker knew each other so well that there was no need for a job interview. There wasn't really anything to catch up on.

"Then you will be getting a call from the president in a few days," Baker said.

Greenspan had pulled his back, and later in the week, Monday, June 1, he was at the orthopedist. Someone in the doctor's office walked in and declared, in a tone that indicated that it surely was a joke, "The president of the United States wants to speak to you."

Alan, said Reagan, I want you to be my chairman of the Federal Reserve Board.

Thank you, Mr. President, Greenspan replied, I'd be honored to do so.

That night, Greenspan attended a birthday party in Washington that his steady girlfriend, NBC television White House correspondent Andrea Mitchell, was having for a friend. After the guests left, he swore her to secrecy and told her that the next day Reagan was going to nominate him. They stayed up much of the night talking.

How do I fill those shoes? Greenspan asked. Paul had really done some heavy lifting.

The next day the White House press corps went on red alert. The president was making an appearance in 20 minutes with an important surprise announcement. Baker didn't want word to get out in advance.

Afterward, Baker said to Greenspan, "We were all watching to see if it was going to leak on NBC."

On August 3, the Senate confirmed Alan Greenspan as chairman of the Federal Reserve by a vote of 91 to 2.

1

On the morning of Tuesday, August 18, 1987, Greenspan walked through the door of his private office and into the adjoining massive conference room at the vast marble Federal Reserve headquarters on Constitution Avenue in downtown Washington, D.C. He had been chairman of the Fed for less than one week. Gathering in the stately meeting room were the members of the Federal Open Market Committee (FOMC), which Greenspan now chaired.

The FOMC is an unusual hybrid consisting of 12 voting members—all 7 Fed governors plus 5 of the 12 presidents from the Federal Reserve district banks around the country.

At its regularly scheduled meetings every six weeks, the FOMC sets the most important interest rate that the Fed controls—the short-term fed funds rate. This is the interest rate that regular banks charge each other for overnight loans, seemingly one of the smallest variables in the economy. Greenspan had come to understand that controlling the fed funds rate was key to the Fed's power over the American economy.

The law gives the Fed power to trade in the bond market. The FOMC can direct the "easing" of credit by having its trading desk in New York buy U.S. Treasury bonds. This pumps money into the banking system and eventually into the larger economy. With more money out there, the fed funds rate drops, making it easier for businesses or consumers to borrow money. Lowering the fed funds rate is the normal strategy for averting or fighting a recession.

On the other hand, the committee can tighten credit by selling Treasury bonds. This withdraws money from the banking system and the economy. With less money out there, the fed funds rate rises, making it more difficult to borrow. Raising the fed funds rate is the normal strategy for fighting inflation.

This buying or selling of U.S. Treasury bonds, so-called open market operations, gives the Fed a brutal tool. Changes in the fed funds rate usually translate into changes in the long-term interest rates on loans paid by consumers, homeowners and businesses. In other words, the FOMC's monopoly on the fed funds rate gives the Fed control over credit conditions, the real engine of capitalism. Though the changes in the rate were not announced in 1987, private market watchers in New York closely monitored the Fed's open market operations and soon figured out the changes. The discount rate was the way that the Fed communicated its intentions publicly; the fed funds rate was the way the Fed actually imposed those intentions.

The FOMC, and now Greenspan, had the full weight of the law and nearly 75 years of history—and myth—behind them. They could work their will if they chose.

The committee members spent several hours in a roundtable discussion, reviewing economic conditions. Then Greenspan took the floor.

"We spent all morning, and no one even mentioned the stock market, which I find interesting in itself," Greenspan said casually, looking down the colossal 27-foot-long oval table.

Greenspan's remark was deeply understated. He meant to convey something significantly stronger: For God's sake, he was trying to tell them, there are factors other than the old classical forces moving the economy. There was more to all of this than consumer or government spending, more than business inventories and profits, more than interest rates, national economic growth, savings, unemployment statistics and inflation. There was a whole other world out there—a world that included the stock market, which had run up 30 percent since the beginning of the year. Wall Street and the financial markets of New York were creating the underlying thrust for a severely overheated economy, the new chairman was certain. The run-up had created more than $1 trillion in additional wealth during the last year. Most of these gains were only on paper, but some people were undoubtedly cashing in and spending more. In any case, many people felt richer—a powerful psychological force in the economy. On top of that, a stock speculation and corporate takeover frenzy was sweeping Wall Street. And nobody had mentioned it. Was the distance between New York and Washington so great?

None of the committee members seemed interested in Greenspan's point about the stock market, but the chairman was convinced of it. By many measures, including earnings, profits and dividends, the stock market was really quite overvalued, he felt. Speculative euphoria was gripping the economy, and the standard economic models and statistics weren't capturing what was happening. Greenspan was concerned about the stability of the entire financial system. During his first week on the job, he had quietly set up a number of crisis management committees, including one on the stock market. The situation, that summer of 1987, had the makings of a potential runaway crisis, he thought.

Greenspan had fully acquainted himself with the law, which requires that the Fed try to maintain stable prices. For practical purposes, that means annual inflation rates—the annual increase in prices—of less than 3 percent. For Greenspan, that rate ideally would be even lower, 2 percent or less. The law also directs the Fed to maintain what is called "sustainable economic growth," a rate of increase in overall production in the United States that can continue year after year while maintaining maximum possible employment. The problem, as Greenspan knew too well, was that annual economic growth above 3 percent traditionally triggered a rapid rise in wages and prices. The Fed was charged with finding a balance between growth and inflation. For Greenspan, any imbalances were warning signs.

The economy in August of 1987 was going too strong. There were no measurable signs of inflation yet, but the seeds were there. Greenspan was sure of it. He saw from economic data reports that the lead times on deliveries of goods from manufacturers to suppliers or stores were increasing, just starting to go straight up. Rising lead times meant that demand was increasing and goods were growing more scarce. He had seen this happen too many times in past decades, so he felt that he knew exactly what he was looking at. The pattern in economic history was almost invariably that you got a bang as prices headed up, resulting in 8 or 9 percent annual inflation—a disaster that would destroy the purchasing power of the dollar. The question now, for Greenspan, was how hard the Federal Reserve could lean against the economy to slow it down, to avoid a drastic series of imbalances. If they tried to put the clamp on with interest rate increases, the system might be so fragile that it would crack under them. The Fed and its new chairman could trigger a recession, defined technically as two quarters, or six months, of negative economic growth.

To Greenspan's mind, they were faced with a challenge similar to trying to walk along a log floating in a river. You sense an imbalance and move slightly to adjust; in the process you may lose your balance, but if you regain it, you end up in a better, more stable place. If you don't, you fall off and crash.

Greenspan contemplated two potential missteps. The first would be to do nothing, which would sanction the overheating. The second would be to take action and raise interest rates. It was quite a bind: acting and not acting each had grave consequences.

The new chairman also felt a mild amount of tension because he didn't want to screw up the formal operating procedures of the FOMC. Before his official arrival at the Fed, Greenspan had met with senior staff members to learn the ropes, to make sure he got it right. A Fed chairman was a symbol, but he was also the discussion group leader. He had to know his stuff. Greenspan's only flub so far had been to mispronounce the name of the president of the Philadelphia Federal Reserve Bank, Edward G. Boehne. It is pronounced "Baney," rhyming with "Janey," and Greenspan had embarrassingly called him "Boney."

Despite Greenspan's apprehension about the economy, he felt confident in his ability to serve as chairman. The key was his private business experience as much as it was his previous government service as chairman of Ford's Council of Economic Advisers from 1974 to 1976. In 1953, at the age of 27, he had founded an economic consulting business in New York City with William Townsend, a bond trader. With a love of mathematics, data and charts, Greenspan had developed models for forecasting based on detailed measurements of real economic activity—from loans and livestock to mobile home sales, inventories and interest rates. Townsend-Greenspan only had about 35 employees, and Greenspan was a hands-on manager, involved in every facet of the firm's work. In addition to his consulting work, he had served on the boards of Automatic Data Processing, Alcoa, Mobil, Morgan Guaranty and General Foods, among others. He believed that he understood the backbone of the American economy from this experience—computers, metal, oil, banking and food.

With a somewhat severe face, bespectacled, a bit hunched, narrow eyed and pensive, Greenspan radiated gloom. He spoke in a gravelly monotone, often cloaking his thoughts in indirect constructions reflecting the economist's "on the one hand, on the other hand." It was almost as if his words were scouting parties, sent out less to convey than to probe and explore.

A cautious man, Greenspan didn't want to overstate his fears about the economy to his colleagues at his very first FOMC meeting. The staff report assembled by the Fed's 200 expert economists headed by Michael J. Prell, a small, bearded Fed veteran, forecast "moderate growth."

"While the staff forecast is in a way the most likely forecast," Greenspan told the FOMC, "I'd be inclined to suppose that the risks are clearly on the upside." Growth and inflation were much more likely to be higher than the staff had predicted. "And my last forecast is that that's likely the way Mike will come out the next time around."

One member suggested, at least half-jokingly, that Greenspan was trying to pressure Prell, whose next report would come in six weeks, just before the FOMC's next scheduled meeting.

"In case there's any doubt," Greenspan replied confidently, "I think *the real world* is going to influence him.

"The risk of snuffing out this expansion at this stage with mild tightening is extraordinarily small," he went on, referring to increasing interest rates that make it more difficult to borrow money. "I just find it rather difficult to perceive a set of forces which can bring this expansion down."

Greenspan could see that the other committee members didn't share the alarm he felt and had somewhat concealed. He realized he didn't know enough yet. And he also didn't think, having been there only a week, that he could walk into the room and expect loyalty and support from everyone. It would not happen. If he had proposed raising the fed funds rate, he could not be sure he would get the votes. It would, he concluded, take quite a while to gain intellectual control of the committee and persuade the members to let him lead them. For Greenspan, it was a sobering moment.

During the next weeks, Greenspan pored over the economic data, attempting to pinpoint the volume in inventories, shipping times, sales and prices that explained the real condition of the economy. He knew where to get the numbers about production and orders for rolled steel, specific kinds of cotton fabric or any other industry he might want to examine. From the data and the charts he could reasonably forecast where the next point on a graph would be plotted, or the general direction and the range of next points. From this, he made his own predictions about how fast the economy was growing. He could see pressures on prices and wages brewing, and he was convinced that momentum in the overall economy was building. It was clear to him that they would have to move interest rates up, sooner rather than later.

Since the FOMC was not scheduled to meet until late September, Greenspan had other options. The seven-member Board of Governors set the other interest rate that the Fed controlled, the so-called discount rate, which is the rate that the Fed charges banks for overnight loans. The economic impact of the discount rate is small compared to that of the fed funds rate controlled by the FOMC, but in 1987 changes in the discount rate were publicly announced and changes in the fed funds rate were not. The discount rate was the Fed's only public announcement vehicle, and changes to it could send a loud public message. It was the equivalent of hitting the gong—exactly what Greenspan was looking for—and declaring publicly that the Fed was worried about possible inflation.

All the Fed governors were full-time and had their offices in the main building, set off wide, attractive marble corridors that seemed a strange cross between a European villa and a funeral parlor. Greenspan made an effort to get to know each governor, seeking some out in their offices or inviting them to his office for unhurried but pointed discussion of the economy. He called this "bilateral schmoozing." Over about a week, he sounded out and convinced the governors to support a discount rate increase. A graceful listener, he nonetheless made it clear what he wanted. In private he could convey more of the urgency he felt.

On September 4, two weeks after Greenspan's first FOMC meeting, the Board of Governors met under slightly unusual circumstances. Two were out of town and there was one vacancy on the seven-member board, so only four voting members were present. But Greenspan was in a hurry. The four governors voted unanimously to raise the discount rate ½ percent to 6 percent. It was the first increase in over three years. The press release announcing the increase said the rate hike was designed to deal with "potential" inflation.

Greenspan went to his office after the announcement. Okay, now, he told himself as he settled into his chair in his brightly lit office.

It was the most risky time for a sharp rate increase, with stock prices so high and the Dow Jones average over 2,500. There was no way to control the secondary consequences of their decision. He turned to the screen on his computer to see how the markets were going to react—the stock market, the bond market, the foreign exchange markets. He knew the reaction would be negative. Had they done too much? Greenspan wondered. There was no way to know yet. He felt tension. He scanned the charts and graphs and numbers he had followed for so long—and suddenly, there before his eyes, he could see the dips he was causing. It was one of the most unusual experiences of his life. As he watched, he felt almost as if an earthquake were occurring and the building were rattling. He didn't know whether the building would collapse, but he hoped the situation would calm down. Finally the markets stabilized, with the Dow Jones down only 38 points on the day.

He got word that Paul Volcker was on the phone.

"Congratulations," Volcker said in his booming voice. "Now that you've raised the discount rate, you're a central banker."

"Thank you," the new chairman said.

Greenspan felt that it was crucial to maintain both the Fed's credibility and his own credibility as an inflation fighter. He did not want to see the unwinding of the Volcker era, when runaway inflation had been effectively slain.

With the discount rate move, Greenspan felt he had put a stamp on his general philosophy of not allowing inflation to take hold. And as he wanted, he had done it earlier rather than later. He felt confident in his knowledge of the markets and the economy, but he was also nervous.

Then he concluded, "If you're not nervous, you shouldn't be here."

Nervousness and doubt were central to the task.

Over the next few weeks, the stock market remained high, with the Dow right around 2500, while long-term interest rates on government and business bonds, which the Fed did not control directly, were also going up. That was rare, Greenspan realized, an unsustainable phenomenon. High interest rates meant higher returns on bonds for investors, which would eventually attract money from the stock market. As investors left stocks for bonds, the stock market should move down accordingly. The higher bond rates or borrowing rates for businesses would also depress business earnings and profits, and that too should have sent the stock market down as investors expected less return. But it wasn't happening. As the prices of stocks went up, their yields in dividends went down. These yields were so low compared to the higher bond yields that it was becoming almost irrational to own stocks.

With the economy running too fast and too hot, Greenspan had little choice but to keep quiet about his concerns. If he talked about the stock market problem in public, he was liable to trigger the very collapse he feared.

What to do?

In 1952, Greenspan met the philosopher and novelist Ayn Rand, a proponent of rational self-interest and radical individualism. The author of *The Fountainhead*, a popular novel about a libertarian architect, took the young Greenspan, then 26, into her circle. Greenspan was a high-IQ mathematician and economic technician who had adopted the philosophy of "logical positivism," which held that nothing could be known rationally with total certainty. He was an extreme doubter and skeptic. The two got into a long series of debates on the issue of values, ethical systems and the nature and origin of morality.

Young Greenspan, intense, with thick, black, slicked-back hair, thought he could outdo anybody in an intellectual debate, but Rand regularly cornered him. It was like playing chess, and all of a sudden, out of nowhere, she would checkmate him. Rand was compelling, and the young man was enthralled.

Rand and Greenspan argued about the nature of society and the power of the state. She pushed him hard. The matters they disagreed on were those that were not provable one way or the other, Greenspan felt, but he believed that the debates and the intellectual rigor gave him a sense of how to determine what was right and what was wrong in his value system. He felt acutely conscious that he would know when he was compromising the market-oriented, pro-capitalist principles he and Rand shared.

After forming Townsend-Greenspan, Greenspan's skill with numbers and data soon had him advising the chief executive officers of major corporations. He became particularly attuned to addressing the anxieties of the person at the top who wanted to know what was going to happen. Yet even when providing his forecasts for high-paying clients, Greenspan's natural precision and doubt stayed with him. He said often that the future is unknowable, and he did not overstate his conclusions. He spoke in terms of most likely outcomes and probabilities.

In 1968, Greenspan became an economic policy adviser to Republican presidential candidate Richard Nixon. His first prolonged contact with Nixon occurred during a meeting of campaign insiders on Long Island. Nixon opened the meeting by uttering more four-letter words than Greenspan knew existed. He was shocked by the contrast between Nixon's public piety and his private profanity and anger. It was no less, he concluded, than Dr. Jekyll and Mr. Hyde. He was the only member of the senior group not to take a position in the Nixon administration.

A "strict" libertarian, as he termed himself, Greenspan was a believer in the efficacy of free markets. Attempts by government to tamper with them or direct them were folly. He was appalled when President Nixon ordered wage and price controls in his first term— the ultimate intervention into the markets, a disfiguration of capitalism by government.

In the summer of 1974, Nixon asked Greenspan to become chairman of the President's Council of Economic Advisers, one of the most distinguished posts in government for an economist.

"There's a very good chance I might feel the necessity of re-signing in three months," Greenspan warned Nixon's chief of staff, Alexander M. Haig. New wage and price controls would trigger his departure. "I physically would not be able to function and I would have no choice but to resign. And I wouldn't want to do that to you and I wouldn't want to do that to me."

Haig and others assured Greenspan there would be no more forays into wage and price controls.

Greenspan finally accepted the post but took an apartment in Washington on a month-to-month lease, figuratively keeping a packed suitcase by the door. In an unusually graphic comparison, he said coming to Washington to advise a president in a free-market economy that might suddenly shift to one with wage and price controls was like a gynecologist being asked to practice proctology.

He stayed on after Nixon resigned in 1974 and Gerald Ford assumed the presidency. Greenspan thought that Ford was bravest and most correct when he didn't meddle with free markets during the recession of 1974–75, even at the risk of his own political future.

Now, Greenspan's job as Fed chairman made him perhaps the federal government's foremost regulator, and the irony was not lost on him. Still, he didn't want to lose his sense of the virtue of keeping his hands off free markets.

At the next FOMC meeting, September 22, 1987, the chairman remarked that the economy was clearly quite strong. He was uncertain, however, about where they might be in the inevitable ups and downs of the business cycle. "There is always something different; something that does not look like all the previous ones. There is never anything identical, and it is always a puzzlement." But, he said, he had not detected what was unusual about this economic situation, though the main problem of overheating was evident. "We do not yet have any evidence of actual inflation," he said, recommending no change in interest rates. The FOMC agreed unanimously. "The actions we are taking," the chairman said, underscoring the point, "basically would indicate that we did nothing at this meeting."

A month later, over the weekend of October 17–18, Manuel Johnson—now elevated to the vice chairmanship of the Board of Governors—spent hours and hours attempting to find a buyer for the largest savings and loan in the United States, the American Savings & Loan Association. American Savings had secretly informed the Fed they were going to have to announce bankruptcy on Monday unless someone took them over. The thrift had a portfolio of so-called junk bonds—bonds that paid high interest rates—and they had taken a severe beating. The price of bonds moves the opposite of interest rates, so as interest rates had soared, the value of their bonds had sunk to the point that the thrift was effectively broke.

Johnson was unable to find a buyer, he reported unhappily to Greenspan. To make matters worse, the stock market had been down on Friday. It looked as though it was going to be a rough Monday.

Greenspan took a professorial approach. Great, if a buyer can be found, he said, but if not, market forces will work it out.

On Monday, October 19, the stock market was down in the morning but then started back somewhat. Greenspan decided to stick to his schedule, which included a speech at the American Bankers Association convention in Dallas the next morning. By the time he left for the airport, the stock market was back down again, by several hundred points, and the situation looked awful. He debated whether to back out and stay in Washington, but he concluded that canceling the speech would send the wrong message, a message of crisis. At midafternoon, he boarded American Airlines flight #567 bound for Dallas.

The plane had no phone, so when he got off in Dallas he immediately inquired about the market.

"It was down five oh eight," replied Jim Stull, a senior vice president at the Dallas Fed who had come to meet him.

"Wow, what a terrific rally!" Greenspan said. The market was down only 5.08 points. Whew!

No, 508.

That meant close to $1 trillion in wealth—more than 20 percent of the stock market's total value—was wiped out for the moment.

"There has never been a decline in one day over 20 percent," Greenspan said soberly. A serious decline in the stock market did not come as a surprise, but the severity of the one-day drop was a shock because it was without precedent.

He had studied the Black Tuesday crash of October 29, 1929, a critical turning point in history. That crash had triggered bank failures and a recession, which led to the Great Depression of the 1930s. The market crash of 1929 had been 11.7 percent, compared with the 22.6 percent drop that had just been reported.

At the Federal Reserve headquarters in Washington, Johnson was the official crisis manager. He was struck by the tomblike hush in the corridors. He contacted the senior staff. Don't go home, he told them, we need to go over this. Everyone gathered in the small library across from the board and FOMC meeting room. Johnson took out a one-inch-thick binder with a pink cover that had emblazoned diagonally across its front a large bold warning: "RESTRICTED—CONTROLLED."

He read, "Summary Papers on Risks in the U.S. Financial System." He turned to the tab on the stock market: "STRICTLY CONFIDENTIAL, STOCK MARKET RISKS." The seven-page section stated that the current prices were "probably unsustainable." The options for action, Johnson read, included open market buying of bonds to keep money in the banking system and short-term interest rates from rising. Some options were extreme. "Try to organize stock purchases by major securities firms," he read. That would be an unheard-of market intervention. Was it that bad? Johnson didn't know. Another option, he read, "an off-the-wall suggestion: targeted Fed lending specifically designed to support stock values." Again, another extreme idea. He wondered how it could be done. Still another option included shortening stock market trading hours or even a trading halt. The papers weren't very helpful.

Greenspan finally reached the Adolphus Hotel in downtown Dallas and held a conference call with Johnson and the others. Some were saying, Well, let's wait and see.

"You people have not been around long enough," Greenspan said. He had been around, around money, around the markets, around people on the verge or in panic, for decades. "This is a shock to the system," he said. "You don't assume it's going to wear off."

Greenspan knew that a crash of that magnitude was like a gunshot to the entire financial system. The full pain would not be felt right away. There would be ripple effects for a long time, a possible convulsion in the economy and in society.

Someone on the phone said that everything might be okay.

"You know what just happened?" Greenspan said. "We just destroyed a huge chunk of wealth in this country."

Drafts of a possible statement by the Fed or by Greenspan were being cobbled together. Without having made a decision, the chairman and others agreed to regroup on the phone the following morning well before the stock market opened.

Greenspan said he would stay and give his speech the next morning. It was important not to appear panicky, he said. The speech was on bank regulation, and he attempted to graft several reassuring paragraphs onto it about the stock market. He was not happy with the result.

No one knew the answer to the main question of why the market had crashed. Was something fundamentally wrong with the businesses whose stock had suddenly plummeted 20 percent? Had the doubt and overvaluing triggered more doubt, starting a landslide of reactive sellers bailing out in anticipation of more declines and doubt? Had the process just been overwhelmed, some self-reinforcing spiral downward unique to the moment?

It was a crisis, a financial Vietnam, but it had happened over a single day, not years, creating the potential for a major economic catastrophe. If the stock market continued down, the system—the relationships, rules and theology that Greenspan had built into his head and that had become a part of who he was—would break apart.

That same day, on the 10th floor of the New York Federal Reserve Bank on the edge of Wall Street, E. Gerald Corrigan, the bank's president, was troubled. Corrigan, a 46-year-old beefy, profane, smart, Jesuit-educated Irishman, was the vice chairman of the FOMC. The open market operations of the Fed—the buying and selling of U.S. Treasury bonds that caused an increase or decrease in the key fed funds rate—were conducted through his bank. Corrigan had personal relationships with the heads of the banks, the investment banking firms and the brokerage houses in the nation's financial capital.

Corrigan had spent nearly his entire career at the Fed. He had been Paul Volcker's aide in D.C. for years and had been president of the Minneapolis Fed before taking over the key New York post on

January 1, 1985. He knew without a doubt that the crash was going to cause major problems.

Corrigan and Greenspan finally hooked up by phone.

"Alan, you're it," Corrigan said. "Goddammit, it's up to you. This whole thing is on your shoulders." Corrigan, an ally, believed there was no time for procrastination and little for analysis. The availability of money in the system would be critical. In one form or another, Wall Street securities and brokerage firms, and their clients, would need bank credit, their lifeline, to cover their losses.

"Thank you, Dr. Corrigan," Greenspan said.

Greenspan knew how the financial system's plumbing worked —an elaborate series of networks involving regular banks such as Citibank, investment banks such as Goldman Sachs, and stock brokerage firms such as Merrill Lynch. Payments and credit flowed routinely among them. The New York Fed alone transferred more than $1 trillion a day. If one or several of these components failed to make their payments or to extend credit—or even just delayed payment in a crisis—they could trigger a chain reaction and the whole system could freeze up, even blow up.

Before Greenspan hung up with Corrigan, he told himself, I'm going to find out what I'm made of. The first challenge: Could he sleep? He did, for roughly five hours. He was amazed.

"Help!" said a new voice on the phone first thing the next morning, Tuesday, October 20. It was Howard Baker, Reagan's chief of staff.

"Something bothering you, Howard?" Greenspan asked.

Baker was feeling pretty lonely. "You've got to get back here," he said. The other Baker, the treasury secretary, was in Europe on a hunting boondoggle with the king of Sweden. "I looked around and there's nobody in town but me, and I don't know what the hell I'm doing."

Greenspan said he couldn't get a flight until after his speech.

"Alan," Baker said, "we've still got airplanes and I'm going to get you back up here." He promised to send a military jet with continuous secure communications to bring Greenspan back to Washington. A Gulfstream was dispatched at once. Greenspan still wanted to give his speech before leaving Dallas to convey a sense of business as usual. Corrigan and Johnson said he had to go to Washington immediately. A routine speech to bankers in the midst of an obvious crisis would send a signal that the chairman was out of touch with reality. Greenspan canceled his speech.

Corrigan had been in his office at the New York Fed since 5 a.m. that Tuesday morning. The 15 phones in his suite of offices were jumping off the hook with calls from the bankers and players in the financial markets. The immediate and pressing question was who would finance or give credit to the banks, the brokerage houses and others in the financial system that needed money. For practical purposes, the Fed was already giving credit in the hundreds of millions of dollars at the current interest rates in routine overnight loans. What were the limits? Would they pull the plug? Would the Fed's lending system be overwhelmed? There were both technical and policy questions.

In a conference call that morning, Greenspan and his colleagues debated what the Fed should say publicly. The Fed lawyers had come up with a lengthy statement.

Goddammit, Corrigan said emphatically, we don't need a scholarly, legalistic thing. We've just got to say in one sentence, We're going to put a lot of money in the market. In part, they had a plumbing problem. Everyone needed to be assured they could get money—in other words, liquidity or credit. The Fed also had to address the confidence problem, he urged. They had to show their hand early.

A key question was whether there was a major hole in the system. Was some firm in trouble and maybe insolvent? In the short run, Corrigan argued, there was no way to tell the difference between just short-term liquidity problems and outright insolvency.

They finally agreed on a one-sentence statement. Greenspan issued it in his name at 8:41 a.m., before the markets opened:

"The Federal Reserve, consistent with its responsibilities as the nation's central bank, affirmed today its readiness to serve as a source of liquidity to support the economic and financial system."

"Alan," Corrigan said in a personal follow-up call to Greenspan, "we're going to have to back this up. I just want you to know that I'm going to start making calls." His phones were still going crazy. He had to talk to the heads of the banks and brokerage houses.

What are you going to say? Greenspan asked.

Corrigan said that he was going to have to talk very tough, and he was going to have to talk in code. He couldn't give them orders, and he couldn't beg.

Greenspan wanted the exact words. They couldn't tell banks to lend to bankrupt institutions; they could be sued for huge amounts of money if shareholders in bank stocks could show that the Fed, a key regulatory agency for banks, had improperly directed unsound loans. How would it work?

Corrigan offered a hypothetical call to the head of a big bank. He would say, "You've got to make your own business and credit decisions. . . . But there is this bigger picture out there. If the system becomes unglued, you won't be insulated. . . . If for God's sake there's anything I should know, let me know." In other words, let him know if you're not going to make your payments or aren't getting payments from others, or if you're in trouble. Corrigan needed immediate, high-quality information if he was to discover a hole that might collapse the system. They couldn't plug a hole they didn't know about, so they would have to address everybody.

Greenspan preferred a more subtle approach. The argument should be more calibrated, assuring the banks that the Fed was not trying to force them to lend on an irrational basis or to take extreme risks. The argument should be: Remember that these people who want money have long memories. If you shut off credit to a customer who has been a good customer for a number of years because you're a little nervous, the customer will remember that. Think of the longer-term interests and the customer relationships. Corrigan should clarify to the banks where their self-interest lay.

Corrigan understood, but he would have to speak in his own voice—and his style was loud and clear. He knew he would have to make sure the payments and credit extensions were voluntary. At the same time, it would be his job to make certain they happened.

Greenspan was aware of how tricky it would be to strike the right balance. With so much power over the banks, they had to be careful about using heavy-handed methods. If they forced actions with implied threats, they could eviscerate the vitality of the banking system, which had to operate freely. At the same time, he knew Corrigan was going to bite off a few earlobes. That was okay. The Federal Reserve needed an enforcer at this moment.

Corrigan, his stomach churning, called Bankers Trust. It was a very tough presentation. Goddammit, you've got to fall in line, you've got no choice.

The bankers on the other end of the phone felt pressured, but they knew that they didn't really have any choice but to do what Corrigan wanted them to do.

Corrigan's call to the Bank of New York was also on the tough side. After some negotiation, they fell in line.

One brokerage house owed some $600 million to $700 million to another brokerage house and was delaying the payment, unsure of the other firm's condition or even its solvency. If they paid, would they in turn be paid what they were owed by other firms?

This was precisely what Corrigan feared—one firm choking, stopping the flow. Rumors were flying.

He argued that there was no insulation for any one bank or firm. If the system came down, everyone would go with it. Clinging to $700 million would not save the firm. Goddammit, he knew what could happen, he said. He tried to sound calm.

The payment was made.

On his way to Washington, Greenspan considered his options. The entire system could crumble. It could happen in 10 minutes.

He particularly didn't want anyone from the Fed to sound like Herbert Hoover, president in 1929, declaring with historically memorable stupidity after Black Tuesday that everything was terrific. Everything wasn't terrific. They were in a real crisis. Failure to acknowledge even this simple state of reality would cause the knowledgeable players in the market to think the Fed ought to go to the loony bin.

After all, the Fed was in charge of the sovereign credit of the United States. They had the legal power to buy up the entire national and private debt, theoretically infusing the system with billions, even trillions, of dollars, more than would ever be necessary to restore liquidity and credit. Of course, the result of that would be Latin American–style inflation.

In addition, there was an ambiguous provision in Section 13 of the Federal Reserve Act, the lawyers told Greenspan, that would allow the Fed, with the agreement of five out of seven members of its board, to loan to institutions—brokerage houses and the like— other than banks. Greenspan was prepared to go further over the line. The Fed might loan money, but only if those institutions agreed to do what the Fed wanted them to do. He was prepared to make deals. It wasn't legal, but he was willing to do it, if necessary. There was that much at stake. At that moment, his job was to do almost anything to keep the system righted, even the previously inconceivable.

Joseph Coyne, the Fed's veteran press officer, was along on the flight. He asked Greenspan how he was able to appear so calm.

"You don't worry about things you can't do anything about," the chairman replied. Until they landed there wasn't much he could do. He returned to his thoughts.

· · ·

By about 11:30 a.m. on that same day, stock in IBM, one of the big blue chip firms, stopped trading. All the trade orders were to sell. There were no buyers. Soon dozens of other stocks stopped trading. A stock is worth only what someone is willing to pay at a given moment. If no one was willing to buy, the stock was, on a theoretical level, worth nothing or heading to nothing. By 12:30 p.m., any ground gained during the morning trading had been lost, and the whole market had tanked.

Corrigan spoke with Johnson in Washington. This was the moment of direst need.

We can't hold it, Corrigan said with real panic in his voice. It's falling apart. There's not enough trust in the market, and it's going to melt down.

He came up with a desperate contingency plan. Instead of just loaning money—guaranteeing liquidity to the banks—the Fed would directly guarantee the payments between brokerage firms. But it would be a last, desperate measure. The plan, and the Fed's willingness to embrace it, had to remain a deeply guarded secret. If word got out, banks and brokerage houses would just seize on the guarantees and use them instead of their own money. It would give everyone an easy way out.

Greenspan's plane had landed at Andrews Air Force Base outside Washington, and the car that was bringing him into town didn't have a secure phone. To hell with it, Greenspan said to himself. He called in to the Fed, even though his conversation might be overheard.

Johnson said that they had just received a call from New York. There was a plan being discussed to shut down the New York Stock Exchange within the hour.

"That would blow it," Greenspan said. The head of the Securities and Exchange Commission, David Ruder, had gone on television and mused that there was a point at which he would favor a "very temporary" trading halt. Ruder later denied that he'd even contemplated a trading halt, but his statement was fact. Awfully dangerous to go on TV, Greenspan thought, if you didn't want to be quoted. Closing the New York Stock Exchange was really not an option in Greenspan's mind. Once it was closed, how would it be opened? What prices would stocks trade at? The Hong Kong exchange had closed once and it had taken a week for it to be reopened. Markets set prices, and if there were no market, there would be no price. It was almost unthinkable.

Johnson worried, if New York shut down, what would happen to the futures market? A futures contract is an agreement to buy or sell something—wheat, gold, bonds, stocks—at a future point. With no basic stock market trading, there would be no future. The stock futures market would collapse. That would trigger general panic, he believed. They were truly about to go over the precipice.

Howard Baker didn't have the foggiest notion what was going on. John Phelan, president of the New York Stock Exchange, had been arguing in favor of a suspension of trading. He urged Baker to have President Reagan issue an executive order suspending stock trading. The 1933 Securities Act gave the president the power to do so.

Baker took the proposal to Reagan.

What do you think? Reagan asked.

"What I think is I don't know," the chief of staff replied. He said his instincts told him it would be a lot easier to suspend trading than to resume it. He proposed that the White House counsel draft an order to suspend trading, just in case. "I'm going to put it in my desk drawer," Baker said, "and I'm not going to bring it to you, and we're going to wait and see how this day goes."

That's fine, the president said.

Phelan kept beating the daylights out of Baker on the phone. He was fierce and certain. Suspend trading. Things are out of control. There's a disconnect. The specialists on the stock exchange floor who kept active trading going for the major stocks were starting to go crazy. If they lost the specialists, they would lose the whole place, Phelan said.

Howard Baker took to the phones. He talked with the heads of General Motors, Salomon Brothers and Merrill Lynch. They all opposed a suspension of trading. Baker reached Donald Stone, one of the most prominent floor specialists on the New York Stock Exchange.

"I owe so much money," Stone said, "I can't count it. This place is knee-deep in panic."

At the Fed, Greenspan reached a key executive in the Chicago options exchange, who said the market there was about to collapse as well.

"Calm down," Greenspan said. "It's containable. Don't worry, don't panic." He was fascinated to see how powerful people functioned under stress. It reminded him of the *Apollo 13* astronauts who successfully repaired their spacecraft in outer space by manufacturing a replacement part they had not brought along. Does your mind or psyche freeze over? he wondered. He was going to find out.

He also spoke directly with a number of big players from the largest financial institutions. Their voices were shaking. Greenspan knew that scared people had less than perfect judgment.

He didn't pray, and he didn't cry—though he admitted later that he would have wept if he had thought it would keep the markets from deteriorating further. If he didn't do something, this crash had the potential to devastate the American economy.

Meanwhile, a number of prominent companies had announced that they were entering the market to buy back their own stock at the lower prices, in effect saying that their stock was such a bargain that the company was willing to put up its own cash to purchase the stock. It was a message of confidence.

At 12:30 p.m., there was very little trading, a sign the system might be freezing up.

Then, about 1 p.m., only a half hour later, the Major Market Index futures market staged its largest rally in history. Several major Wall Street firms bought a mere $60 million in future contracts on stocks, and the action sent a shock of brief optimism through the market. Because the buyer of futures contracts had initially to put up only a small portion of the money, the cost of these transactions was only a fraction of that $60 million. But the positive movement apparently triggered a significant number of buy orders in the underlying stocks. Some big institutions or wealthy investors had perhaps decided to gamble in order to stabilize or even save the market. Soon the Dow itself rallied, ending the day up 102 points, a record gain.

Howard Baker had lived through one of the tensest days of his life. He sensed but did not know—not a soul ever told him—that some big companies and investors had gone into the market to buy stocks and drive the prices up. By law and tradition, the White House, Treasury, the Securities and Exchange Commission, the free markets, the New York Stock Exchange and the Fed all had a role in solving the problem. There was no single stock market czar, a person or institution fully in charge. Baker was pretty sure it was one of those moments when fractured responsibility made it as dangerous as it ever got.

But the greatest achievement, Baker believed, was Greenspan's one-line press release. The Congress could have met in extraordinary session and passed legislation without hearings to reassure the markets, but that would have had little impact. The president could have suspended trading or acted somehow, but that too would have done little. There was only one part of the government that could have turned it around, and that was the Fed offering unlimited credit. In the end, money talked—or, at least, the Fed's openly stated willingness to provide it.

Treasury Secretary Jim Baker had flown back to the United States on the Concorde. He too thought the one-sentence statement was brilliant. They were lucky to have Greenspan at the Fed. Baker wasn't sure that Volcker would have been so quick to act.

Corrigan never figured the whole thing out, and part of him didn't want to know. If it was a major miracle rescue of American capitalism, several people or firms might have operated in concert to manipulate the market. That was technically a scheme, and possibly illegal. And if someone in the government or the Fed had given tacit approval, encouragement or even just a wink, that would make it worse. Corrigan decided that he didn't want to pursue the matter.

For all Greenspan knew, it might have been a handful of individuals who made the move. There was no telling whether the transactions were made out of knowledge or desperation, skillful calculation or serendipity. Was it possible that American capitalism was given a reprieve by the strategic—or accidental—investment of several million dollars? It was possible, of course. Or perhaps the bottom had been reached and the market had pulled out naturally. Whatever the answer, Greenspan's largest realization was they hadn't known what to do. They could set up a crisis committee, confer, send messages to the financial markets, seek intelligence, talk tough or smart, look at the data until they were blue in the face and try to project, but they were all novices given the problem they faced.

That wonderful, nebulous space between the free markets of capitalism and regulations of government was the land of the unknown. It was Greenspan's first major lesson at the Fed, and he had been chairman only 72 days.

Greenspan set up a crisis command post in his office. He, Johnson and some of the others stayed round the clock for the next several days. They were eating crummy sandwiches and keeping in constant contact with Corrigan in New York, the other bank presidents and market people from around the world.

On Thursday, October 22, the president of the Chicago Fed

called with a new crisis. First Options, a subsidiary of Continental Illinois, a giant bank, was broke and could no longer provide loans to the options market.

The Fed, as the regulator of banks, had insisted that Continental keep a firewall between its depositors' money and its subsidiaries, such as First Options. The firewall was there to protect the bank from being drained while supporting a failing subsidiary and to protect depositors from losing their money. Continental now wanted relief from the firewall in order to keep First Options afloat.

William Taylor, head of the Fed's bank supervision enforcement division, rushed into Greenspan's office as the chairman and Johnson were sitting at a small oval coffee table.

"We have to shut them down," Taylor said. They had to follow their own regulations and protect Continental Bank and its depositors. They could not let First Options bleed the bank.

Taylor didn't have the big picture, Johnson knew. The failure of First Options would send the options market into paralysis and perhaps trigger another stock plunge. He looked at Greenspan, who seemed to signal agreement.

"Let them do it," Johnson said to Taylor. "Don't block it. Let the money go. We'll clean this up later."

Greenspan just nodded.

Things weren't fixed, he realized again. There was no mathematical way to figure out what was happening, let alone what had already happened, no way to remove the many elements of uncertainty. It was more sobering than ever.

2

"PASSING A TEST: Fed's New Chairman Wins a Lot of Praise on Handling the Crash," read the headline in the *Wall Street Journal* five weeks after the stock market crisis. Federal Reserve Bank presidents, Wall Street analysts and staffers gave Greenspan credit for a cool and quick reaction.

For his part, Greenspan felt he had dodged a bullet that was still flying through the air. He continued his analysis of what precisely had happened on Wall Street and why. In January 1988, a government commission headed by Nicholas F. Brady, chairman of the old-line Wall Street firm Dillon, Read & Co., released its 340-page report on the crash. Brady, who had served briefly as a Republican senator from New Jersey, criticized Wall Street's computer-driven trading practices that automatically dump large blocks of stock when prices drop significantly, amplifying declines. The commission recommended so-called circuit breakers to halt price movements automatically. The report also recommended one overarching regulatory structure, because stocks and the ancillary futures and options exchanges were in reality one market.

"The financial system came close to gridlock," the report said, adding that "the experience illustrates how a relatively few, aggressive, professional market participants can produce dramatic swings in market prices." Continuing, it said, "Monday, October 19, was perhaps the worst day in the history of U.S. equity markets," noting that the next day—the so-called Terrible Tuesday of October 20—was equally unnerving, when trading was halted in 175 stocks, including some of the biggest names.

Some banks that borrowed extensively from the Fed at the discount rate during the crash were now perceived to be in precarious financial shape because they had needed so much money. In general, the Fed expected banks to borrow at the discount rate—usually a below-market rate—only after all other sources of funds had been exhausted. The Fed monitored who borrowed at the discount rate and chastised those who came too frequently, which usually kept that borrowing at a minimum. In the wake of the crash, discount rate borrowing became even less popular and less important as banks didn't want to appear to be weak. So the fed funds rate became increasingly important, giving the FOMC and their decisions more significance than ever before. The FOMC had eased the fed funds rate very slightly since the crash, and in January the rate stood at 6¾ percent. At the committee meeting on February 10, after hearing lengthy presentations about the economy, Greenspan turned to interest rate policy.

"One thing about this meeting, which I think is pretty important," Greenspan said, "is that we have to find the mechanism by which we are perceived to be in a general consensus." Reagan was in his last year as president, and the administration was winding down, he noted. "There are elections coming up and we are turning out to be the only people who are minding the store." Everyone else was playing politics with the economy—at a time when the stock market was still relatively high and the economic situation highly unstable. In Greenspan's view, it was an important time for the Fed to speak with a single voice, even if no one was totally comfortable with the final decision. The markets were still healing from the stock market crash, and any rash move by the committee might cause further damage. "If we were to indicate that we were tightening," Greenspan added starkly, "the shock to the markets I think would break the stock market."

The others expressed a wide range of views, and Corrigan could see that Greenspan had been clairvoyant in anticipating disagreement and asking for consensus preemptively. The committee engaged in a prolonged, torturous technical discussion but seemed to agree that, in delicate conditions of economic uncertainty, the chairman needed a great deal of flexibility to make interest rate changes between the scheduled FOMC meetings every six weeks.

After listening, Greenspan presented a plan that would give him authority to make, on his own, minor adjustments to the fed funds rate between meetings. The FOMC would take no official action, but Greenspan would have the flexibility to ease rates down slightly. Technically, this was called an asymmetric directive toward easing. Since Greenspan's unilateral action would not be publicly announced, there would be no immediate public impact. Fed watchers would know what had happened, but the impact of the rate move would seep into the markets largely unnoted by the general public. The vote in favor was unanimous.

"My congratulations to you, Mr. Chairman," Ed Boehne said, referring to the unanimity. "You have performed a miracle."

"I don't know where it came from," Greenspan replied, and the meeting ended.

The answer, in part, was fear. With the stock market crash just four months earlier, the country had been about as close to financial disaster as it dared ever come.

Earlier in the year, one of Treasury Secretary Baker's assistants had sent a letter to the Fed arguing that the economy would weaken and interest rates should be lowered. Greenspan told the FOMC that he resented the pressure and promised to "use a sledgehammer" to stop it.

The letter eventually became public, and on February 24, Greenspan told the Senate Banking Committee that he had raised his sharp objections with Baker. If such pressure to cut rates continued, Greenspan said, "we will feel the necessity to do the opposite."

The next day's headline in *The Washington Post* read: "Greenspan Tells Administration to Stop Pressure."

Nonetheless, Manuel Johnson thought Greenspan was too passive. The aggressive, ambitious board vice chairman thought Greenspan ran his own office and the Fed too much like an academic department. The new chairman was obviously the best numbers man around, but he seemed an expert in being obtuse, too frequently declaring at their committee meetings that the situation was murky. In the interest of prudence, Greenspan would often argue that he wanted the future data to direct their next action. Most often, that meant the committee would vote for asymmetric directives, which let the chairman make changes between meetings. What Johnson seemed to miss was that Greenspan's apparent passivity meant he had the power to determine the timing of interest rate changes. It was exactly what he had done at the February meeting. The FOMC was basically ceding operational control to Greenspan. Throughout the spring, the committee continued to give the chairman the power to raise rates through an asymmetric directive.

Greenspan feared an outburst of inflation. Lower interest rates for an ailing economy could soon become the disease. As the economy grew, businesses would raise prices and workers would receive higher wages. This chain of events would spark dangerous, even debilitating, inflation. As he often said, inflation destroyed the purchasing power of the dollar and eventually led to lower economic growth and lost jobs. He wanted to keep focused on the law, which said the Fed was to maintain stable prices—no, or low, inflation—and economic growth that could be sustained year after year. It was tricky.

Inflation was now hovering around or above 4 percent, higher than Greenspan wanted. By June, he had raised the fed funds rate to 7½ percent.

Though Johnson had been appointed as part of Jim Baker's effort to put Reaganauts who favored lower rates on the board, by the late summer of 1988 he saw the need to raise interest rates even more. The evidence showed that the economy was overheating and pressures from workers for potentially inflationary wage increases were growing.

At the June 30 FOMC meeting, Corrigan spoke with some passion about his fear of skyrocketing inflation. "If the inflation rate, however measured," Corrigan said, "were to get in the area of 5 percent or more, just getting it back to 4 percent—much less price stability, whatever that means—is going to involve enormous costs to the economy." The obvious cost would be a Fed-induced recession to drive inflation down, achieved by large rate increases to slow the economy.

Greenspan argued for no immediate rate hike but for continuing the asymmetric directive. He won by a vote of 8 to 3, but the district bank presidents were pushing for higher rates. By July, the next month, 9 out of 12 of the bank presidents had submitted requests for a discount rate increase because of their fears of inflation.

Greenspan and Johnson devised a subtle strategy. They would attempt to persuade the board to grant the less important but publicly visible discount rate increase, hoping that the public announcement impact would reduce pressure from the bank presidents for FOMC action to increase the key fed funds rate.

Greenspan had some missionary work to do to persuade the reluctant board members.

On Friday evening, August 5, Johnson attended a ceremony and parade at the Marine Barracks in Washington, D.C., honoring Jim Baker, an ex–marine officer. Baker was resigning from Treasury to take over the management of the presidential campaign of his longtime friend Vice President George Bush. Though Bush was assured the Republican nomination after his primary victories, his campaign seemed to be in trouble. Much attention was focused on the Republican National Convention later that month.

Johnson approached one of Baker's deputies to say they were having some tense moments at the Fed. It's not clear how it's going to come out, Johnson hedged, but the outcome could be a discount rate *increase*.

Oh my God, the deputy replied, what are we going to do? How do we deal with that?

On the morning of Sunday, August 7, Baker appeared on NBC television's *Meet the Press* and said he did not think the Fed was sending signals that a rate hike was coming soon.

On Tuesday, August 9, about 7:30 a.m., Greenspan dropped by the office of board member Martha R. Seger, a Reagan appointee from Michigan who generally opposed rate hikes. She had felt neglected and pushed around during the Volcker era, and she was keenly aware of the devastation to manufacturing in her home state caused by previous recessions.

Greenspan argued that they had to worry that inflation would not just rise but come roaring back, making it impossible to extinguish without significant rate hikes in the future. In addition, they had to demonstrate their public commitment to inflation fighting. Such a demonstration with a discount rate hike would diminish inflation expectations and help keep price increases down. He badly wanted a consensus.

Seger finally agreed.

Several hours later, at a special early morning meeting, the Board of Governors voted to raise the discount rate ½ percent. The vote was 6 to 0.

Greenspan knew Jim Baker was not going to be pleased. Bush was behind 7 points in the polls, and the economy was a growing issue in the campaign. Greenspan and Baker had been friends for 12 years, and Greenspan owed Baker a lot—in some respects, no less than the Fed chairmanship. Greenspan also respected and admired Baker for his political and social skills. He often said that if he were ever in serious legal trouble, he would hire Baker as his attorney in a heartbeat.

Greenspan believed that Baker deserved to be told about the rate increase. He decided to go over to see Baker to break the news before it was announced.

At Treasury that Tuesday afternoon, Greenspan tried to come straight to the point.

I'm sure you're not going to be happy, he said, looking Baker in the eye, but we've decided that it was necessary and we're announcing a rate increase within the hour.

"You know," the treasury secretary said, "you just hit me right here." He indicated his stomach.

"I'm sorry, Jim," Greenspan said.

Baker flew off the handle and began screaming bloody murder.

Greenspan thought it was a simulation of anger, not genuine, a display of Baker's showmanship. He felt he could see through Baker. The treasury secretary would perhaps need to be able to tell Bush, their political associates or the media that he had blown his top and taken Greenspan to the woodshed. Greenspan had long since dissected Baker's well-honed verbal style. He knew that a word delivered with a certain spin or manner could change the whole meaning.

Baker's rant lasted only about 20 seconds. "What shall I say?" he then inquired. He asked for specific advice on what the proper public response should be.

The rate increase, Greenspan said, was essential for the long-term stability of the economic system, and they could not have avoided doing it. A discount rate increase was the best way to send a public message that they were vigilant about inflation.

Years earlier, Greenspan had learned a rule of institutional survival: Bring the bad news yourself. He didn't believe anyone else could convey such delicate messages the way he wanted them conveyed. It was important to look people in the eye, to lay out the facts that would soon emerge and to be as direct as possible. The chairman had found that there was no alternative if he wanted to have future relationships with those like Baker. But it wasn't just a matter of survival. Bringing the news personally gave him power—he was the one who had and would share the still-secret decision—and further cemented his relationship.

At 9:45 a.m. the Fed announced the increase.

"You goddamn traitor!" Baker was soon screaming at Manuel Johnson, launching a brief, vehement attack. He was joking, but worried, too.

"Now give me a chance to explain," Johnson said. This is in the interest of the economy and ultimately in your interest and that of Bush. It would keep inflation under control.

"You're probably right," Baker said, "but your timing sucks."

He calmed down. "I know you guys have a job to do, but this is ridiculous."

"There is no good time to do this," Johnson replied, noting it was much better now than, say, in late October right before the presidential election.

Later that day, Treasury and the White House issued statements voicing disappointment in the rate hike but overall approval of the Fed and Greenspan. White House spokesman Marlin Fitzwater said there was "a sound reason" for the hike, and the Fed was "doing a good job" keeping inflation low and under control.

That week, Fed Governor Kelley's wife of 34 years, Ellen, died. His longtime Houston friend Jim Baker, who had him appointed to the Fed, invited him over to dinner.

Baker and his wife, Susan, were sympathetic and warm as they ate, but Baker couldn't avoid bringing up the discount rate hike. Now in full swing as the Bush campaign manager, Baker said that it was killing them. He didn't see how it was necessary. While he wouldn't ask for any special favors for the administration or for Republicans, he sure as hell didn't think it was right to kick either the Republicans or the Democrats in the teeth. And the Fed had kicked them in the teeth, Baker added, in his pleasant but grinding, insistent drawl. He just couldn't imagine how they could do that.

Kelley didn't expect to have his ass chewed out so thoroughly, especially at this moment in his life, but he answered. The Fed didn't intend to kick anyone. Their decisions were an effort to make the economy better in the long run.

Baker made it clear he didn't believe it.

Interest rate worries soon subsided, and Baker and Greenspan were soon very happy. Bush was elected president in November.

After he was chairman more than a year, Greenspan's operating style was beginning to emerge—intellectual engagement, tempered by emotional detachment; near obsession with economic data, tempered by a steady stream of doubt and uncertainty over the impact; indirectness as a means of achieving a desired outcome, tempered by sudden directness and a desire to have it his way; and a pronounced deference to political power.

Greenspan had learned to adapt early on. He was born in 1926 in New York City to Rose and Herbert Greenspan, both of whom were Jewish. They divorced when Greenspan was about three, and Greenspan, their only child, moved with his mother to her parents' home in the Washington Heights section of upper Manhattan. She worked as a furniture store salesperson. He responded to the stress and confusion by losing himself in baseball. He became a master of the stats and wanted to become a ball player himself.

In 1935, when Greenspan was eight, his father, Herbert, a self-educated stock market analyst, published a book called *Recovery Ahead*, predicting that the New Deal would generate an economic and stock market recovery the next year. Greenspan's father was an adherent of Keynesian economics, which held, in part, that government spending could stimulate an economic recovery. Herbert Greenspan's forecast initially came true in 1936, but then the market collapsed in 1937.

Herbert put a handwritten inscription in the copy of his book that he gave to his son. It read: "May this my initial effort with a constant thought of you branch out into an endless chain of similar efforts so that at your maturity you may look back and endeavor to interpret the reasoning behind these logical forecasts and begin a like work of your own. Your Dad."

It was as if the father passed on to his son a tendency toward convoluted prose and wandering sentences. Perhaps the son also saw the value of obscuring the message, particularly if your own conclusions and sentiments were not clear or were best not revealed. In the mature Alan Greenspan, the result was a verbal caution that could be maddening, a series of loose boards and qualifications in sentences that would allow him an exit ramp from nearly everything he said.

Greenspan attended George Washington High School on West 192nd Street, three years behind Henry Kissinger. He loved math but was average in most of his other course work. A lifelong lover of music, he decided after graduation to enter the Juilliard School of Music—then known as the Institute of Musical Art—where he studied clarinet and piano. After two years at Juilliard, he dropped out and joined the Henry Jerome Band, a 1940s-style big band noted for its bebop stands in New York City and on tour across the country. He played tenor saxophone, but he also doubled on clarinet and flute—and he always played "by the sheets," meaning that he wasn't a good improviser. Like many musicians, he thought of becoming a conductor, but it wasn't his style to stand up front and lead. Greenspan also dabbled in composition, ending up with what he called "crazy stuff on piano" that never really went anywhere. By the end of his run with the Henry Jerome Band, he knew that he was a skilled musician—but he also knew that exceptional talent was innate.

During his stint with the band, Greenspan rediscovered his own talent with numbers. While other young musicians drank, smoked dope and stayed up all night, he read economics and business books and eventually became the band's bookkeeper. After a year touring, he enrolled at New York University to study economics. He graduated summa cum laude in 1948 and went on to complete a master's degree in economics at NYU in 1950.

After NYU, Greenspan began a doctorate in economics at Columbia University, where he studied under Arthur Burns, whose staunch views about the evils of budget deficits influenced Greenspan strongly.

"What causes inflation?" Burns once asked his students in a seminar. Everybody in the room got a turn to provide an answer, and then Burns revealed his own.

"Excess government spending causes inflation," he said. That lesson was not to be lost on Greenspan. Deficits create more money to chase the same amount of goods—a classic precursor to inflation.

Greenspan discontinued his doctoral work to go to work for the National Industrial Conference Board, an economic research group, where he started off as a steel industry analyst. In 1952, he married Joan Mitchell, a painter. Less than a year later, the two realized that their expectations were incompatible, received an annulment and remained friends. It was Mitchell who introduced Greenspan to Ayn Rand.

At one point, Greenspan argued to Rand's circle that his own existence could not be proven beyond doubt. Absolute certainty was impossible. All that one could count on were degrees of probability. Rand and Nathaniel Branden, one of her disciples, came to call Greenspan "The Undertaker."

Branden wrote in his memoir that Greenspan had finally conceded his existence. He told Rand the news: "Guess who exists?"

"What?" Rand exclaimed. "You've done it? The Undertaker has decided he exists?"

Greenspan was never a complete Rand acolyte. He had a separate career and identity, which caused some to mistrust him. He was a dedicated networker who liked to attend social functions in New York. Branden wrote that he and Rand admired Greenspan's mind but sometimes thought of him as too much of a social climber, too occupied with worldly status. For Greenspan, it was critical to be in contact with people, and social events were an efficient medium of exchange—even though he was visibly uncomfortable and mingled reluctantly, often making a beeline for someone he knew.

· · ·

In 1957, after his move to Townsend-Greenspan, Greenspan attempted to determine how much steel inventory was in the hands of steel users or manufacturers so that he could forecast steel production for the next year. Using data and methods from the government's controlled material plans in World War II and the Korean War, he evaluated raw materials, inventories and consumption, discovering that shipments of steel were higher than consumption. That meant inventories were increasing and less production would be needed. Greenspan forecast a sharp reduction in steel production for 1958.

It was a shocking prediction to some of his clients. The chairman of Republic Steel told Greenspan, then 32, that what he'd done was interesting but that Republic did not see it that way at all. In 1958, things fell apart in a recession and steel production was down some 20 percent. Though the Republic chairman had disagreed, Republic had been cautious about how much raw material—coke and iron ore, for example—they purchased. It was perhaps Greenspan's best forecast, and he continued to work with Republic until they merged with another company years later. He learned that bad news, if it was accurate, could be as important and useful as good news.

As he worked his way through the business and political world, Greenspan discovered that avoiding confrontation served him well. Confrontation only empowered his opponent. Robert Kavesh, Greenspan's former classmate at NYU and a friend, saw Greenspan display this trait on the tennis court. "He was almost too good a loser," Kavesh said. "Sometimes you like someone you beat to smolder. He didn't smolder. He would just shower and go back to work." Greenspan didn't have screaming matches with colleagues, and he very rarely, if ever, raised his voice. Sober explication and a kind of studied nonchalance were his only armor.

Greenspan had long had the habit of reaching out to the politically powerful. In 1974, when he went to work as Ford's CEA chairman, Greenspan quickly ingratiated himself as both friend and adviser to Ford, elevating the CEA to a status not seen since the Kennedy years. Greenspan used his experience with advising CEOs of major companies to figure out how to make himself indispensable to the president. Once, at a White House lunch for the world's finance ministers, Ford noticed that Greenspan's seat was empty.

"Where's Alan?" the president asked.

An aide said that Greenspan was testifying before Congress and then offered to go and get him.

"No, don't get him," Ford responded, sounding like a concerned parent. "I just want to know where he is!" The finance ministers went home recounting that the president of the United States couldn't turn his head without knowing Greenspan's whereabouts.

Greenspan's increasingly personal relationship with Ford had its downside. His one-on-one meetings with Ford caused friction with colleagues, who thought Greenspan circumvented the established process of group decision making. Some saw him as conspiratorial, willing to climb in through the Oval Office back window for time alone with the president.

In the late 1970s, NYU finally awarded Greenspan his Ph.D. for a collection of previously published writings.

Greenspan cultivated relationships with any number of people involved in politics, always making people think that he was on their side. "I felt in him a kindred philosophical spirit," wrote David Stockman, Reagan's first budget director, in his 1986 memoir, *The Triumph of Politics*. Greenspan's attentiveness—his willingness to take a phone call immediately, arrange breakfast or a private meeting the next day—left many with the feeling that they had an exceptional relationship with the chairman. He had dozens of such relationships.

_____

AFTER BUSH's election, Greenspan and the FOMC continued to raise rates, each time by ¼ percent. The fed funds rate was up to 9 percent by the beginning of 1989.

"I frankly don't recall an economy that at least on the surface looks more balanced than the one that we have," Greenspan said happily at the FOMC meeting on February 8, 1989, during the third week of the new Bush administration. Supply and demand for goods and services were in healthy balance. Inflation was still too high, at more than 4 percent, so he said he anticipated that they would have to continue to raise rates—but he was willing to wait, given some differences that had surfaced within the committee. He proposed that the committee hold off but adopt an asymmetric directive toward tightening, granting him the authority to increase rates if data came in during the next six weeks showing some signs of inflation.

Like a decision to raise or lower the fed funds rate, the asymmetric directive was not made public, and it did not commit the chairman to action. The directive simply indicated that the entire committee was leaning toward increasing rates and that the chairman could move the rate slightly—tradition dictated that it usually be no more than ¼ percent—during the intermeeting period.

Fighting inflation had to do with their credibility, Greenspan said. Doing a little cheerleading, he added that their credibility was building.

"I think it is very important for the credibility of this committee to try to find some consensus," the chairman said.

"It would be very useful if we could find a means to accommodate each other in such a way that we can have a policy that we all can essentially go along with, though we all may not feel fully comfortable with it. So I've said my piece."

After a long discussion, he won 10 to 2. He raised the fed funds rate ¼ percent several days later.

On February 22, in testimony before Congress, Greenspan issued a blunt warning. "If inflation worsens, a recession will move up on us more quickly than you can imagine, and it will be prolonged." Consumer prices had risen in January about .6 percent—an annual rate of more than 7 percent. Using his authority the next day, February 23, Greenspan quietly raised the fed funds rate ½ percent to 9¾ percent—the most he had ever moved the rate on his own. The rate was now the highest it had been in four years. It had been a long march up since the crash.

Over the next months, when Greenspan analyzed data, he saw that the future orders were down in a wide range of businesses. That meant that demand for goods was falling and economic growth was slowing.

Greenspan tapped into his network of business contacts in New York. One was E. F. "Andy" Andrews, who wrote the monthly National Association of Purchasing Management Business Survey for 19 years. Greenspan knew Andrews from back in the 1970s, when Andrews had made the survey available to Greenspan, who was then a private citizen, a day in advance. From the survey and his contact with Andrews, Greenspan gained an understanding of who was buying what and in what amounts in a wide range of businesses.

He also phoned the purchasing managers at various companies, including some former clients. To his delight, he was now able to get information from his clients' competitors as well, information previously off-limits to him. Those competitors were now more than happy to respond to the Federal Reserve chairman, and he pledged to keep the information confidential.

Another of his regular contacts was Robert P. Parker, 49, the associate director for national income, expenditure and wealth accounts at the Bureau of Economic Analysis in the Department of Commerce. He had known Parker for 18 years, going back to his New York and White House days, and they had kept in touch. Parker had been struck that Greenspan was the only private forecaster who had produced a monthly gross national product statistical series for his clients. Greenspan had also been the first to notice that houses, which had shot up in value in the late 1970s, were being sold for large gains—and the profits used for consumer spending. It was a statistic that the government didn't measure, but the gains and the spending that resulted from them created additional inflationary pressures.

Greenspan also phoned Jack Welch, the CEO of General Electric. GE had its tentacles just about everywhere, Greenspan found. Welch provided sales data on current products—light bulbs and the like—and also on long-lead products, such as engines, that were helpful to Greenspan.

Sounding out his long list of contacts took a great deal of time, and Greenspan eventually set up a system in which Fed staff members would formally call a long list of companies each week to get their real-time numbers.

Only a small fraction of Greenspan's information came to him orally, though he listened to the British Broadcasting Corporation. Reading was more efficient, and he kept up with the newspapers and specialty magazines such as *Aviation Week*. He tried not to over-schedule himself, making only three or four appointments or meetings a day. The rest was for study and reading.

As he looked at the economy in the spring of 1989, it was clear to him that the economy was slowing, reducing inflationary pressures. It was quite a turnaround from earlier in the year. The optimism of only a few months earlier was quietly turning into anxiety.

At the May 16 FOMC meeting, the committee took no action on rates but agreed that Greenspan might need to lower rates on his own between meetings. On June 5, 1989, after the release of some discouraging employment numbers, Greenspan notified the committee he was effectively lowering the fed funds rate to about 9½ percent. He didn't know if it was the right move. "If we had complete capability of seeing into the future, this would be an easy job," he said, "but we obviously don't have that."

By the July 6, 1989, meeting, it was clear the economy was even weaker.

"I'm concerned that the worst thing that can happen to us," Greenspan said, "as far as policy is concerned, is that we are perceived to be easing too fast and in a manner which would open up the possibilities of inflationary expectations." He proposed another small ¼ percent cut in the fed funds rate, and the committee agreed 11 to 1.

On Sunday, August 13, Greenspan was relaxing at the home of Senator John Heinz, the Pennsylvania Republican, and his wife,

Teresa, on the island of Nantucket, off Massachusetts. The heir to the Heinz 57 fortune had a perfect retreat, with cool breezes and an ocean view. Heinz had been on Greenspan's Social Security Commission in the early 1980s and had voted for the commission's consensus compromise.

Greenspan tuned in to the morning television talk shows. Richard G. Darman, Bush's budget director who had recently been described by *Newsweek* as "the most brilliant intellect and political gamesman in the government," was on NBC's *Meet the Press*. Nine months earlier, when Bush had announced Darman's appointment, Greenspan had phoned Darman. "When your appointment was uncertain, I was thinking of tearing up my tickets to the inaugural," Greenspan had said flatteringly, indicating that he thought Darman's role was crucial to a Bush presidency.

Darman had been Jim Baker's top assistant in the White House and later his deputy treasury secretary. There was no finer mind in the Bush administration. Greenspan had in recent months urged Darman to come up with a federal budget that would cut the mounting inflationary federal deficit. Darman in turn had been urging lower interest rates to help the economy.

On *Meet the Press*, when the Federal Reserve came up, Darman said he feared the Fed "may have been a little bit too tight," adding, "If we do have a recession, I think it will be because they erred on the side of caution."

"What!?" Greenspan shouted at the television set. It made no sense. Public bashing by the president's top economic advisers would only encourage the opposite of what they wanted, forcing the Fed to assert its independence and delay lowering interest rates. In addition, the Fed's interest rate policy had to be credible. A particular fed funds rate had to be seen by the markets as the best rate for the economy, not as an artificially low rate influenced by political pressure.

Darman went on a binge of criticizing the Fed. He flooded Greenspan with memos and faxes. His core argument was that the Fed was mismanaging the money supply.

Technically, the Fed raised or lowered interest rates by decreasing or increasing the money supply in the economy. They did this by buying or selling government bonds in open market operations. Debates in academic and economic policy circles had raged for years about whether it was possible any longer to measure money supply accurately. How much money was out there? Cash, bank deposits, checking accounts, money market funds? Economists weren't sure.

Many people were moving money to mutual funds, which made it almost impossible to track and measure the money supply.

Greenspan thought Darman had some sadly out-of-date notions. The Fed couldn't even measure the money supply accurately, let alone control it. The Fed's policy was increasingly set by targeting specific interest rates, though they tried to tinker with money supply numbers.

Darman also argued that Greenspan was mismanaging the psychology of money. A public declaration that rates would be lowered would give the economy a needed boost. As a top White House aide, Darman had seen the political force of Reagan's optimism. Persistent, repeated declarations of hope by the president had generated incredible popular support and momentum. Darman wanted Greenspan to serve the same function for the economy.

For Greenspan, this verged on silliness. In some respects, Greenspan didn't want too much uncontrolled hope. It was precisely that psychology that generated the spending and investing sprees— whether by government, business or individuals—that could make reasonable, sustainable economic growth difficult. Greenspan wanted all the players in the economy to feel confidence, and that included a determined sense that the Fed had a tight and consistent rein on inflation.

But Darman was very smart, and he had influence with the president and Jim Baker, now the secretary of state, who retained his portfolio as the new president's chief political adviser. So Greenspan engaged in cautious debate with Darman. He was never as dismissive as he wanted to be, always willing to continue the seminar, engaging the budget director in a range of technical discussions. The approach was simple—hear him out, wait him out, always be open, make no enemies—and make your own decisions.

For his part, Darman felt that Greenspan was a political animal who would respond to public pressure. Look at the results, he said to others, noting that Greenspan continued to lower the fed funds rate slowly.

On Friday, October 13, the Dow Jones fell 190 points, nearly 7 percent, the largest drop since the 1987 crash. Johnson, the vice chairman, wanted Greenspan to agree to let it be known that the Fed would supply the necessary liquidity on Monday to head off another stock market crash. In 1987, the Fed had promised liquidity after the Monday crash. This would be a preemptive declaration.

Greenspan wanted to wait.

Johnson was in charge of the crisis management committee at the Fed. Convinced he was right, he took matters into his own hands and leaked to *The New York Times* and *The Washington Post* that the Fed would be ready to supply liquidity, as it had during the 1987 crash. Sunday's papers, put out before the world markets would open, had front-page stories quoting a Fed official who asked not to be identified. "Fed Ready with Cash to Cool Market Fears," read the *Post* headline. The *Times* said, "Federal Reserve Moves to Provide Cash to Markets."

Greenspan told Johnson that it was a mistake, bad judgment. The stock market decline was not that significant, and they had only a limited amount of ammunition to deploy. Don't go shooting in the dark, he said. The leak made them look panicky rather than cool. Detached and careful was the way Greenspan wanted to manage the Fed. The markets had to find their own natural level. The reason to supply liquidity was to ensure that the payments system flowed freely. Johnson's leak made it look as though the Fed were moving to keep the stock market up—precisely what the chairman did not want to do. It was important that the Fed be levelheaded.

At a Monday morning FOMC conference call, Greenspan said that the weekend leaks had not been authorized. Corrigan blasted the leaks as "amateurish."

Greenspan urged restraint and indicated they might make some technical adjustments of little consequence. "I think any official policy position that we initiate can be held off for a few days until this whole thing simmers down and we know pretty much where we are," he said.

Nonetheless, because of the leaks, Greenspan and those who managed the open market operations felt forced to supply more money to the system. It was designed to be carried out in such a restrained way as not to signal another rate cut, but the action had the practical effect of cutting rates another ¼ point.

The Dow Jones ended the day up 90 points.

Greenspan did not say or do anything about Johnson's unilateral action. The damage was done. A blowup would be contrary to his desire to let the incident just fade away.

As the sluggish economic conditions continued, the FOMC cut rates twice more in ¼ percent increments before the end of the year, taking the fed funds rate down to 8¼ percent.

The first year of the Bush presidency did not bode well for the economy.

It was also increasingly clear that the collapse of nearly one-third of the savings and loans in the country—due to speculative real estate and high-yield junk bond investments—was delivering yet another jolt to the economy.

Savings and loans (S&Ls), known as "thrifts," had been established in the 1930s in order to promote home construction during the Depression, and they were federally insured. Initially, thrifts could issue only fixed-rate 30-year mortgages to homeowners within 50 miles of their own offices. Over time, it became clear that if short-term interest rates went up higher than the rate the thrift collected from its investments, the S&Ls were going to start losing money.

In order to make S&Ls more competitive with other types of investments, many of the restrictions on thrifts were slowly pared down during the 1960s, 70s and 80s. S&Ls began to invest in non-residential real estate and junk bonds—and since a deposit with an S&L was federally insured, investors could seek high returns without substantial risk. Extensive fraud ensued, as single investors ran high-risk S&L ventures with enormous amounts of leverage—as much as $100 invested for every $3 that the S&L actually owned in deposits. And large numbers of these bloated, overextended S&Ls began to fail.

William Seidman, the man who chaired the Resolution Trust Corporation (RTC)—the government organization that managed the assets of failed thrifts during the S&L bailout—said of S&Ls, "Crooks and highfliers had found the perfect vehicle for self-enrichment.

"We provided them with such perverse incentives that if I were asked to defend the S&L gang in court, I'd use the defense of entrapment," he said. The government bailout was going to cost taxpayers some $100 billion.

Greenspan had a problem. Five years earlier, in 1984, a New York law firm had hired him as a private consultant—to make an assessment for Lincoln Savings and Loan Association and its owner, Charles H. Keating. Keating had since become the poster boy for S&L excesses, fraud and political influence buying. The federal takeover of Keating's S&L alone was expected to cost $2 billion.

At Townsend-Greenspan in 1985, Greenspan had written a seven-page letter stating that, under Keating's leadership, Lincoln "had transformed itself into a financially strong institution that presents no foreseeable risk" to federal regulators. He recommended that Lincoln be given an exemption that would allow them "to pursue new and promising direct investments" in ventures that earned higher rates of return. It was consistent with his view that investment restrictions on S&Ls loaded down with 30-year mortgages at fixed rates would eventually fail, because they had to pay depositors short-term rates that fluctuated significantly. Federal regulators had not granted Keating the exemption. John McCain, the Arizona Republican, and four other senators, known as "the Keating five," were now under investigation for helping Keating, who had given them large campaign contributions. McCain cited Greenspan's prior endorsement as one of the reasons that he decided to help Keating with federal regulators.

Greenspan was alternately embarrassed, forthright and defensive. He granted unusual on-the-record interviews to *The Washington Post* and *The New York Times*. "Of course I'm embarrassed by my failure to foresee what eventually transpired," he told the *Times*. "I was wrong about Lincoln. I was wrong about what they would ultimately do and the problems they would ultimately create." At the same time, he voiced consternation that the senators would cite his 1985 letter as grounds for support lent to Keating in 1987. "How could anyone use any evaluation I would have made in early 1985 as justification more than two years later?" Greenspan asked. "No one ever called saying, 'Do you still hold these views?' It's almost as bad as saying, 'I just read a report written two years ago that Amalgamated Widgets is a good stock to buy.' It just doesn't make sense."

The issue of Greenspan's involvement with Keating soon died.

Privately, Greenspan believed he would do it the same way again, given the information he had in 1985. When he reviewed Keating's balance sheets, he found them both quite impressive and fiscally sound. Keating had not done anything wrong at that point, or if he had, it wasn't detectable. Greenspan just hadn't anticipated that Keating would turn out to be a scoundrel.

"Listen, you don't need to write letters about your concerns," Greenspan said to Senator Connie Mack, the Florida Republican who had just joined the banking committee. "Just pick up the phone and we'll talk about it." Mack, 50, whose grandfather of the same name was the famous owner and manager of the Philadelphia Athletics baseball team, had been a Florida banker. He had recently signed a joint letter to Greenspan from some Republican senators complaining about interest rates. Greenspan made it clear he was available to Mack at any time. When they did talk, Greenspan said, "Why don't you and I just plan to talk more often."

Mack was soon speaking to Greenspan whenever he wanted, and the two had breakfast or lunch a couple of times a year. He found Greenspan's I'm-on-your-side tone reassuring and his willingness to listen and confer about the economy nearly endless.

For Greenspan, this wasn't just the care and feeding of the banking committee. He made himself available to any member of the House or Senate who seemed interested or whom he found interesting. Such private phone conversations or lunches were a source of important information. He could take small bits he picked up from these sessions or his frequent stops on the Washington social circuit and, almost like a professional intelligence officer, assemble those bits into a mosaic—a picture of which way the political winds might be blowing.

Greenspan went to lunches at the Business Council, an organization of business leaders, and listened to the CEOs of America's largest corporations. As soon as they saw he wasn't going to disclose much or press his own conclusions on them but instead wanted to listen, they poured out their anxieties or latest good news. Greenspan insisted that he nearly always learned more from the people who came to hear him speak than they learned from him.

"I know that if you really want to get something done that you go one-on-one privately but *never* publicly," he once said—privately, not publicly.

4

_____

ON AUGUST 2, 1990, Iraqi President Saddam Hussein invaded and took over neighboring Kuwait. President Bush declared, "This will not stand," and it looked as if the nation were on the verge of war.

Greenspan had done enough work on the economics of the Vietnam War to know it took months or more to build up forces and supplies to fight a war on a far-off continent. He consulted with his longtime friend Secretary of Defense Dick Cheney, who had been the White House chief of staff during the Ford administration. Despite the saber rattling, war was far off in time but likely at some point, Cheney said, essentially giving Greenspan a top-secret summary. The gravest problem was the vulnerability of the initial small wave of U.S. troops who had been sent to the Middle East. They could be crushed by Saddam's forces.

Greenspan convened the FOMC August 21, 1990, at a time of incredible tension, uncertainty and speculation about military action. The Mideast crisis had also sent oil prices surging.

"The odds of an actual war in the Middle East are 50-50," Greenspan said, refining the top-secret assessment, one of the best available to anyone at the time. "We are bringing in fairly significant tactical offensive weapons," he added. The chances that Saddam would back down were low. A serious question was the vulnerability of the vast oil fields in Saudi Arabia, near Kuwait. He then gave a precise account of the geography of the oil region. Some of these Saudi oil fields were vulnerable to "a couple of kamikaze raids, which some Iraqi pilots have already volunteered for," he said, drawing in part on further sensitive top-secret intelligence.

"It's extremely unlikely that anything will be triggered until we are in position. We are nowhere near there because of the lead times it takes to move our equipment and troops."

Turning to the ongoing negotiations between the Bush administration and the Democratic congressional leaders on a possible budget agreement to reduce the federal deficit, Greenspan said, "We are in a sense in economic-political policy turmoil. In that type of environment, it is crucial that there be some stable anchor in the economic system. It's clearly not going to be on the budget side; it has to be the central bank." And with grammatical pedantry, he added, "It's got to be we!"

In those circumstances, he urged a more modest view of what they could accomplish. "I don't think it is in our power to either create a boom or prevent a recession," he said. "I would suggest that perhaps the greatest positive force that we could add to this particular state of turmoil is not to be acting but to be perceived as providing a degree of stability," he added, rounding out his argument against taking any action on interest rates at the present time. He proposed a directive that was asymmetric toward ease, to indicate that though the FOMC wasn't moving rates down now, they were in all likelihood headed in that direction.

The committee members voiced support for Greenspan's proposal, but they were all over the lot. Some of the bank presidents wanted to lower interest rates slightly, arguing that it might give a psychological boost and create confidence that they were acting to prevent a recession.

"I don't think I have asked specifically for support in a large number of meetings going back a number of years," Greenspan said. "I'm not saying that people should violate what they think are their principles.

"But," he continued, "if you can find your way clear, this is the type of meeting in which it would be helpful if we had a very substantial consensus."

He won the vote unanimously.

By September it looked as if the Bush administration and the Democratic Congress had reached a budget agreement that would lower the deficit by $500 billion over five years.

"There is a lot of 'real stuff' in here," Greenspan told the FOMC approvingly on October 2, 1990, in reference to the pending budget deal. Though there was some inevitable smoke and mirrors in the numbers, he said, the agreement was substantial enough that "we have to find some mechanism to ease." He proposed "an under-

standing that if the budget resolution passes we go down ¼ percent."
It was unusual to tie an interest rate drop to action on the federal
budget, though the impact of a real budget agreement could help.
Less deficit spending would reduce inflationary expectations, so
purchasers of bonds would be willing to accept lower interest rates.
Lower long-term interest rates would enable businesses and consumers to borrow for less.

One of the bank presidents thought it would be bad precedent
to tie an interest rate move directly to political developments.

"I don't see how we can get around not responding to a real
budget agreement," Greenspan replied. An agreement would mean
that government spending was going to be cut significantly, which
would slow the economy.

Some spoke up in support of the chairman's proposal. Martha
Seger, a Fed governor generally known to favor lower rates, advo-
cated an immediate ¼ percent cut to be followed by another ¼ percent cut as a "reward to the boys on the Hill for doing the budget."

Several voiced opposition and surprise, and some outright dissent. "It is not a good precedent to have a linkup with fiscal policy,"
said Wayne Angell, a Fed governor from Kansas, in reference to the
budget deal. "I cannot support this policy action." Other members
of the committee were uncomfortable that inflationary pressures
were too high to ease, while still others demanded that if the Fed
moved, they publicly link the move to economic conditions and not
to the budget agreement itself.

Greenspan held his ground. "I would recommend," he said,
"asymmetric toward ease, with the presumption that if the budget
resolution passes both houses, there would be a ¼ percent decline in
the funds rate on Tuesday morning or Wednesday." After that, he
wanted to remain tilted toward further easing, but nothing other
than the initial ¼ percent drop would be done without consulting
the other members of the FOMC on a telephone conference call.

Corrigan cautioned the chairman. "I thought there was a lot of
wisdom in the suggestion that several people made about not tying
this unduly to the budget resolution in your public statements. The
more I think about that, the more I think it would be embarrassing."

"No," Greenspan agreed, "I would say that the budget agreement would not be a relevant reason to move were it not for the fact
that there was a weak economy." But he held firm. "If the Congress
passes the budget bill, I would intend to implement the easing."

Greenspan won somewhat narrowly, 7 to 4.

• • •

Later in October, Congress passed a somewhat different version of the $500 billion deficit reduction package after protracted negotiations. This version had more tax increases, including a jump in the top income tax rate from 28 to 31 percent. Signing it would put President Bush in the position of breaking his 1988 campaign pledge, the famous "Read my lips: No new taxes."

A furious debate erupted within the administration. Bush's more political advisers argued that signing the bill with the visible tax increases would betray the anti-tax conservatives and jeopardize his reelection chances in 1992.

Dick Darman argued that signing the deal was the only responsible course, with deficits heading up and up.

Another key player in the Bush administration, Treasury Secretary Nicholas Brady, agreed. Brady, a longtime Bush friend who had succeeded Jim Baker in 1988, liked to remind people that he had once been captain of the Yale squash team—even though he was only the seventh-ranked player on an eight-player team. The team won the national championship, and Brady liked to point toward his captainship as proof that he knew how to get things done.

As treasury secretary, his performance had been closely scrutinized and criticized. Darman called Brady a "dolt" who couldn't pass an introductory economics exam at any American university. He thought Brady was probably the weakest treasury secretary in the history of the country. Whatever his stature as treasury secretary, Brady was quite close to Bush.

The continuing U.S. military buildup for the Kuwait-Iraq crisis in the Persian Gulf required that the government show it could reach agreement, Brady said. The most important argument for signing was that the budget deal would give Brady significant ammunition in persuading Greenspan to lower interest rates. Lower interest rates would mean lower costs for new loans, and would also allow businesses and consumers to refinance debts or mortgages at lower rates. Since homeowners increasingly used refinancing as a source of consumer credit, they would be able to buy more automobiles, appliances, home furnishings and a whole variety of consumer goods. That would help the sluggish economy.

An improving economy was key to assuring the president's reelection, Brady argued.

Bush finally signed the agreement but later said publicly that there were parts that made him "gag."

When the budget agreement finally passed, Greenspan ordered the ¼ percent cut on October 29.

Two weeks later, at the November 13, 1990, meeting, the FOMC faced clear signs of a still greater downturn in the economy. Greenspan remained focused on inflation, which had been running high during October and had only quite recently begun to falter. "Slowing inflation is now finally becoming credible," he said. But at the same time, he said, "It's very clear to me that if we are perceived as responding excessively easily to all the other signs that would induce central bank ease, that the risks of the system cracking on us are much too dangerous." He recommended only a ¼ percent drop—and that, he said, would have to be done reluctantly. He won unanimous support.

Greenspan was facing another problem, which was perhaps even bigger, but partly secret. The nation's banks, the foundation of the credit system, were in big trouble. Bad loans, especially those made in real estate and in Latin America, were taking their toll. Some of the largest commercial banks were on the verge of going under. The depth of the problem was a big secret within the Fed, which had a regulatory role. But it wasn't just the banks. A number of big securities firms and insurance companies were in trouble as well. Greenspan was so alarmed that he rose at 6 a.m. each morning to check the overnight financial news on TV. He was deeply worried about a collapse in the financial markets. It was very disturbing— "The fall of '90 was the bottom!" he would later declare.

Surveying the situation from his paneled office at the New York Fed, Gerald Corrigan could see the making of an economic calamity for the entire financial system and the nation.

Citibank, which six years earlier had been the biggest, strongest and most powerful bank in the world, was closest to collapse. The Federal Deposit Insurance Corporation (FDIC), which insured deposits, examined Citibank and on their grading scale gave it a 4. A 5 was the lowest grade and indicated complete insolvency. Headed by John S. Reed, a problem-solving manager of some genius, the bank had gone through a vast expansion. Now the stock had fallen to a new low because of bad real estate and foreign loans. Corrigan arranged a come-to-Jesus meeting with Reed and informed Greenspan of his plan.

Greenspan didn't second-guess Corrigan and gave his tacit approval.

The day before Thanksgiving 1990, Corrigan met with Reed. They got into a big argument about Citi's likely losses. Reed insisted that the bank's losses would total only $2–$3 billion.

"Goddammit," Corrigan shouted, it would be $5–$6 billion and Reed had better get used to it. Corrigan figured that Citi had about six months to raise $5 billion in capital, or else they'd go under. At that time, raising $5 billion was almost unheard-of, virtually impossible.

Leaving the meeting with Corrigan, Reed seemed to cross a psychological threshold and realize he had to put Humpty-Dumpty back together again. Hey, he said to himself, this is a guy who's been in the business a long time, and he's seen a lot of banks in trouble. Maybe he knows more than you do. Reed realized that Corrigan was probably right, and that Citi needed more help than he'd thought.

Prince Alwaleed bin Talal, a young, flamboyant Saudi Arabian of extreme wealth who already owned a considerable amount of Citibank stock, was willing to invest another $1.2 billion. It would give him about 14 percent of the Citibank stock and make him by far the largest single stockholder.

Corrigan flew to Saudi Arabia for a secret meeting with the prince. During a two-hour meeting, he laid out the rules. The prince had to understand he was a passive investor. He had to agree to an extraordinary set of restrictions: he would not attempt to influence management, take over the bank or the board or try to influence the dividend, loan or credit decisions of the bank. Corrigan made it clear he would not look kindly on any infringement, and in his role as president of the New York Fed he would learn if there were any.

Reed wrote a 600-page memorandum of understanding outlining his plans to improve performance and cut costs dramatically. He shared a copy with the Fed, which, along with the FDIC and the comptroller of the currency, acted as Citi's overseer and de facto board of directors as Reed tried to save the bank. Eventually, Reed turned the bank around.

Central to the bank rescue mission, both Greenspan and Corrigan knew, was bringing the short-term fed funds rate down—which would bring down other short-term rates as well. This would enable many banks to borrow at lower rates, creating a larger spread between short-term rates and the long-term rates at which the banks had already made loans to customers. This would mean more bank profit, the key to saving the banking industry and building bank capital. But it would be a long road back. The bad condition of the banks had created a so-called credit crunch, which meant that banks were either unwilling or unable to extend enough credit to meet demand for loans. Businesses that needed loans in order to grow had a harder and harder time finding them, which resulted in yet another significant drag on the economy.

On top of the problems with the banks, the separate savings and loan collapse had depressed the real estate market. Greenspan was on the board of the Resolution Trust Corporation, which was the government agency created to dispose of the insolvent S&Ls and their real estate. He applauded and supported the eventual effort to unload a large block of real estate—billions of dollars' worth from all around the country—to get the real estate market primed. There had to be significant real estate sales to revive the market and get prices up. That meant bargain-basement prices, creating vast fortunes for those who got in on it.

The largest buyer of RTC assets was Joe Robert, a Washington, D.C.–area entrepreneur. He spent about $8 billion and ended up making a total $3 billion profit. It was a practical application of old-fashioned Ayn Rand capitalism in the money jungle. As Greenspan said in a private meeting, "We endeavored to galvanize on the greed of a number of people in the business, who when seeing their counterparts making big profits, dived in, and they virtually cleaned out our inventory." The real estate market was recovering.

The bank and S&L problems, along with the credit crunch, were not going to go away quickly, Greenspan knew. It might take years. So his major focus was the economy, which was now headed toward, if not already in, a recession. By the December 18, 1990, FOMC meeting, Greenspan acknowledged this. Real estate prices were down and retail sales were down.

"But recessions always end," he said almost coldly. They would probably have to lower rates some. But only some. His concern: "We'll succeed beyond our wildest dreams. . . . I think we also have to be prepared for the fact that we may, and probably will, overdo it." Reluctantly, he recommended another ¼-point cut to 7 percent, and he won unanimously.

5

"WE'RE IN a slowdown economically in this country, if not recession," President Bush said in a television interview on January 2, 1991. "In some areas, we're clearly in a recession. . . ." It was among the most dreaded pieces of political news a president had to convey and face. The prospect of war in the Gulf only heightened the uncertainty.

Less than a week later, operating under the asymmetric directive approved by the FOMC to reduce rates on his own, Greenspan on January 8 lowered the fed funds rate by ¼ percent. At the conference call of the FOMC the next day, he announced his action. The Fed's technical experts on the call acknowledged that Greenspan had based his decision on partial data, compounded by the difficulties of sorting out seasonal patterns at the end of the year.

After half a dozen members had spoken, Roger Guffey, president of the Kansas City Fed, said he also had some concern about the data—and then he laid down almost a challenge. "It seems to me that it is pretty soft information to be taking a policy action on. But beyond that, it seems to me that almost everything that was expressed this morning by the various participants was based upon uncertainty. And I don't think we should be making policy on uncertainty. So, I hope that we hold steady for a period of time in the future."

Greenspan merely inquired, "Any further comments or questions?"

Greenspan asked his friend Secretary of Defense Dick Cheney for a heads-up before offensive operations began in the Gulf, because of the potential impact on oil prices and the economy. On January 16, the day the air strikes were to begin, Cheney gave Greenspan a top-secret briefing. The prospects of dislodging Saddam's forces from Kuwait were excellent, Cheney said, but it would involve weeks of round-the-clock bombing and an inevitable ground offensive some weeks or months down the road. They were entering a period of immense uncertainty and international instability.

Greenspan stayed in his office the night the bombing began. He wasn't sure how the financial markets would take it. As the first air strikes appeared on CNN about 7 p.m., he watched oil and other prices gyrate wildly.

On February 1, two weeks into the air war, Greenspan decided to lower rates by ½ percent. The economy, now obviously in recession, needed big help.

When he convened a conference call later that day to inform FOMC members of the second rate decrease, some of the bank presidents mildly questioned Greenspan's failure to consult them.

"I don't know whether you consider this a technical point or not," said Tom Melzer, president of the St. Louis Fed. Speaking of the rate cut, he asked, "Should that be an action taken by the FOMC?"

Greenspan responded by saying that the directive given him left him enough room to do what he'd done.

Dick Syron, the president of the Boston Fed, agreed with Greenspan's actions but asked if the chairman might want to conduct a formal vote of the committee, so that it would not appear that Greenspan was acting unilaterally. A story had run in *The New York Times* on January 11 alleging that Greenspan wanted to ease but the bank presidents, a "dissident faction," were standing in his way. Syron wanted to give Greenspan a chance to have a vote in which the presidents supported him, so that it would not look as if he were out there on his own.

Greenspan declined, saying that taking a formal vote might lead the markets to believe that the Fed was trying to make a bigger statement than it actually was. Although the ½ percent cut was a big one, a formal FOMC vote—possibly calling for everyone to meet in Washington—would have more of an impact than a quiet unilateral action by the chairman.

At the February 5 full FOMC meeting in Washington four days later, Greenspan appointed a number of Fed economists to a task force to determine exactly how much authority he had under an asymmetric directive to move without consulting the other members of the FOMC. After a brief discussion, nobody mentioned it again. At the end of the meeting, when he recommended that the committee keep rates where they were but issue another asymmetric directive toward easing—giving him precisely the same latitude he had previously enjoyed—the members voted unanimously to support him.

On March 26, at the next FOMC meeting, the task force presented its findings. They proposed a method of "enhanced consultation." Greenspan would provide prior notice to committee members of the action that he was contemplating and include an opportunity, via telephone, for some discussion before the action was taken. A number of members voiced concern that the meaning of "enhanced consultation," and the precise circumstances that warranted it, were slightly unclear. Despite the ambiguity, the issue of what the chairman could do in between meetings was seemingly put to rest.

But some of the FOMC insiders carried their complaints to the media. Manuel Johnson, who had left as vice chairman the previous year and had joined a private international consulting firm, heard that *The Wall Street Journal* had prepared a big front-page story. It was going to show that the hawkish bank presidents had slowed Greenspan down and, on one occasion, had even defeated him, forcing him to hold off on a rate cut.

Johnson spoke with some of his former colleagues. Several grumbled about Greenspan and voiced more concern than they had to the chairman directly or at FOMC meetings. Johnson believed he had confirmed the story and that his business and international clients were entitled to learn of the scoop in advance of the *Wall Street Journal* story. Johnson wrote in his newsletter on April 2 that the Fed was "in a unique state of gridlock," adding, "Much of the current policy stalemate stems from a series of brutal confrontations between the Chairman and members of the FOMC over the Chairman's discretionary control over the fed funds rate."

Greenspan's style—a patient, almost total willingness to listen respectfully and openly to others—tended to diffuse potential confrontation. Nonetheless, the mild discontent was out there. *The Wall Street Journal* ran a short article on April 4 titled "Dispute Flares Up at Fed Over Greenspan's Authority," which stated that the bank presidents had stood up to Greenspan's discretionary rate decreases.

The next day, the *Journal* ran its long front-page article headlined "The New Fed: Democracy Comes to the Central Bank, Curbing Chief's Power." Greenspan was quoted saying that accelerating or delaying rate increases by a matter of weeks as a result of listening to others would have had no meaningful impact. Rather, he said, it was the cumulative direction and thrust of interest rate policy that mattered. "The Fed cannot effectively be run by executive fiat."

Greenspan complained privately to the *Journal* and to Johnson, who eventually concluded he had seriously overstated the intensity of the debate. During the next few days, however, the furor grew. More stories appeared in *The New York Times*, *The Washington Post*, and *The Wall Street Journal* alleging that Greenspan's authority had been curbed and that he faced a severe internal struggle in his efforts to lower interest rates. Some of the FOMC members clearly felt discomfort, if not discontent, with Greenspan's agenda.

Wayne Angell, a Fed governor from Kansas who had a regular Sunday afternoon tennis game with Greenspan, was concerned that during the first three months of 1991 Greenspan had pushed hard, maybe too hard, for lower rates. Angell, a small, scrappy, outspoken banker and farmer, was concerned that the rapid interest rate cuts were converging with the question of whether Greenspan would be reappointed by President Bush to another four-year term as chairman. Greenspan's term expired on August 11, and in Angell's view the Bush administration was engaged in a dangerous, unseemly game of dangling the reappointment and suggestively tying it to lower rates.

On April 10, *The Wall Street Journal* ran a story quoting the White House spokesman saying that Greenspan had done "a fine job," but that Bush hadn't yet made any decisions on reappointment—and, by the way, the president and his economic advisers wanted lower interest rates.

The day after the *Journal* story, Angell had a long phone conversation with Greenspan. Angell was a strong supporter of Greenspan's, but he thought it was important to have more collegial discussions at the FOMC and among the Board of Governors. Even more careful listening and consensus building was essential.

Greenspan told Angell that they had to decide whether to lower rates even more but insisted that he was unsure and open to hearing what all of the others might think.

Angell said that he too was open about what to do.

The next morning, April 12, Greenspan convened an early conference call of the FOMC, sometime before 8:30 a.m.

Angell was surprised.

"Good morning, everyone," Greenspan said. The consumer

price index (CPI) for March was going to be released later that morning, and it was down significantly—the first decrease in five years. The drop meant that inflation pressures were easing even more. "That is probably going to cement expectations, which are pretty general at this stage," he said, "that we are in the process of moving to an easier policy.

"Twenty-four hours ago," the chairman said, "I frankly would have preferred not to do anything. But we are potentially in a position at this stage where if we don't move, the markets could break." There was some evidence that economic growth might be stalling even further, and the market expected the Fed to move. Failure to move, Greenspan believed, risked a crisis of confidence in the bond and stock markets.

Angell was astonished at the change, and even more at Greenspan's strident insistence that a failure to cut rates would entail such a risk. But he waited for his turn to speak.

They could either do nothing, Greenspan continued, or they could do what he proposed—a ½ percent cut in the discount rate and a ¼ percent cut in the fed funds rate. "I'd be curious to get people's views," he said. He then called on Corrigan, his vice chair.

"I, for one," Corrigan said, "would favor a ½-point discount rate cut and a ¼-point funds rate reduction."

Like clockwork, Angell thought.

Next, three bank presidents spoke in full support of the proposal. Bang, bang, bang—in lockstep. All of a sudden, it looked like a railroad job to Angell. Five yes votes for the rate decrease, even though the day before Greenspan had talked about openness and listening.

"I'm very interested in what I'm hearing," Angell said when his turn came. He proceeded slowly. "I guess I'm going to express caution and a real preference not to move," he said. He noted that the last six months of rate cuts were in anticipation of causing the very CPI drop that they were witnessing. Now to cut rates again on the announcement made little sense and was slightly disconcerting. "I may indeed be in a minority," he said.

Several bank presidents and governors immediately chimed in, agreeing with Angell and voicing reluctance and reservations. It sounded as if Greenspan had no more than the five initial votes. Angell was even more astonished.

"So, gentlemen," Greenspan finally said, "what I hear at this particular stage is a mixed view or willingness to do perhaps a ¼ point." Rather than summarize his own embarrassing position or call for a vote that he might lose, Greenspan simply adjourned the conference call, asking the governors to stay on the line.

With the governors alone on the line, he again made a strong case for a discount rate cut.

Angell couldn't believe it. He said he thought there was no support for cutting the discount rate, either. The other governors agreed with Angell.

Afterward, Angell thought Greenspan had made a significant mistake. Failing to take a vote in the FOMC conference call, which would make a public record of the decision, only exposed the Fed to further suspicion that it was a cloistered, remote financial priesthood trying to prop up the bond market and protect the investments of the rich—the kind of argument made in William Greider's 1987 best-selling book on the Volcker Fed, *Secrets of the Temple*. In addition, the law specified that the Fed keep a record of any "action" and the "reasons underlying the action" and report those to Congress annually. Rejection of a proposal by the chairman surely merited recording, but a summary of the April 12 conversation did not appear in the Fed's annual report to Congress for 1991.

Some of the other governors believed that the April 12 conference call was more an informational conversation than a formal meeting of the FOMC, and Greenspan didn't like to take formal votes on conference calls. But Greenspan realized he may have made a mistake in trying to move impulsively on the basis of one CPI drop.

On the most sensitive issue of whether there was any connection between Greenspan's efforts to push for lower rates and the pending reappointment decision, Angell decided he had too much respect for Greenspan to even think about it. At the same time, he knew that the temptation to make deals was always there.

Angell was often an extreme voice for tight money on the FOMC. He was not afraid to dissent from the majority, and he enjoyed standing apart from the others, playing what he called "the polar role." He thought that his positions broadened the debate within the committee and gave Greenspan more room to work. At the same time, Angell felt that he actually had more influence at the FOMC when he voted with Greenspan's majority than when he dissented. When he voted with the majority, Angell felt, it was because Greenspan was able to create a consensus that was broad enough to accommodate his views.

During their regular tennis matches, Greenspan and Angell

often talked shop, though their discussions were seldom very long. Greenspan thought of Angell as a straight shooter—a bit quirky, maybe, but someone who didn't prevaricate or mislead. At one point as Greenspan's reappointment was up in the air, the two sat up in an alcove at Greenspan's private tennis club in suburban Virginia after a match and had another talk.

"Alan," Angell said, "I want you to know how proud I am to be serving in the Greenspan Fed. I know that in terms of achieving what I want to achieve, you are the instrument of doing it.

"I don't want to do anything that lessens the chances of your reappointment. I don't want to do *anything* that makes it more difficult for you during this period."

It was a subtle circling of the wagons around the chairman.

On April 18, *The Washington Post* ran a front-page story quoting three Fed bank presidents, Corrigan of New York, Lee Hoskins of Cleveland and Robert Black of Richmond, disavowing on the record that there had been any revolt against Greenspan. They all insisted that Greenspan's authority was fully intact.

Less than two weeks later, on April 30, Greenspan unilaterally lowered rates ¼ percent to 5¾ percent. He convened a conference call of the FOMC to explain his action. Auto sales and consumer spending were still off, he said, and several other economic indicators were down as well. "In my judgment the inflationary pressures are easing very considerably," he said. No one questioned or challenged him.

He had done more than simply assert control. To those inside the Fed, he had proved it.

"Look, we've got to decide on Greenspan," Michael J. Boskin, the chairman of President Bush's Council of Economic Advisers—the position Greenspan had held under President Ford—said to his White House colleagues at the end of June. "Do we reappoint him? Do we put someone else in? There's such a thing as impact on the markets about whether the Fed chairman is going to be reappointed." The decision about whether to reappoint Greenspan had been languishing for months, and Greenspan's term expired in about six weeks.

Infighting and turf wars in the Bush administration had reached the point where Treasury Secretary Brady and John Sununu, Bush's chief of staff, were not on speaking terms. Both very proud men, neither would go to the other's office to have a meeting on the subject. Boskin finally assembled the key players in his office in the Old

Executive Office Building, next to the White House. Brady, Darman, Sununu and Boskin had a long, intense meeting. None could come up with a viable alternative. A widely reported poll of New York money managers in April and a *Wall Street Journal* poll of financial decision makers in May both found that about 75 percent of the people on Wall Street favored Greenspan's reappointment.

Greenspan was pretty sure Brady was looking for an alternative, someone else to appoint to the chairmanship. Normally patient, Greenspan was increasingly disturbed and decided that if he didn't get an answer soon, he was going around Brady to Jim Baker, now the secretary of state.

Bush's economic advisers agreed on a series of questions about the economy that Brady was to ask Greenspan. After months of inaction, the treasury secretary and the Fed chairman finally sat down to talk.

Greenspan responded to Brady's questions by providing his estimate of what the economy might look like over the next year or year and a half. He gave what he considered to be a pretty pessimistic view of the economy, although he did suggest that he thought growth would pick up. He did not figure that he was being interviewed for a job. He had his own relationships with Bush and Baker, and he knew that Baker's influence was great, particularly on political matters. And nothing was more political than the condition of the economy. Greenspan didn't think his future was in Brady's hands, and he wasn't going to negotiate with him. He could see that the treasury secretary was trying to extract a tangible promise on rates in exchange for reappointment.

Brady took Greenspan's remarks as a virtual guarantee that Greenspan would act to lower interest rates even faster if he were reappointed, and he reported the good news to the president and the economic team. Bush's advisers were somewhat skeptical that Brady had accomplished everything that he said he had. "Brady is the wrong person to have in there to close a deal," one of them said.

In Greenspan's eyes, all he had done was offer his economic forecast.

On June 30, Greenspan went over to the White House and met with Bush and some of his economic advisers in the Oval Office. It was the chairman's first visit with the president in six months.

What's going to happen next with the economy? someone asked.

The economy was improving more than he had previously thought, Greenspan replied. "I'm not believing what my staff is telling me," the chairman added, "but we could have growth of 4, 4½ to 5 percent the next quarter. I can't believe this." Greenspan knew that the initial data weren't reliable. There simply weren't enough resources being put into the process of forecasting overall national economic growth, so he was suspicious of the numbers he'd seen. The situation was getting better, but not nearly as fast as some of the forecasts had predicted. In all, though, the recovery was under way. He urged the others not to tell anyone what he'd said, adding that there was really nothing they could do about it anyway.

For the White House, this was positive news. The Gulf War had been won in March, Bush's approval ratings were sky high, and now it looked as if there were a lock on high economic growth during the year before his reelection bid—if not Greenspan's high numbers, at least something in the realm. The effective message to Bush: Don't touch the steering wheel, don't fix what isn't broken.

Just before 6 p.m. on Wednesday, July 10, Bush called a press conference in the briefing room at the White House with Greenspan at his side.

"Just to top the day with a very important announcement," Bush began, "I want to say that it is my intention to send, as soon as possible, to the Senate my intention to reappoint Chairman Greenspan as chairman of the Federal Reserve.

"It gives me great pleasure," Bush continued, "to move forward at this time, quite a bit in advance of the expiration of the term." "Quite a bit" was a slight exaggeration; Greenspan's term was up in a month, and Bush had cut the decision very close.

"It's a job of great pressure," Bush said. "He has done an outstanding job."

"I thank you very much, Mr. President," Greenspan said when he stepped to the podium. "I look forward to another four years.

"It has certainly been an honor to work with you," he said to the president.

Asked about the recession, Greenspan said, "I think the evidence is increasing week by week that the bottom is passed and the economy is beginning to move up. We still do not yet know how rapid the recovery is, or the underlying strength of it, but I think it's a pretty safe bet at this stage to conclude that the decline is behind us and the outlook is continuing to improve."

"Mr. President, did Chairman Greenspan, in effect, save his job with these interest rate cuts early this year?" a reporter asked Bush.

"No," Bush replied. "His job wasn't in jeopardy. The Fed is an independent—sometimes very independent—organization over there, and he's got to lead that important enterprise the way he sees fit."

In response to another question, Bush said, "I've expressed my interest in lower rates from time to time, and I can't say there have never been differences of how we look at a problem. My view is to keep the interest rates as low as possible without getting inflation out of control, and to see this country grow. And I'm satisfied that in a broad sense Chairman Greenspan shares those goals."

Do you see any signs of emerging inflation? another reporter asked.

"Not yet," Greenspan said.

"That's not to say we should not be concerned about their being reignited at some point," Greenspan went on characteristically, "but really examining the existing state of data gives one some confidence that inflation is well contained at this stage."

"What are you going to do differently in your next term?" someone asked, the last question of the conference.

"I haven't a clue," Greenspan said.

Two days later, in an editorial called "A Stiffer Spine for Mr. Greenspan," *The New York Times* said that "the question arises why the renomination—coming barely a month before Mr. Greenspan's current term ends—was so tardy and grudging. The obvious inference is that the White House hoped to strong-arm the chairman into lowering interest rates, delivering a temporary boost to the economy. . . .

"Mr. Greenspan knows his business," the editorial concluded, "yet doubts remain about his independence."

Six days later, on July 16, Greenspan testified before Congress. "At this stage, we are well on the path of actually achieving the type of goals which we've set out to achieve: a solid recovery with the unemployment rate moving down to its lowest sustainable, long-term rate, with growth at or close to its maximum long-term sustainable pace, with inflation wholly under control." He intimated that the Fed's current policy position was "a posture of watchful waiting," implying that he wouldn't move rates anytime soon.

In a sense, Greenspan was saying the Fed had done its job, the recession was over, and the economic forecasts were for solid growth of 3 percent or more for the rest of 1991 and into 1992.

Toward the end of his testimony, Greenspan put in a good word for Bush. "He's very knowledgeable about these issues," Greenspan said. "A lot of times you think you're giving him new information, and he's heard it 10 times before, and he often knows a good deal more about certain issues than you do."

A story on the front page of the business section of *The New York Times* the next morning clearly understood what Greenspan was trying to accomplish: "Mr. Greenspan's forecast and the tone of his comments could hardly have been sweeter music to a President gearing up for a run for re-election in 1992."

Over the next five months, the economy took a nosedive. Business and consumer spending were depressed, and employment fell sharply. On October 28, Greenspan told a business conference audience in Rhode Island that "the economy is moving forward, but in the face of 50-mile-an-hour headwinds." He indicated that he was frustrated that previous rate cuts hadn't turned the economy around. He suggested that the credit crunch, with the banks still in trouble and reluctant to make new loans, had caused the recovery to falter. The Dow Jones rose that day as the markets began to expect the Fed to lower rates.

"I think it's time to ring the bell," Gerry Corrigan said to Greenspan during a coffee break at the December 2, 1991, FOMC meeting. Corrigan had been listening to the others on the FOMC all morning, thinking to himself that another kind of plain vanilla rate cut probably wasn't going to achieve much. Greenspan seemed still to be thinking only of ¼ percent incremental drops. As president of the New York Fed, Corrigan was not a member of the Board of Governors and technically he had no say in what went on with the discount rate, but he recommended that Greenspan persuade the Board of Governors to step up and cut rates significantly, perhaps a full 1 percent. The public announcement effect would send the needed message.

David Mullins, who had replaced Johnson as board vice chairman four months earlier, approached Greenspan a few minutes later and urged a big discount rate drop as well. Mullins, 45, a former Harvard Business School professor, was particularly close to Nick Brady. He had served as a top adviser to the commission that had investigated the 1987 stock market crash and then had been an assistant treasury secretary to Brady. He had been Bush's first Fed appointment.

Attempting to act neither as Bush's nor as Brady's man at the Fed, Mullins had nonetheless been pushing for a big rate cut for a few months, arguing that there couldn't be any real risk of reigniting inflation in the current sour economic environment. He observed Greenspan's leadership style carefully. The chairman tended to provide leadership by supporting, adopting or appearing to adopt the views of others on the board or FOMC. Because Greenspan was so deferential, allowing everyone their argument, he was able to pull a very large consensus along on the ultimate decisions. Let's take a major step, Mullins said now. The short-term interest rates, both the fed funds rate and the discount rate, could be safely moved lower than the inflation rate. That would mean businesses and consumers would have real interest rates that would be less than zero, which should provide a giant stimulus to the economy. Greenspan had been resisting, but with Corrigan pushing, too, the chairman began to consider it more seriously. Both the FOMC vice chairman and the board vice chairman were saying essentially the same thing. They had a point, Greenspan concluded, and it was important to preserve consensus—even if it formed around the proposals of others.

The Board of Governors could change the discount rate only if at least 1 of the Fed's 12 regional reserve banks requested it. Soon after the December 2 meeting, Corrigan convened the New York Fed's board of directors and talked to them about a big rate cut. He was careful to say that although he didn't have the slightest idea how the board would respond to it, he wanted to put something on the table that was unconventional—a real statement. Some people voted for a plain vanilla incremental move first, but in a second vote he got a request from his board for a full 1 percent decrease.

Corrigan informed Greenspan of the New York Fed's request. Greenspan was in Chicago, where he and the president of the Chicago Fed were having a similar conversation. The Chicago bank soon requested a full point decrease as well.

Greenspan knew that he had some convincing to do to get the other governors to go along. He knew that the markets were becoming increasingly weak, and that a dramatic rate decrease—unthinkable two months earlier—would most likely not risk an inflation outburst. But he wanted unanimity, or at the least a clear majority. He talked to all of the governors, seeking their support.

On December 19, 1991, the Board of Governors voted 6 to 1 to lower the discount rate a full 1 percent to 3½ percent, the lowest it had been since 1964. Angell was the lone dissent.

The announcement made a splash on Wall Street and at the White House. *The Washington Post* quoted Scott Pardee, chairman of a securities firm in New York, saying, "It's sort of Merry Christmas and Happy New Year from the Fed." Bush issued a public statement praising the Fed move, and the next day Greenspan went to the White House, where Bush and his advisers were very happy.

Several days later, *The Wall Street Journal* published a long front-page story about the new bold Fed that extended the holiday metaphor. "It was a Christmas Eve conversion to rival that of Ebenezer Scrooge," the account began. Greenspan was cast as the stingy old man who led his colleagues but also allowed himself to be led at times. Mullins was portrayed as the hero, the one who "laid the intellectual groundwork" for the 1 percent decrease. Because of the rate cut, the article said, indebted businesses and homeowners would be able to refinance loans and optimistically projected that billions of dollars would go to consumers—"as swiftly and surely as a tax cut."

On the day after Christmas, December 26, Greenspan met with Bush again.

Over the course of 1991, in ten separate moves, the FOMC had also lowered the fed funds rate from 7 percent to 4 percent, a sure sign that the economy was in trouble.

6

_____

GREENSPAN HOPED that Bush would win reelection in 1992. As a citizen he was allowed to have his preference, but as Fed chairman he wasn't supposed to involve himself in politics. It was delicate. When he met with the president, he conveyed his support. Budget Director Darman, who had been present at several sessions, was hoping to use Greenspan's obvious leaning to convince him to cut interest rates more and faster.

Darman was increasingly convinced that Greenspan was grossly mishandling the money supply. He also believed Greenspan was wrong to insist that the economy could not grow more than about 2½ percent a year without producing inflation. He had charts and his Harvard Business School education to reinforce his arguments. There was an immutable law, a mathematical formula, about the relationship of economic growth and inflation to the money supply.

Greenspan didn't disagree with the formula, but the key variable, the velocity—or number of times money changed hands—could no longer be measured accurately for a variety of reasons that were accepted by most economists. That was why the Fed was essentially just setting the fed funds rate, not attempting to target the money supply directly. Greenspan reiterated his view to Darman that the Fed had been unable to control or even accurately measure the money supply for years. The notion that it was possible was outdated.

Darman persisted, convinced that Greenspan wanted to go into the history books as the super–inflation fighter, at almost any cost, including Bush's reelection. He sent Greenspan memos and faxes urging lower rates.

After several years of sparring, Darman had begun to take Greenspan's obstinacy somewhat personally. He began telling associates that the chairman resembled the character Woody Allen plays in his movies, a man of some intellect but simultaneous insecurity. Greenspan wasn't leading. Darman wanted him to get up and declare, "I'm lowering rates. Your Fed is with you. I'm not going to let this happen to this country."

Darman also found it odd that Greenspan said he telephoned his mother almost daily and visited her weekly, traveling on the shuttle to New York. This was not ordinary in Darman's mind, and he suggested sarcastically that there were parallels with Norman Bates, the mother-obsessed character in Alfred Hitchcock's *Psycho*. We can't be sure the mother exists, Darman joked. In any case, he suggested that Greenspan's mother had a strange and unnatural power over her son. And he and the administration seemed to have too little.

Darman would not go away. He argued to Greenspan that the chairman of the Fed was a crucial character in the confidence game of building support and national optimism. Greenspan had almost an obligation to cut rates—perhaps just for two or three months, as a vote of confidence in the economy, in Bush, in America. That would be a near-zero-risk operation for Greenspan, Darman said. If the chairman would get up and say, We are confident the economy can grow, and then act accordingly, it would.

Greenspan listened but did not budge. He disagreed with Darman. That was just not how the economy worked.

Darman started whispering around town that Greenspan was to blame for the 1990–91 recession—or at least, as the budget director put it, anywhere from 50 to 80 percent of the blame belonged to Greenspan.

Treasury Secretary Brady picked up where Darman left off. If the money supply were managed properly, interest rates would be much lower. He wanted the fed funds rate, which was now at 4 percent, down to 1 percent or even lower. Inflation was under control, the government was cutting its spending and the Fed should keep feeding the money supply.

Brady considered lower rates to be an insurance policy. Why aren't you flooding the economy with money? The downsides are negligible. If inflation popped up, the Fed could tighten. Brady warned Greenspan: You're going to get into a cul-de-sac where you can't get out, and you're going to be a day late and a dollar short with rate cuts. Then the economy will tank and it will take dramatic rate reductions to help bring it back.

The risks as you view them are wholly different from the risks I see, Greenspan replied. Once inflation began, the genie would be out of the bottle and it would take months or more to clamp down. The economy had to grow on its own. The Fed couldn't make it happen—perhaps artificially for a few months, but the benefit would be so small compared to the risk.

Brady, who had risen to head Dillon, Read, had probably been a good market person, Greenspan concluded charitably. His knowledge was subliminal, making the right moves and judgments about markets. "I feel it in my bones" was a frequent Brady refrain. But when he tried to articulate it, the words could sound like hash. Perhaps his state of knowledge was not at a level where it was verbal, Greenspan concluded. In any case, Brady's words made no economic sense.

"Look, Nick," Greenspan finally said, "don't complain to me. Call the board members. I have no objection."

So Brady took to the phone. He called board member Kelley, Jim Baker's old friend. The Fed should ease more aggressively, he urged.

"Thank you very much, Nick," Kelley said. "I appreciate your call. It's nice of you to take your time to communicate with us, and we'll certainly take that into consideration." Period. Good-bye.

Several governors mentioned to Greenspan that Brady had called them. If Brady kept it up, Greenspan concluded, he might trigger a vote to *raise* rates. The problem with the treasury secretary was that he didn't realize that, and he didn't know how the economy really worked.

By March 1992, Greenspan had not lowered rates for three months, and Brady canceled his weekly breakfast or lunch with him. "You only get his attention if he's not included," Brady said at one White House discussion. He agreed with Darman that Greenspan was a political animal, subject to manipulation if he perceived himself excluded. He soon concluded he would have to go further, playing on what he believed was Greenspan's status anxiety, his concern about his social standing. He cut off all regular social contact with the chairman—no parties, no dinners. "Whoosh! Boom! Stop!" Brady said. "The only way to really get his attention is to sort of make him an outcast."

As the treasury secretary, Brady was the senior economic spokesman for Bush. He would not allow Darman or any other person less senior to have regular meetings with Greenspan. In no way would he accede that important turf to Darman, whom he thought brilliant but immature and self-important. Bush's economic advisers were so divided that Bush himself had to take over the Greenspan account. In the spring, the president began meeting with the chairman to make the case.

"I don't want to bash the Fed," Bush said at one meeting. The president, who had majored in economics at Yale, said he had heard from businessmen that the Fed should be increasing the money supply. A lot of people are saying this is a problem. How should I be looking at this? Bush asked.

We're as concerned and frustrated sometimes as you, Greenspan replied. Rates were at a historic low, and normally the money supply should be way above where it currently was. Because of the collapse of the savings and loan industry and other technical issues, the Fed was struggling with the money supply, Greenspan acknowledged. Our ability to control the money supply is not as facile as it used to be.

The president said that he just wanted to understand what the Fed was doing.

It was not an adversarial discussion, and Greenspan left feeling better. He thought Bush had a legitimate right to know what was going on. The chairman was delighted to deal with Bush. Though the president's undergraduate degree in economics did not make itself overly apparent in these discussions, Greenspan found Bush, as he put it carefully, "not unknowledgeable."

In Greenspan's first 18 months at the Fed, Ronald Reagan had never wanted to know any of these things.

On June 23, in an interview with *The New York Times*, President Bush said, "I'd like to see another lowering of interest rates."

At the FOMC meeting a week later, only one member of the board, Lawrence Lindsey, a former Harvard economics professor appointed by Bush, mentioned Bush's remark. He said he didn't like it.

Greenspan didn't say anything about the public comment, but he proceeded with an extra dimension of caution. He noted that the extended discussions by the members were very mixed concerning the economy, and he admitted his own confusion. The gloomy data from the most recent weeks could turn out to be "phony," he noted. Yet since they had eased rates 22 times since May 1989, "which has to be some sort of record," at some point the economy could start to show "some significant vibrancy."

The chairman proposed what he called "a mildly asymmetric directive toward ease, but with the requirement that before any action is taken there be a telephone conference to explain why." He was being exceedingly careful. "I am not sure that captures everybody; I suspect it probably does not. But having thought about trying to find where the central tendency is—where one captures the largest number of views and concerns of this committee—that's pretty much where I come out." The FOMC approved his proposal by a 10–2 margin.

The next day, July 2, the Labor Department released unemployment data. The unemployment rate had risen to 7.8 percent from 7.2 percent, an alarmingly sharp increase. The Board of Governors immediately voted 7 to 0 in favor of a ½ percent cut in the discount rate. Greenspan convened a conference call of the FOMC to propose a ½ percent cut in the fed funds rate as well. There was no dissent.

On September 4, Greenspan lowered the federal funds rate by another ¼ percent, two months before the presidential election. That move put the fed funds rate at 3 percent, the lowest it had been in 20 years. The normal medicine was not working. The extreme reduction to 3 percent, with inflation at about 3 percent, meant that the real interest rate was effectively 0 percent. In some respects, it was a bold decision to overstimulate the economy.

On October 6, *The Wall Street Journal* published a front-page article that gave a great deal of credit for the rate cuts of the last two years to Vice Chairman Mullins. With its trademark black-and-white etching of the scholarly, bespectacled Mullins, the article quoted an unnamed official saying of the vice chairman, "He's like the wave washing against the shore. He's constantly pounding against Greenspan."

The FOMC convened that day. The economy was growing, but at a subdued pace, and the outlook for future growth was uncertain.

Mullins attempted to make a modest case for a rate cut, saying that he expected negative data in the coming weeks. "We likely will be confronted with a persuasive case for a rate cut," he said. "Indeed, I think the case is fairly persuasive now. The timing and execution are difficult."

"This has to be one of the most difficult periods for policy making that I remember," Greenspan said after the others had spoken. "We have a very touchy problem here. I'm aware, as you all are, that everyone expects us to ease, and that becomes a self-fulfilling activity. While the case for easing right now is quite strong, I would be far more inclined to wait for a short while." He moved for an asymmetric directive toward ease, aware that the committee might have to lower rates in the very near future.

"I say this without a great conviction because anyone who has a great conviction at this stage about what the economy is doing or what proper policy is, I think, is under a mild state of delusion.

"I wish we had the luxury to sit back and do nothing until after the election, as is the conventional procedure. I don't think we have that luxury. However, I don't think the markets have been viewing anything we have been doing as politically motivated. There are obviously those who make those statements, but I don't think that's a serious issue confronting us. So, I would dismiss that as a consideration." If the economy didn't pick up, they would have to move toward ease no matter what.

"Let me just say something that I think is important for us to focus on," Greenspan added after hearing from everyone. "This is a very close call here, and what I don't want to do is convey a sense that I have some strong conviction as to what is involved here. I want to make certain that we're not getting a committee vote which merely acquiesces in a view that I have stipulated because, as we have all indicated around this table, this is an extremely difficult period. I want to make certain that we get a vote which is essentially a committee vote rather than acquiescence to the position of the chairman.

"Ordinarily," he added, "I would never say such a thing!"

The members laughed.

"I want to read off my notes to be *sure* that I have gotten everyone's view and priorities correctly. Accordingly, I'm going to poll each of you."

Greenspan finally got to the wave that was supposedly pounding constantly against his shore. Governor Mullins? he asked.

"I think there's a case," Mullins began, "for ease now, but I—"

"But," Greenspan cut in, "that's not the question."

Mullins said he would go with Greenspan's asymmetric proposal.

"That there is a case for ease now is unquestioned," Greenspan continued, "but what's your priority?"

He made Mullins say it twice: He would go with the chairman. Greenspan finally declared, "There is a majority for asymmetric toward ease in the form which I originally stipulated it." He then called for the vote, and his proposed directive won 8 votes, including Mullins's. Four were against. The shore had won.

"Okay," Greenspan said. "Let's go have lunch."

Four days later, October 10, Greenspan attended the fall meeting of the Business Council at the secluded Homestead resort in Hot Springs, Virginia. Although traditionally the Fed didn't act in the month before an election, he rejected the idea that the Fed would hold off out of any fear of appearing to bow to pressure from the Bush administration.

"This would be an irresponsible action on our part," Greenspan said. "I wish to emphasize that we at the Federal Reserve will continue to observe and evaluate the economy the way we always do and will not, if we believe it is necessary, abstain from taking actions largely or solely because there is an election and a campaign under way."

But he did not cut rates.

On Election Day, Tuesday, November 3, 1992, Arkansas Governor Bill Clinton beat Bush, with only 43 percent of the popular vote. Bush had 38 percent and Texas billionaire Ross Perot 19 percent. All the polls and most of the analysis showed that the main issue in voters' minds was the economy. Clinton had promised presidential action to fix it. Bush seemed out of touch.

It was tragic, Greenspan felt. Bush, who Greenspan believed had done a flawless job on the nation's most important policy issues—the confrontation with, and eventual collapse of, the Soviet Union and also the Gulf War—deserved reelection. Of course, Greenspan thought, it was exactly what had happened to Winston Churchill, who had been thrown out of office after victory in World War II.

David Mullins thought the Bush loss had much to do with a failure of the administration to address the wreckage of the 1980s that Bush had inherited. He had a list of 10 negative economic conditions that Bush had faced in January 1989 when he took office: 1. lots of debt for government—the federal deficit plus state and local deficits; 2. high business and consumer debt; 3. commercial real estate overbuilding; 4. the so-called junk bond collapse; 5. Department of Defense budget cuts after the fall of the Soviet Union; 6. a Democratic Congress that wouldn't give Bush much maneuvering room; 7. American business restructuring and layoffs; 8. the Japa-

nese economic troubles; 9. decrease in exports; 10. an uncoopera-
tive Fed.

Mullins felt in retrospect that Bush should have gotten out the
bad economic news early in his administration, perhaps with a call-
to-arms speech about the trouble. He could have taken the political
hit up front and diminished expectations right away. But Bush
hadn't wanted to do anything that would imply criticism of his political godfather, Ronald Reagan. In addition, Mullins thought that
Brady hadn't faced up effectively to the economic problems at hand
in the fall of 1991. Brady had recognized that there was a long-term
problem, but he wanted to gut it out rather than acknowledge to the
public that there would have to be a period of adjustment and slower
growth. This failure to explain the situation—both to the president
and to the public—was one of Brady's greatest failures as treasury
secretary, in Mullins's view. Mullins thought that the personal closeness between Bush and Brady had freed Brady from having to persuade the president with logical or politically viable arguments. And
so, in some sense, Brady's philosophy of hope and optimism as a
cure had become Bush's. Over time, the cure had become the disease. The result was a hands-off economic policy, which to many
voters appeared as indifference.

Bush and Brady had failed to engineer their survival, but
Greenspan had succeeded in engineering his.

When President-elect Clinton invited Greenspan to visit him
in Little Rock on December 3, the chairman jumped at the chance.
As they talked alone in the Governor's Mansion, Greenspan found
himself quite taken with the new young leader. Clinton was totally
focused, as if he had no other care in the world and unlimited time.
They ranged over topics from foreign policy to education, and
Greenspan saw that Clinton's reputation as a policy junkie was richly
deserved. The president-elect seemed not only engaged but totally
engrossed, as best Greenspan could tell. He saw an opening to give
an economics lesson. The short-term interest rates that the Fed
controlled were at 3 percent, as low as they could practically go in
these economic conditions, he said. But they could keep them there.

The long-term rates—the 10-year and longer rates—were an
unusual 3 to 4 percent higher than the short-term fed funds rate, at
about 7 percent. The gap between the short-term rate and the long-
term rate, Greenspan lectured, was an inflation premium being paid
for one simple reason. The lenders of long-term money expected
the federal deficit to continue to grow and explode. They had good

reason, given the double-digit inflation of the late 1970s and the expanding budget deficits under Reagan. They demanded the premium because of the expectation of new inflation. The dollars they had invested would, in the near and distant future, be worth less and less.

Perhaps no single overall economic event could do more to help the economy, businesses and society as a whole than a drop in the long-term interest rates, Greenspan said. The Fed didn't control them. But credible action to reduce the federal deficit would force long-term interest rates to drop, as the markets slowly moved away from the expectation of inevitable inflation. Business borrowing costs, mortgages and consumer credit costs would go down. Clinton was so sincere and attentive, and full of questions and ideas, that Greenspan continued. Establishing credibility about deficit reduction with the markets would lower rates and could trigger a series of payoffs for the economy, he said.

Greenspan outlined a blueprint for economic recovery. Lower long-term rates would galvanize demand for new mortgages, refinancing at more favorable rates and more consumer loans. This would in turn result in increased consumer spending, which would expand the economy.

As inflation expectations and long-term rates dropped, investors would get less return on bonds, driving investors to the stock market. The stock market would climb, an additional payoff.

The federal deficit was so high and cumulatively unstable, Greenspan said, that increased government spending to increase jobs—in accordance with the traditional Keynesian model—no longer worked. The economic growth from deficit reduction could actually *increase* employment—a critical third payoff.

Greenspan noted that the economy was rebounding, but there was no telling if it would last. As had happened in the past, he said bluntly, the recovering economy could fall on its face. Getting the long-term rates down and keeping them down with a strong deficit reduction program could sustain and increase economic growth even more than the conservative estimates that were circulating in the government or privately.

This extraordinary conversation continued for two and one-half hours. Greenspan had not intended to stay for lunch, but he did. From the beginning he sensed a kind of academic atmosphere, which he liked. To his mind, Clinton was close to being an intellectual, inclined and willing to talk about abstract ideas. He was different from the four Republican presidents Greenspan had seen up close—Nixon, Ford, Reagan and Bush. The chairman left the meeting thinking, Either this guy has a lot of the same views as I do, or he is the cleverest chameleon I have ever run into. The first would be a compliment, Greenspan thought. The second: Oh, wow, this guy is something if he can fool me.

Clinton's conceptual ability was impressive, but Greenspan wondered whether Clinton was *too* thoughtful—whether he might know too much on both sides of the major questions of the day. Might the new president be indecisive, like Hamlet, incapacitated by endless debate and doubt?

On the five-hour trip back to Washington, Greenspan tried to assess what he had observed. Clinton was a politician and a notorious schmoozer. Had the session been some kind of show? That, Greenspan felt, would really be impressive. If it was a show, it had been a remarkable one. No, he concluded, it was straight and sincere. Clinton was what Greenspan termed an "intellectual pragmatist." He didn't necessarily like to use the term because it was slightly pejorative, but he couldn't think of another that captured Clinton. It fit, and it also applied to Greenspan himself. Part of Clinton's campaign promise included tax increases on the wealthy, a violation of Republican orthodoxy. But increasing taxes reduced the federal deficit—and those deficits, Greenspan thought, were such a threat to the future of the economy that it might just be worth it to support Clinton's proposal.

One of the main paradoxes, Greenspan realized, was that by running up the federal budget deficits, Reagan had effectively borrowed from the period that was now going to be the Clinton era. In his era, Clinton would have to pay it back by paying down the deficit in some way. The irony was that Clinton probably wouldn't have been elected if Reagan hadn't created the deficits. Reagan had bequeathed Bill Clinton his major problem, but he had also given him his opportunity to win the presidency.

Clinton was happy that Greenspan had not made the typical Republican plea against raising taxes on the rich.

"We can do business," Clinton told Vice President–elect Al Gore after the Greenspan meeting.

7

PRESIDENT-ELECT Clinton named Thomas "Mack" McLarty, his friend from kindergarten in Hope, Arkansas, as his White House chief of staff. McLarty, 46, the small, gracious CEO of the Arkansas-based natural gas company Arkla, had succeeded by cultivating personal relationships. He was soon identified as the new president's main man. Mullins, also from Arkansas, knew McLarty from high school football. Mullins's father had been president of the University of Arkansas when McLarty had been president of the student body.

Greenspan asked Mullins to arrange a private dinner for the three of them at the Metropolitan Club. The downtown Washington establishment was so old world that members were not allowed to use working papers or conduct business at the tables in the main dining room. Greenspan was a member.

Mullins was happy to act as a go-between for such powerful figures. Obviously Greenspan felt vulnerable and out of touch with an incoming Democratic president. At dinner, Mullins noticed that Greenspan was attempting to soften his image as a conservative intellectual. The chairman turned on the charm and schmoozed. Hillary Rodham Clinton was going to oversee a health care reform program, and Greenspan said he would be delighted to talk to her about the issue. He invited McLarty to address the boards of directors of the district banks when they came to Washington. The boards comprised some of the United States's most prestigious businesspeople.

Greenspan's real connection to the new administration was going to be Lloyd Bentsen, the former Texas senator who was now

Clinton's treasury secretary. They were close friends and regularly played tennis together. Greenspan thought that the aristocratic and leathery-faced Bentsen, 71, looked and acted like a president. Bentsen had beaten George Bush in 1970 for the Senate and later had run unsuccessfully as the Democratic vice presidential candidate in 1988.

Though a partisan Democrat, Bentsen had been the powerful chairman of the Senate Finance Committee and was conservative on fiscal and money matters. Greenspan considered him more Republican than Nick Brady.

Bentsen arranged for Greenspan to see Clinton on Thursday, January 28, the eighth day of the new administration. Greenspan told the president that it would be dangerous not to confront the deficit very soon. The problem would not make itself immediately apparent during the next several years, because defense spending cuts would obscure the ballooning deficit. After 1996, though, the data showed—as persuasively as any numbers could—that the deficit and interest on the federal debt would become explosive.

"You cannot procrastinate indefinitely on this issue," Greenspan warned. Without action, he forecast "financial catastrophe."

Clinton made it clear he had received the message.

Greenspan thought Clinton and his team were learning that campaigning for president was a great deal easier than being president. Campaigning was just identifying the problem—like a practice swing in golf, without a ball. Everyone could do it well. But governing was real, and it was all a lot harder with the ball on the tee.

Bentsen urged the president to develop a personal relationship of trust with Greenspan and to listen to him on the critical question of cutting the federal deficit. He also emphasized to Clinton the importance of deficit reduction as a catalyst for lower long-term interest rates.

With Bentsen, Greenspan went further. He urged the new administration to set ambitious deficit reduction targets for the federal budget. On February 5, the White House economic advisers sent Clinton a 15-page memo that summarized budget options and Greenspan's analysis.

It read, in part: "Greenspan believes that a major deficit reduction (above $130 billion) will lead to interest rate changes *more than offsetting*" the contraction to the economy caused by less government spending. This meant the long-term rates would come down if the deficit reduction was sufficient to have credibility in the financial markets, not that Greenspan would lower the fed funds rate.

On his copy, Bentsen had written with his lead pencil referring to Greenspan, "He urges 140 or above," meaning Greenspan thought a $140 billion reduction in the economic plan four years out (1997) would be more credible than $130 billion. It revealed their most private, confidential talks. In a sense, Bentsen and Greenspan were using each other. For Bentsen, Greenspan's view on a specific deficit target was a potent weapon in the Clinton administration deliberations. For Greenspan, a big reduction in the federal deficit would make his job immensely easier, because lower deficits would likely mean lower actual inflation. Bentsen, and perhaps Clinton, could help Greenspan fight inflation.

Greenspan didn't worry that the president or Congress would cut the federal deficit so much as to induce economic chaos. He recalled that Paul Volcker had once said that no one was kept awake at night for fear that Congress would overdo deficit reduction.

Bentsen and all of Clinton's other top economic advisers recommended the $140 billion target. Some of Clinton's populist political advisers, such as James Carville and Paul Begala, unaware of Greenspan's indirect role as ghostwriter, thought it was too much deficit reduction, and they fought hard for less—perhaps just $5 billion less. But it was as if the $140 billion target, which included spending cuts and tax increases to add revenue, were carved in the sacred tablets, and Clinton adopted it. Bentsen told President Clinton that they had effectively reached a "gentlemen's agreement" with Greenspan.

When Clinton unveiled his economic plan at his first State of the Union address to a Joint Session of Congress on February 17, Greenspan was there in the gallery, in seat A6—right between Hillary Clinton and Tipper Gore, the vice president's wife, on full display as the national television cameras swung over to get reaction. The First Lady had invited him to sit in her box for the speech, and Greenspan had accepted on the basis that protocol dictated he not refuse her invitation.

As Clinton spoke, Greenspan applauded stiffly. He believed the White House had given him enormous power, because if he chose to criticize the Clinton economic plan, he could do substantial damage—even perhaps do it in. They had elevated him in the power structure very significantly, he believed. But the large deficit reduction portion was in part his own design, and he was hardly going to shoot it down.

Greenspan was due to testify before Congress in two days about the plan. To make sure he was on solid ground, he canvassed the FOMC to make sure there was not so much as a razor-thin bit of difference between his views and those of the other committee members. On February 19, in testimony before the Senate Banking Committee, Greenspan said that the Clinton plan was "serious" and "credible," making major headlines with his support.

Greenspan thought that Clinton had broken the gridlock on dealing with the deficit. He couldn't say it publicly, but he believed the president had displayed an element of political courage. He was taking a stance that some in his own party would fight him on. In Greenspan's view, Clinton deserved commendation if there was any justice in the crazy town of Washington.

It had been a remarkable four months for Greenspan. His impact on the new Democratic president was real and positive—a degree of influence he had not begun to approach during the more than five years he had been chairman under Reagan and Bush.

Within a week, long-term interest rates began to fall, and Clinton said in a speech, "Just yesterday, due to increased confidence in the plan in the bond market, long-term interest rates fell to a 16-year low." The yield on the 30-year bond had dropped below 7 percent.

Bentsen was delighted. He was all over Greenspan, peppering him with questions about the chairman's forecast and projections for the bond market. The long-term bond rate was the new talisman in the Clinton administration.

On March 10, Greenspan was in his office, sitting at his desk, staring into the computer screen. "The Buck Starts Here," read a large plaque nearby.

He glanced at the summary on the screen. The fed funds rate was at $2^{15}/_{16}$ percent, just below the Fed's target of 3 percent. Slight variations in the market were inevitable, and the $^{1}/_{16}$th percentage point lower meant the market was calm. With a stroke of button A on his computer, Greenspan moved on and checked the Treasury bill market, where demand for Treasury bills was up slightly. From there, it was on to a minute-by-minute breakdown of the Dow, which was down 4.31 points. He hit more keys, which took him through the foreign currency exchange markets—the yen, the deutsche mark—which were updated every 15 minutes and had daily numbers all the way back to January.

Greenspan then checked the relationship between the British pound and the deutsche mark, which was a vital indicator of what was happening in the European markets. He called up the commodities market and looked at spot gold prices, then moved on to the Eurodollar deposit rates in London for short-term instruments—three months, six months and a year. He checked the important international interest rates and then moved on to oil prices.

In all, Greenspan accessed about 50 charts by using button A on his computer. He hadn't programmed the computer himself, but he had made sure that all of the information he wanted was always a click or two away. It was a calm day, so he checked the charts only once every half hour or so. He always checked regularly, because, as he liked to put it, he could never know for sure that something was *not* happening.

Greenspan felt that a growing part of his task was to anticipate the unexpected. He was increasingly convinced that the unexpected, in one form or another, would occur. He knew that what seemed impossible at first was often what happened, so preparation for dealing with the inconceivable was a necessary part of his job.

The way he read the history of the 1950s and the 1960s, the Fed had been able to have a fairly expansionist, low–interest rate policy that helped the economy grow without significant inflation. There was almost a presumption that the system would not allow inflation to take hold. As a result, the key long-term interest rates important to businesses and consumers were always modest to low. The cost of the Vietnam War eventually cracked the system, and the deficits blew up in the late 1970s. Greenspan recalled one period in 1979 when long-term interest rates went up an incredible 5 percent. This was the runaway inflation that his predecessor Paul Volcker had tackled.

The lingering residue of that runaway inflation was that an inflation expectation, which had been nonexistent prior to Vietnam, was now apparently built into the system. One result was a psychology of inflation that was, at least initially, more important than real inflation. At any sign that inflation might be coming or that the Fed wasn't vigilant, the long-term rates would shoot up in response. As Greenspan had told Clinton and his advisers, the magic bullet of any successful economic plan was to keep those long-term rates down.

Of course, reducing the inflation expectation in the economy made it easier to keep actual inflation down. In a sense, the president and Congress, with their reduced spending, were taking on some of the inflation-fighting role of the Fed.

To a large extent, that meant catering to the bond market. Businesses and government had trillions of dollars in outstanding debt in bonds, having borrowed the money at fixed interest rates for specific time periods. Bondholders would benefit as rates dropped and the value of the bonds that they held increased. But Greenspan believed he had argued successfully to Clinton and the Congress that there was a much bigger payoff for the overall economy and society. In the end, if they did it right and kept inflation in check, both the bondholders and the wage earners would gain. The income skewing of the 1980s, when the rich got richer and the poor got much less, would start to reverse, he believed.

On the evening of April 19, 1993, Greenspan laid out some of this history in a speech to the Economic Club of New York.

"Regrettably," he said on page 12 of his speech, droning on, "the inflation excesses of the 1970s still condition the inflationary expectations of today." The wide gap between short-term rates and long-term rates—the inflation premium—"reflects deep-seated investor concerns that inflation will significantly quicken in the latter part of this decade and beyond." He said he didn't think that inflation would occur, because the banks and the financial lenders were still recovering from the early 1990s—meaning that business expansion was not likely to get out of control and overheat the economy. But, he cautioned, "We need to be especially vigilant not to be mesmerized by the current tranquillity of the inflation environment." Just 10 days earlier, the consumer price index for the previous months had shown a mere 1/10 percent increase, indicating no real problem with inflation.

"Suppressing inflation over the past decade, and more, has obviously not been without cost. To fritter away this substantial accomplishment by failing to contain inflationary forces that may emerge in the future would be folly."

Lest anyone miss the message, he added, "A society's central bank is rarely popular."

On May 13, the Labor Department released the April consumer price index. It had bounced up 7/10 of a percent, an unexpected surge that foreshadowed inflation. Greenspan was troubled. What was happening?

If he was forced to raise interest rates, Greenspan could shatter Clinton's deficit reduction plan, which was limping through the Congress with no Republican support.

Since the middle of 1989, Greenspan had felt at least conceptually in control of what was going on in the economy. His numbers and forecasts hadn't always been right, expected trends had been off a little, but there had been no significant surprises. By the Keynesian models of the 1960s and earlier, a weak economy and inflation could not coexist. The 1970s had shattered that construct. When Greenspan had been Ford's chief economist in 1974, the consumer price index had risen 12 percent as the economy slid into a recession. Then in 1979 and 1980, so-called stagflation—a coincidence of high inflation and low or negative economic growth—struck again, with the CPI up above 12 percent and an economy that had ground almost to a halt.

Now the chairman summoned three top senior staff members to his office. They were confronting a situation that he likened somewhat to Galileo's problem, he told them. Galileo, the famous 17th-century Italian astronomer, mathematician and physicist, had stuck to his conclusion that the earth revolved around the sun, despite the accepted wisdom that the earth was at the center of the universe.

Greenspan said that things were being observed in the economy that shouldn't be happening. Either measurements were wrong, or they were measuring the wrong things, or the old models weren't adequate to explain what was occurring. It would be unacceptable for them not to come up with an explanation. Though it was possibly just a short-term aberration or the result of faulty seasonal numbers, Greenspan said they had to deal with the possibility that new forces were at work. Suppose, he said, in two months inflation had continued to increase? "What could have caused us to be wrong? What is wrong with our structure of analysis, our body of concepts, which can explain it? In other words, I'm not asking you to construct a concept which forecasts. I'm asking the reverse." Let's shake ourselves up, question everything.

The data indicated that some businesses, particularly small, non-incorporated businesses—the mom-and-pop shops of the world—were using their own resources to grow, instead of borrowing money. That did not constitute a classic inflationary environment. Inflation was usually the result of increased demand for credit and loans as businesses attempted to finance their growth through borrowing. If inflation continued without rising demand for loans and credit, it would be a kind of "immaculate conception," Greenspan said. It would be the first time significant inflation had ever occurred in such a low-credit environment. Was there an assumption they were making that they hadn't identified? Greenspan asked. The situation was both mystifying and dangerous. It could mean that the economy was out of control and in worse long-term shape than he and they had imagined.

The harsh reality was that they were responsible for the economy, not for whether they got the data right. If they made the wrong choice, there would be no forgiveness.

Greenspan and his team went into crisis mode. It was as if the CIA had suddenly discovered that the Russians had developed a secret weapon that could undermine the American military. The top Fed officials bounced ideas off each other, about inflation psychology and about what factors could possibly be causing an inexplicable surge. The Fed's vast statistics and research operation started cranking out forecasts incorporating some of the conflicting data, using a large computer model that didn't actually forecast well but was still useful in establishing consistent, logical interrelationships among all the elements of the economy. Greenspan also called on a number of specialists at the Fed to ascertain what could possibly be going on that the Fed had not yet detected. None of the explanations satisfied him.

At 9 a.m. on Tuesday, May 18, 1993, Greenspan convened the full committee.

"I think you are all aware that what will be going on here today has very considerable interest outside," he said. The stakes were high. Public and media expectations that the Fed might increase rates were palpable. He urged that no one talk or leak. "Let's be cautious, and I think we can fend off the clever endeavors on the part of a lot of our media friends on the outside who will try to infer how this meeting came out."

He summarized a meeting he had just attended in Switzerland with the world's leading bankers. "There was quite an extraordinary number of subdued people in Europe; there is an underlying fear that that system is continuously eroding," he said. "Even among the Brits a slightly hollow cheerfulness is evolving." The European economies were also under stress.

Turning to the perplexing inflation signs in the U.S. economy, Greenspan worried aloud, long paragraph after long paragraph. The increase in steel prices didn't make any sense. Perhaps the subtle rise of efforts to protect American industry from foreign trade had emboldened the makers of steel to increase prices, he speculated. Whatever the case, Greenspan said that the chances of choking off inflation in these economic circumstances were nearly impossible. "I would say that history tells us the chances of doing that are *zero* short of a 2 or 3 or 4 percent rise in interest rates." He went on, "But I will tell you that at this stage we are pretty much testing the limits of our theoretical knowledge as to what the actual inflationary process is really doing."

One bank president suggested that the recent spate of bad weather might be a factor. Yes, but only in fruit and vegetable prices, others answered.

The members used words like "puzzled," "disturbing," "a mystery," "uncertainty," "uncomfortable" and "very disturbing." One old hand recalled how they had been good at explaining away inflation in the 1970s and then had waited too long and eventually ended up with sky-high inflation. Another asserted that the Clinton health care proposal being drafted under the supervision of Hillary Clinton would be inflationary. One noted that if they increased the fed funds rate, they could kill the Clinton deficit reduction and budget discipline efforts. Greenspan knew only too well. Another spoke of a remote possibility of a new recession.

Wayne Angell said they had to increase rates at this meeting. "The longer we go with this situation, the more we'll have to increase rates and the higher long-term rates will go." He gave a passionate speech and said a move up was essential. "I don't feel very strong about it!" he declared when he finished, mocking his own excited rhetoric. The others laughed.

David Mullins argued that the sooner they raised rates the better. With rising inflation unchallenged by the Fed, the long rates would go up.

After a coffee break, Greenspan told his colleagues that he sensed a pessimism about the ability of the political system to solve problems such as the deficit. He said he had contemplated the overall picture as much as possible. Given all the alternatives, he proposed that they agree to an asymmetric directive to tilt in favor of increasing rates. That directive would be made public in six weeks when summary minutes were released.

"I would have no intention of acting on that directive without full consultation of this committee because it's a very important move." He promised they would have a telephone conference call.

Corrigan said that it was important to leave the chairman maneuvering ability. The directive tilting toward a rate increase, he said, would show that they were watching inflation carefully. "I think institutionally that makes us look better," he said. "In other words, the signal is still there that we weren't insensitive to what was going on."

Mullins agreed, "We can only look good."

Greenspan stepped in. "I think we ought to try first to find a means by which to separate what policy is and then to discuss the issue of how we wish to be perceived." They were different issues, he noted gently. "And from what I can judge, I think most of us would be willing to do that."

As they went around the room, three committee members, including Angell, spoke for an immediate rate increase that day. Mullins, a possible fourth vote to raise, said, "I wouldn't be opposed to moving now." Several others spoke against an immediate increase.

The chairman had a sharply divided committee. He couldn't let it float. Over his years as chairman, he had heard in detail how Bill Miller, Jimmy Carter's first Fed chairman, had let the committee members vote as they wanted, without much guidance or influence from the chairman. He felt such a course was weak and ineffective.

Greenspan reminded them again that they had not moved interest rates up since 1989. "This committee is going to be highly visible," he said. "It's going to be quite important for us to be as close as we can to each other." He emphasized their shared philosophy. "I think it would be very tragic if a group of this extraordinary capability . . . were perceived to be in disarray.

"If it ever gets to the point where this committee is either in disarray or perceived to be in disarray, there is no other institution in this government that can substitute for us.

"It is crucially important that we stand tall as a group and try to find the means by which we can merge our differences," he said. He reminded them that he had made this plea only two or three times in the past. By his reading, the consensus was for a directive that would empower him to raise rates before the next meeting, but he again promised a telephone conference before that happened. He added that he hoped the conference call wouldn't be necessary and that the data that would come in over the next six weeks would be "benevolent"—but the chances of that happening, he said, were "less than 50-50."

He believed he knew how each FOMC member would vote. "I could take the vote myself if I had to, and I bet I'd get it on the nose three times out of four!" He then asked for the vote on his recommendation.

It was 10 to 2 in his favor, with only Angell and Philadelphia Fed president Boehne dissenting.

Six days later, *The Wall Street Journal* scooped everyone with an inside story reporting accurately that "Federal Reserve officials voted to lean toward higher short-term interest rates." *The New York Times* wrote that the Clinton White House "would view such action as a declaration of war. And it would probably direct its heavy artillery at Mr. Greenspan."

Greenspan wanted to avoid war between the Fed and the White House at almost any cost. He spoke with David Gergen, a longtime communications adviser to Republican Presidents Nixon and Reagan, who had just joined the Clinton White House staff in the same capacity. Greenspan had been friends with Gergen for years, part of his Washington network. Gergen urged the chairman to give Clinton a pep talk. Polls showed Clinton's approval rating at 36 percent, the lowest of any new president in his first four months. Greenspan needed to encourage Clinton to continue to push his deficit reduction plan.

On Wednesday, June 9, Greenspan went to the White House to see the president. The chairman was upbeat. The new consumer price index due out the next day was expected to show an increase of only $\frac{1}{10}$ percent, suggesting inflation was in check, he said. They could feel some relief. The long-term economic outlook was the best and most balanced in 40 years, he told the president. He confirmed the authority his committee had given him to raise rates.

"If I have to do something, it will be very mild," he assured Clinton. A small increase would signal to the markets that the Fed was on top of the situation, and it was likely that the long-term rates would come down.

Clinton spoke yet again with such depth and passion about his deficit reduction plan that Greenspan concluded once more that unless Bill Clinton was the best actor ever, the statements were genuine.

On Friday, June 11, White House spokesperson Dee Dee Myers was asked at a White House press conference to comment on the consumer price index.

"Obviously, it's good news," she said. "Producer prices did not go up in May, inflation was zero. We think that that will help keep the long-term interest rates low.

"We're going to continue to press to get the president's economic plan through Congress. We think that the deficit reduction included in that plan has helped bring interest rates down. And we think if we get the plan passed, it will help keep them down."

Hallelujah, Greenspan said to himself when he read Myers's comments. The world had indeed changed. He was amazed that economic lessons had penetrated so deep into the new administration. He had spent a good deal of time explaining to them that the Fed was not working out of a black mystical box. The goals of the Fed and the administration, he had argued to them, were exactly the same—to get maximum sustainable economic growth and to restore the system. He had even offered that if the administration had any better ideas on how to achieve this, he wanted to hear them. But if long-term interest rates started up now, the housing markets would fall apart and the substance of the economic recovery would disappear. It might even be worse than a recession, Greenspan believed.

That's the most interesting op-ed I have read since I have been here, Greenspan remarked to Senator Daniel Patrick Moynihan, the New York Democrat.

Moynihan had written a long, somewhat scholarly article in *The Washington Post* on Sunday, June 6, about Baumol's disease, named for William J. Baumol of New York University. Baumol argued that jobs in which productivity does not increase substantially over time tend to wind up as part of government. Moynihan cited, among these, the police, the postal service, sanitation services and the performing arts as fields that were once entirely private but now depended on government funding because they had not been able to become more productive. To Greenspan's amusement, Moynihan had cited a Mozart string quartet as an example of how some fields cannot become more productive. In 1793, a Mozart quartet required four players, four stringed instruments and roughly 35 minutes to play, and it was just the same in 1993.

As socially useful enterprises ceased to become more productive and lost out in the marketplace, the government took them on in order to keep them going—thus increasing its obligations.

Moynihan and Greenspan worried that Hillary Clinton's new health care initiative might prove the same thing about health care. Greenspan was quite concerned about the health care plan and its possible consequences for the federal deficit. The more entitlements there were, the more spending there would be. He was quite happy to see that Moynihan had some of the same concerns. Greenspan thought Moynihan's article was quite clever, and he felt a kinship with the professorial senator from New York. He was also aware that Moynihan, as chair of the Senate Finance Committee, would be critical to any Clinton deficit reduction program, and he liked to keep in touch.

By July, Greenspan realized that the earlier inflation data had been a false signal.

At the July 7 committee meeting, one of the major topics was the leak of their earlier decision to *The Wall Street Journal* and a more precise leak, with the 10–2 vote, to the television network CNBC. Greenspan noted that the reporting had changed, that reporters were more aggressive and often competent in economics. When he had been President Ford's economic adviser in 1975–76, he told the committee, "You could just feed them pabulum and they pretty much accepted it. That clearly has changed quite dramatically." He demanded discipline. If there were another leak, he would ask for a voluntary sworn statement from everyone in the room that each had not talked with reporters.

"Just remember that there was an organization called the Plumbers," he cautioned, recalling the notorious group in the Nixon White House that tried to plug leaks and eventually became the Watergate burglary team, "and the last thing we need in the Federal Reserve is a 1993 version of same."

Soon several Democratic senators suggested publicly that Clinton drop his five-year deficit target. This was precisely the wrong message, Greenspan felt, and on July 20 he testified before the House Banking Committee with unusual directness, "If you appear to be backing off, I think the markets would react appropriately, negatively."

Clinton's hands were effectively tied. He stuck with his deficit reduction plan, though Bentsen had to bat down an effort from populist advisers to trim it some more.

In August, Clinton's deficit reduction plan passed Congress by the narrowest possible margins, 218 to 216 in the House, and 51 to 50 in the Senate, with Vice President Gore breaking the tie. Not a single Republican had voted for the plan, which cut $500 billion from the deficit over the next four years by increasing taxes and cutting some federal spending. The only real Republican support had come from Greenspan.

In September, Greenspan was huddled with the latest government statistics. He settled into the newest monthly 11-page Commerce Department report called "Current Industrial Reports, Manufacturers' Shipments, Inventories, and Orders." Chock-full of tables and charts, it was released September 2, but the chairman usually received the data a day or so early.

New orders for manufactured goods were down 2.1 percent for July, the most recent month for which data were available. Poring over columns of figures, Greenspan noticed two big numbers, dramatic *increases* from the previous July. Computer and office equipment orders up 21.6 percent. Communications equipment up 19.8 percent. Except for a few explainable aberrations in shipbuilding and tanks (up 461 percent), these were the biggest numbers among hundreds of measured new orders. He had noticed the same pattern for months. That meant businesses and their plant managers were spending billions of dollars more for high-technology equipment. Why?

He knew from his business days in New York that such expenditure bursts normally occurred at the beginning of an economic recovery. But the United States was more than two years into its recovery, a time when such capital expenditures would normally be going down. These increases would not be made month after month unless something was happening, unless the businesses were getting significant returns from the large investments or perceived they soon would. But what was happening?

From his study of Albert Einstein's theories, Greenspan knew the importance of finding discrepancies—light bending, time slowing, light being both a wave and a particle.

It looked as though the discrepancy might be more productivity growth—more output per hour for workers. But that was only a theory, and Greenspan knew it could dissolve with the next month's statistics.

He examined the Labor Department unemployment statistics out September 3. For the latest month, August, the unemployment rate was down to 6.7 percent. In the last year nearly 2 million more people had joined the workforce, and they were working a half hour more a week when compared with figures from the 1990–91 recession.

Next he examined the Labor Department's productivity statistics, which measured the changes in output per hour for the second quarter of 1993. Released September 9, the department's report showed that productivity had decreased by 1 percent in the business sector during the second quarter of 1993—the same rate of decline as the first quarter.

Something was in error. More high-technology investment, more workers, more hours and *less* productivity? Prices weren't rising that much, and business profits were increasing. A business could not hold prices relatively stable, have a less efficient workforce and make more money. It was mathematically impossible.

At the FOMC on September 23, Greenspan said that the interest rate policy question was pretty easy. They didn't need to raise or lower rates. Everyone agreed. But something else was bothering him—the very statistical foundation for their decisions.

"There is something wrong with the numbers we are looking at," he said.

"Now, I don't know what is going on in the statistical system, but I'm almost certain that out in the real world in an economy that is growing, the thought that we are having declining productivity just doesn't square with my understanding of the real world."

He continued to pick apart the data. "Something is wrong with the data system . . . the numbers just don't square."

Greenspan finally let the matter rest, and the FOMC voted unanimously to keep interest rates the same. But he was sure there was a missing link. The "Survey of Current Business" from the Bureau of Labor Statistics, one of his favorite monthly publications, indicated that business inventories were shrinking significantly while the economy was growing, suggesting that the new computer technology was allowing just-in-time orders. Instead of stocking products weeks or months in advance, businesses could keep detailed track of what was needed and order within days. In addition, competitive pressures were also forcing quality control.

At the November 16 FOMC meeting, Greenspan said, "I think the argument has to be that the missing link in all of this is the inventory patterns." The result was better-quality products. "The finding of fault in a particular product or a particular element in the fabrication process means that it can get fixed relatively quickly. In other words, you don't have two months' worth of widgets which are slightly off. If it's just-in-time, you have three days. So you don't lose the quality and you don't lose the production."

But much of this argument was theoretical and tentative, he knew. He was noticing discrepancies, but he was a long way from explaining what they meant, if anything.

Just before Christmas, on Tuesday, December 21, the FOMC met again. Angell and Lindsey wanted to raise rates at once, and several bank presidents were leaning that way. David Mullins noted that the unemployment rate had dropped over 1 percent in the last 18 months, and overall economic growth had been a very high 5 percent in the last three months.

"In short," he said, "the world has changed. The fed funds rate has not changed." He said he did not favor raising the rate right away, but it needed to go up at some point in the near future.

Greenspan remarked how extraordinary it was that a full 2 percent of the economic growth was coming just from motor vehicle sales. Still, the recovery was accelerating and had some legs. "All this leads me to conclude, as a number of you have concluded, that the days of accommodation have got to be over."

Angell passed Mullins a note: "We've won."

Greenspan said that sometime over the next year they would probably have to raise rates. "When do we begin? I don't see any material reason to begin today." He recommended an unchanged policy and won 10 to 2, with Angell and Lindsey dissenting.

"We have one additional item on the agenda," Greenspan said after the vote. For years, the FOMC meetings had been secretly tape-recorded and a verbatim transcript kept. The existence of the transcripts had been kept secret not only from the public, but from the Congress and even some of the FOMC members. Greenspan maintained he had not learned about it until a year before. He had disclosed the existence of the system and the transcripts in testimony to the House Banking Committee two months earlier, as the members knew. Committee chairman Henry B. Gonzalez, an old-style Texas populist Democrat, had launched a crusade to get the tapes.

The FOMC had spent hours discussing the matter, including an hour-and-a-half conference call of the FOMC on October 15. Gonzalez now wanted the transcript and tape of that discussion. He was alleging that the FOMC had conspired to hide the tapes.

"There is deep-seated suspicion of this institution," Greenspan said. "It's regrettable, but I guess it comes with the turf." The matter would not be put to rest very quickly. He proposed that they allow a senior staffer from the Gonzalez committee to come to the Fed and listen to the full tape of their October 15 discussion. He had listened to it himself, and there was no conspiracy. "There are a few sentences which, out of context, could very readily be employed to raise an issue," he said. He wanted to make sure that a senior Republican staffer also attended the session so nothing would be taken grossly out of context.

Greenspan was not entirely comfortable with this idea. It could set a bad precedent. But he knew that failure to disclose that session could fuel efforts to force out all the tapes and parade all of their debates and remarks before the public. The only antidote was full disclosure of this tape to prove they were hiding nothing.

After much discussion, the members agreed. The House Banking Committee staffers listened to the tape, and the issue subsided. The Fed agreed to release a lightly edited transcript of each year's FOMC meetings five years after they occurred.

Soon the chairman came to see that providing the public and the markets with more information about the Fed and its interest rate decisions not only brought more attention and timely focus on their work, it also gave him more power. The Fed had always been viewed as a temple of important secrets. Revealing some of them drew the press and others in, which in turn magnified the importance of the Fed's decisions. As interest rates became more closely monitored, they also became more important as a critical indicator of the state of the economy to an increasing number of Americans.

8

SOME SUBTLE and some less subtle signs of a major expansion in the economy became apparent to Greenspan in early 1994. The banks had been saved. Credit was easing, and businesses could get loans. The system had been "liquefied," as he liked to say. High inflation could not be detected, but he suspected it was around the corner. He was almost sure.

For years, there had been discussions in the media and elsewhere of the possibility that the Fed could execute a so-called soft landing, taking preemptive action to increase interest rates months before actual inflation showed up. This could take the top off the coming boom, moderate and stabilize the economy and prevent inflation—and a recession.

Greenspan followed the discussion of this theory scrupulously. There was no doubt that the raising or lowering of interest rates worked with a lag, having an impact on the economy as much as a year or more later. Milton Friedman, the Nobel Prize–winning economist, had taken the extreme position that the Fed was always 180 degrees wrong—meaning that they raised rates too late, when the economy had already turned down, or they lowered rates when the economy had already turned back up. He argued that the average lag was about half a business cycle.

Greenspan thought Friedman wasn't exactly right, but there was persuasive evidence that the Fed needed to be ahead of the game. Rates would have to be increased in anticipation of actual inflation. But when? And by how much? Effective early action could prolong the expansion. Eliminating the wild highs could eliminate the lows. Not only would a preemptive soft landing be good for the economy, it would eliminate some of the social unrest that accompanied a recession. But this was all theory, yet untested. Earlier efforts at a soft landing had failed, including the Fed's effort in 1988.

Greenspan was willing to give it a try. If the soft landing succeeded, he could see no downsides for the economy. Normally *any* action, he believed, had a price or a downside, even if it succeeded. This did not. But if they failed, they might hamper or even strangle the economic recovery—and that was a huge risk. Because it was untested and because it was not a concept rooted in economic theory, Greenspan recognized that it was very risky. To him, it was like saying, Let's jump out of this 60-story building and land on our feet.

On January 21, 1994, Greenspan went to the White House to meet with President Clinton and his economic advisers to warn them that rate increases were likely. "We've got a dilemma, and you should understand," the chairman said. "We haven't made a decision, but the choices are, we sit and wait and then likely we'll have to raise short-term interest rates more. Or we could take some small increases now."

"Obviously," the president said, "I want to keep interest rates low, but I understand what you may have to do."

Treasury Secretary Bentsen saw that the president was reluctant. Clinton was swallowing about as hard as he could.

"We've been flat so long," Greenspan said, referring to some 15 months of a 3 percent fed funds rate. "We almost have to show that we can do something, that we're willing to move."

"Wait a minute!" Vice President Gore interjected. "What about the possibility that you introduce uncertainty?" Historically, the Fed moved in a series of stair-step increases. Gore noted that in 1988–89 the fed funds increases had gone from about 6½ percent up to nearly 10 percent in a dozen small moves. With that expectation in the market, long-term rates could be driven back up, the opposite of a soft landing.

It was an interesting point, Greenspan said, but the long-term rates were high because of the inflation expectation, which the administration was addressing with their deficit reduction plan. Even if long-term rates went up initially, he did not think they would stay up.

Clinton and his advisers now had to face what potentially could be a profound change in their relations with Greenspan. Politics was often a matter of choosing sides. Which side was Greenspan on?

For that matter, it was difficult to determine exactly which side Clinton was on. The president's economic policies were difficult to label. He tended to talk liberal, especially as he pushed for his wife's health care reform, which would extend universal health care insurance to more than 40 million Americans. But his actions so far had been a blend. The term Clinton liked was "New Democrat," meaning someone who was pro-business but concerned as well with the middle class and the poor. But his policies also included the more visible deficit reduction, bond market, free-trade Eisenhower Republicanism that was more in tune with Greenspan than Clinton wanted to acknowledge.

The blend was embodied in Robert E. Rubin, the former head of Goldman, Sachs & Co., the premier New York City investment banking firm, who was director of the White House National Economic Council, the administration's coordinator of economic policy.

Rubin, a slight man with soft eyes and a gentle, at times even shy, manner, was fabulously wealthy, but he wore inexpensive suits and could be taken for a staffer. Forged in the crucible of the nerve-racking bond arbitrage market on Wall Street, the 55-year-old Rubin had advised the president to hold Greenspan even closer. Perhaps one of the most careful listeners on the planet, Rubin had built a strong relationship with Clinton, and he reinforced Greenspan's and Bentsen's arguments that the first order of economic business had to be deficit reduction. Rubin had also argued successfully to the president that the administration would topple itself if it were perceived to be anti-business and anti–Wall Street. One result had been that the administration was widely seen to have adopted a deficit reduction plan that was dependent on the financial markets.

Like Greenspan, Rubin believed nothing could be known for certain—that everything was "probabilistic," as he put it. No matter how good your information or judgment might be, you can always turn out to be wrong. He liked to offer the example of someone from another firm who had called him at Goldman Sachs, saying that he'd found a takeover deal that couldn't go wrong.

I'm buying enormous amounts of stock in the company that's being bought out, the banker said.

I think you're right, Rubin said. I think this is very good, but there's nothing that can't go wrong and everything is "probabilistic."

No, the other banker said. We can't lose on this one.

Rubin bought tons of the same stock, but not so much that any potential losses would sink his firm. The other banker was not quite so careful. When the situation ultimately did go bad, Rubin lost a great deal of money for Goldman but stayed at his firm for 20 more years and eventually ran it. The other banker lost his job. Since then, Rubin often reminded people that even the best-looking deals could go wrong on the basis of things that you could not anticipate. It was necessary to take risks, but it was important to recognize your fallibility.

With interest rate hikes coming, Rubin urged Clinton to hold off on any public criticism of the Fed. First, he said, criticism would not be effective. The Fed considered itself almost religiously independent, and any effort to influence it could be counterproductive. The Fed wouldn't listen, so short-term rates would stay the same. The financial markets *would* listen, and they would see such criticism as motivated by politics. If the markets grew distrustful of the administration's motives, long-term rates would go up. If the administration refrained from criticizing the Fed, it would enhance the administration's and the Fed's credibility.

Bentsen argued to the president that it was better for the Fed to move now, in 1994. Given the one-year lag in the impact, any economic slowdown would occur in 1995, with a pickup in 1996. If the Fed waited and raised rates in 1995, the slowdown would be in— Before Bentsen could get "1996" out of his mouth, the president had grasped the point.

Greenspan was certain that if they did not raise rates, history and experience both dictated that at some point in 1995–96 there would be a recession. That Clinton would be running for reelection in 1996 obviously made it easier for Greenspan to sell an attempted soft landing. He would be taking economic growth from 1994— lopping off the top of an expected boom of excessive growth—and saving it for 1995 and 1996. That is, if it worked. He also wanted to send a message to the markets that the Fed would never again allow the runaway inflation of the 1970s.

Making it work had a lot to do with timing, which in turn had to do with economic forecasting, an imprecise science that did not approach the mathematical certainty Greenspan loved. There was no alternative to forecasting, which at least incorporated some data. It wasn't guessing or fortune-telling, but the forecasters, including himself, were going to be wrong some of the time.

On January 31, Greenspan appeared before the Joint Economic Committee of the Senate and House. He testified that Fed interest rate policy "must not overstay accommodation" and "short-term interest rates are abnormally low." Unless there was a prolonged weakening of the economy, he said, "We will need to move them to a more neutral stance." Though it was oblique and somewhat veiled, Greenspan believed his testimony made it clear that interest rate increases were coming. It had been five years since any rate increase, and he did not want the Congress, the public or the markets to be surprised. The more he thought about it, the more he believed he was beating the drums quite loudly, sounding a warning. But there was little reaction. Where's the parade? he wondered. It was remarkable. He felt as if he were walking around, banging on a pot, "Hey, you know, we're going to raise rates!" Still, there was little reaction.

The FOMC met on the morning of Friday, February 4.

As he listened to the reports of economic conditions in the various Fed districts, Greenspan saw his colleagues all over the place. Because they hadn't moved rates in a long time, it was going to take longer to arrive at consensus. He didn't have a lot of data to hang his conclusion on.

"We are at the point where we finally have to start moving," he said. "We haven't raised interest rates in five years, which is in itself almost unimaginable.

"The presumption that inflation is quiescent is getting to be a slightly shabby notion," he went on, concluding, "I would put on the table my preference that at this meeting we move up ¼ percent."

One bank president voiced his preference for a ½ percent increase.

Greenspan replied that he had thought about that. "But I think it may be very helpful to have anticipations in the market now that we are going to move rates higher because it will subdue speculation in the stock market; at this particular stage, having expectations hanging in the market that we may move again, and move reasonably soon, could have a very useful effect." Simply put, "If we have the capability of having a sword of Damocles over the market, we can prevent it from running away."

Another bank president said that he too had a mild preference for ½ percent.

"Well," Greenspan responded, "I've been around a long time watching markets behave, and I will tell you that if we do ½ percent today, we have a very high probability of cracking these markets. I think that would be a very unwise procedure. . . . To go more than ¼ percent at this point I think would be a bad mistake." The announcement of a rate increase was going to be a very big move. "Look," he said, "the stock market is at an elevated level at this stage by any measure we know of." The Dow was nearly at 4000, a record high.

Greenspan could see that a caucus favoring ½ percent had formed as more members spoke. Coming into the meeting, he had thought he might have to argue hard to get any kind of rate increase. He had not had the time to canvass the whole committee and line up the votes. He was now defending ¼ percent as enough, something he had not expected. He was going to have to reshuffle the deck very quickly. Control seemed to be slipping away.

"You know," Greenspan finally said, "I rarely feel strongly about an issue, and I very rarely sort of press this committee.

"Were we to go the ½ percent with the announcement effect and the shock effect, I am telling you that these markets will not hold still." Then, pulling out all the stops, he said, "I've been in the economic forecasting business since 1948, and I've been on Wall Street since 1948, and I am telling you I have a pain in the pit of my stomach." He noted that in the past he had listened to his instincts and that they had been right.

This pain in the stomach was a physical awareness Greenspan had experienced many times. He felt he had a deeper understanding of the issue—a whole body of knowledge in his head and a whole value system—than he was capable of stating at that moment. If he was about to say something that wasn't right, he would feel it before he was intellectually aware of the problem. It was this physical feeling, this sense in the stomach, that he believed kept him from making dangerous or absurd statements that might appear on the front page of the newspapers. At times, he found his body sensed danger before his head. As he walked down the street there would be an approaching car, and his body knew to stay out of its way before his head.

"I am telling you," the chairman continued, "and I've seen these markets, this is not the time to do this. . . . *I really request that we not do this.*"

In the near future they could do a couple of ½-point jumps when the markets were acclimated to what was happening, he said. And he wasn't through.

"I also would be concerned if this committee were not in concert because at this stage we as a committee are going to have to do things which the rest of the world is not going to like. . . . If we are perceived to be split on an issue as significant as this, I think we're risking some very serious problems for this organization."

Two of the bank presidents challenged the chairman, asking for assurance, as a kind of compromise, that the committee would convene a telephone conference call before the next scheduled meeting. The implication was that the FOMC could then raise the rate another ¼ percent.

Greenspan bristled. "I've been chairman of this committee now for over six years. I hope I have enough credibility to know when a telephone call is appropriate."

"But there will be a phone call?" Lindsey insisted.

"Yes," Greenspan replied.

"I think it's demeaning to the process," said William McDonough, the New York Fed president who had taken Corrigan's place, "to the nature of this committee, to say to the chairman, 'I'll vote for what you want, but we've got to have a phone call.'"

Greenspan went all the way. "I don't request often that we try to stay together," he said. "As I listened these last two days, I didn't sense any significant difference within the committee on the purpose and the goals of what we're doing. I would request that, if we can, we act unanimously. It is a very potent message out in the various communities with which we deal if we stand together. If we are going to get a split in the vote, I think it will create a problem for us, and I don't know how it will play out. I rarely ask this, as you know." He realized he was asking for nothing less than a vote of confidence. He requested a call of the roll on his proposed ¼ percent increase.

John LaWare, a Reagan appointee on the board, found the chairman's warning sobering—it was one he would remember for years.

The vote in favor was unanimous.

"I thank you for that," Greenspan told the committee. He believed it was the first time he had ever been so openly grateful to the committee. "I think in retrospect when we're looking back at what we're doing over the next year, we'll find that it was the right decision."

They agreed that, for the first time in the history of the Fed, they would publicly announce a fed funds rate increase. No more covert moves subject to misinterpretation. Greenspan had a sense that they had created unnecessary secrets, and it was better to be up front with the public and the markets.

Later that day, when the ¼ percent rate hike was announced, the Dow Jones dropped nearly 100 points to 3871. It was the largest single-day loss in two years.

. . .

Three weeks later, during a February 28 FOMC conference call, Greenspan expressed pride in their earlier decision. "I think we partially broke the back of an emerging speculation in equities," he said, noting they also had pricked a bubble in the bond market.

On March 22, the committee voted to raise rates another ¼ percent, then voted for another ¼ percent increase on April 18.

At the May 17 committee meeting, Greenspan once more addressed what he called "the financial bubble," noting that the economy was probably stronger than they all suspected.

"I think there's still a lot of bubble around; we have not completely eliminated it. Nonetheless, we have the capability I would say at this stage to move more strongly than we usually do without the risk of cracking the system.

"The chances of our breaking the back of the economy at this point," he said, "have to be pretty low." He recommended a ½ percent increase and received unanimous support.

Personally, Greenspan was less than confident. To his knowledge, a soft landing had never been carried out successfully. He retained the image of jumping out a 60-story building, hoping to land on their feet. In any case, he felt they were grappling—or plummeting—through a fog.

At the White House, the president was increasingly restless. Was this necessary? Was Greenspan going too far? Did he know what he was doing?

Rubin and Bentsen insisted everything was okay.

Clinton grew angrier and angrier. When he blew up about rising interest rates, as he frequently did, the members of his economic team let him blow off steam and then urged him to continue to confine his distress to the privacy of the Oval Office. Any reasonable Fed was going to have to pull the foot off the accelerator, they told him. The low fed funds rate had been pumping up the economy, so interest rates were going to have to go up to cool things off. All the economic models built on years of history showed there was a limit to how high growth could go without triggering inflation. To complicate matters, the economists believed—and recent American economic history showed—that there was a level of so-called full employment. There was a limit on how low the unemployment rate could go without triggering inflation, and it was thought that the range was 6 to 7 percent. This lower limit was called the NAIRU—the non-accelerating inflation rate of unemployment. The unemployment rate had started the year above 6 percent and was heading down.

Even Rubin insisted that there was an optimum full employment rate of growth.

The president was skeptical and even outraged. So the problems were too much economic growth and too many people working! It was ridiculous, he seethed.

Rubin believed that the president had chosen correctly with an economic plan of deficit reduction and fiscal discipline. As a Democrat, Clinton was going to have more difficulty getting credibility from the business community and Wall Street than a Republican. There were lingering reservations about tax-and-spend Democrats, and the key was to build confidence, stick to the plan. It would take time, because during the last 12 years of Republican administrations there had been little fiscal discipline. In the overall picture, the Fed's role was to help create that discipline. The president had to let Greenspan do that job.

Once, when Greenspan had an appointment to see the president, Clinton and his economic team were assembled in the Oval Office. As they waited for the chairman to arrive, the president had launched into a comedic imitation of the chairman. Speaking in a gloomy, deep voice, he mimicked Greenspan drumming on inflation. Inflation! Inflation was all-important. Inflation was the center of the universe. Inflation! Inflation! It was a pretty good caricature, and his advisers were in stitches. One checked nervously to make sure the soundproof Oval Office doors were shut tight so the chairman wouldn't hear.

Now there were no jokes coming out of the Oval Office about Greenspan.

Worse, the bond market had gone to hell. The long-term rates were shooting up, nullifying the gains from the 1993 deficit reduction plan. Where was the payoff? the president wanted to know.

Mortimer B. Zuckerman, the wealthy real estate entrepreneur and the owner and editor in chief of *U.S. News & World Report*, launched a campaign against Greenspan's rate increases as unnecessarily choking the economy. In his magazine column, Zuckerman kept up a week-by-week drumbeat that mocked phantom "inflationary expectations" and Greenspan's "Delphic utterances." In Zuckerman's view, the Fed chairman had failed "to understand that huge productivity and efficiency gains have restructured the U.S. economy and fundamentally transformed the prospects for inflation."

After a number of these critical columns, Zuckerman ran into Greenspan.

"What do you know about monetary policy that I don't?" Greenspan asked disparagingly.

Zuckerman said that he regularly talked with people in the real economy in a wide range of businesses—largely his own.

How many do you think I speak to? Greenspan inquired, noting the organized effort throughout the Fed's 12 districts to speak with hundreds of sources of information.

Zuckerman invited Greenspan to come speak to the *U.S. News* editorial board. He found Greenspan's talk there the single most brilliant exposition of the economy that he had ever heard—but continued to pound on him nevertheless.

9

_____

Get some Democrats on the Fed, President Clinton instructed his economic advisers. The entire board was made up of Reagan and Bush appointees. But now board vice chairman David Mullins was resigning to go make money, and Governor Angell's term had expired. Clinton could name two governors to the seven-member board, his first Fed appointments. With interest rates rising, he wanted Treasury and the White House staff to move fast. The instructions weren't quite "Sink Greenspan," but the president wanted some counterweight on the Fed.

The search began for two academic economists who were Democrats and who would be at least sympathetic to Clinton's overall economic policies.

Rubin sought out Alan Blinder, the deputy on the president's Council of Economic Advisers, one of his allies in the White House.

How about being the Fed vice chairman? Rubin asked.

A little over a year earlier, Blinder, who was the pride of Princeton's Economics Department and author of numerous economics books admired for their scholarship and clarity, had given President-elect Clinton what Rubin saw as a critical briefing on the economy. Blinder, 48, a tall, thin, balding academic with thick glasses, had the uneasy erudition of many professors, but he also had a sense of humor that demonstrated he knew how dry and pedantic economics could be. In a lecture loaded with charts and economic theory, Blinder had argued that an aggressive deficit reduction plan might lower long-term interest rates—the key to building a strong economy—and raise the standard of living for everyone. As the implications of Blinder's words dawned on Clinton, the president-elect turned red and, in a critical moment of self-awareness, declared: "You mean to tell me that the success of the program and my reelection hinges on the Federal Reserve and a bunch of fucking bond traders?" The uncomfortable answer was yes.

Blinder kept one foot in the traditional mainstream liberalism that looked out for those on the bottom of the economic ladder, but he was a Democrat who didn't use the class-warfare rhetoric Rubin detested. In Rubin's view, Blinder was just about the right mix.

Blinder had earlier declined appointment as one of the Fed's seven governors, but now he thought hard about Rubin's offer. The job at the Fed meant a step up in the Washington pecking order. A Fed governor was C list, anonymous politically and socially, which was about where Blinder was with his current White House position. Vice chairman of the Fed would put him on the B list. As he thought about whether to take the job, Blinder admitted to himself that he had a human foible, shared by many in Washington—status.

Blinder figured that the vice chairmanship would offer him a seat at the table and a hand in the great interest rate game. Part of his job at the Council of Economic Advisers had been to phone Greenspan a day in advance of the release of the various Commerce and Labor Department economic statistics. He marveled at how Greenspan wallowed in the numbers, frequently asking questions that sent him deep into the charts. Greenspan and he would be number one and two at one of the most important arms of the most important government in the world. After about a day, Blinder told Rubin yes.

When Greenspan got word that Blinder would be coming as the new vice chairman, he asked Mullins to conduct a due diligence review, to check out Blinder's previous publications and statements. Just so we have no surprises, the chairman said.

Mullins dug into columns that Blinder had written for *Business-Week*, old articles and books. Blinder had criticized Volcker for clamping down too hard on inflation, declaring at one point that the American economy was not like a Vietnamese hamlet that must be destroyed in order to be saved. In his 1987 book, *Hard Heads, Soft Hearts*, Blinder wrote that there was too much hysteria about the evils of inflation. Inflation was more like a head cold than a serious disease, and you don't prescribe a lobotomy for a head cold.

Several days later, Mullins, looking worried, came to see Greenspan.

"It's not perfect," he said.

Greenspan grimaced.

"Don't worry," Mullins said, "it's not like he's a Communist or anything. It's just in his early publications he's noticeably soft on inflation." He provided chapter and verse.

Greenspan quipped, "I would have preferred he were a Communist."

Before he joined the Fed, Blinder had several encouraging conversations with the chairman. Greenspan indicated that the board was shorthanded, needed help and would welcome Blinder. The chairman provided him with a very frank assessment of the strengths and weaknesses of the various other board members.

In the period after his nomination, Blinder followed his own press clippings carefully. The initial press coverage was flattering. Though a piece in *The New York Times* characterized Blinder as an inflation dove who "does not see inflation as a problem," most of the stories, like the Associated Press piece on the day of his Senate confirmation, noted that the appointment "could put him in line" to succeed Greenspan as chairman. Other stories dubbed Blinder Greenspan's "likely successor," and one story in *Investor's Business Daily* included a brash prediction from the chief economist at a large Wall Street firm: "A new coalition will form around Blinder. I think this is the beginning of the end for Greenspan." Because Blinder was the first Democratic appointee to the Fed in more than 12 years, the press simply assumed that Blinder would vie for the chairmanship with the Republican Greenspan, whose term was set to expire in March of 1996.

Blinder knew that no vice chairman had ever ascended to the chairmanship. When the press began to talk about him as Greenspan's heir, Blinder said little to fan the flames, but he also made little effort to extinguish them. He said nothing about the press coverage to Greenspan, and the chairman, who had been following the news reports, did not raise the subject.

On the morning of June 27, the day after his official confirmation in the Senate, Blinder and his wife, Madeline, arrived at the Fed building on Constitution Avenue. Greenspan swore Blinder in as vice chairman, and photographers snapped pictures of the new Fed leadership team. After the ceremony ended, the chairman said he had arranged for two governors and some staff to take Blinder to lunch—and then walked out the door. Good-bye.

Blinder wasn't sure what to make of it all, but his wife told him that the reception seemed ominously cold. On day one, minute one, the chairman was out the door as soon as he could be. What could it mean?

Several days before Blinder's second FOMC meeting on August 16, Greenspan's secretary called him to say that the chairman was coming over to see him.

Greenspan appeared promptly. "This thing," the chairman said, referring to the overall economy, "is heating up." He made it clear that he wanted to raise rates ½ percent at the next meeting.

Blinder said that he thought ¼ percent would be sufficient. That was the standard Fed increase, and Blinder saw no need for more, given that the Fed had already raised rates four times since the beginning of the year.

Greenspan disagreed. The economy was hot. The chairman indicated, in no uncertain terms, that more than the normal increase was required.

Blinder was less concerned about individual rate increases than he was about where the Fed would wind up in this series of increases. Where was this going? How much was enough? What would tell them when to stop? Blinder was in favor of keeping inflation low, but he was worried that the Fed might be headed toward overkill, a crash instead of a soft landing.

The FOMC didn't like to accompany its rate decisions with any clear wording, Blinder knew. Zero wording—implying that the rate decision could speak entirely for itself—was beautiful in the world of the Fed. But Blinder thought that the Fed needed to explain itself if it were going to raise rates by ½ percent. He asked Greenspan, If the ½-percent raise were inevitable, would it be possible to issue a statement declaring that the Fed would go to the sidelines after the rate hike, indicating that no immediate additional rate increases would be forthcoming?

Greenspan said a statement would be possible.

Blinder said he thought a statement would be essential if the entire committee were going to vote for a ½ percent hike.

After about 15 minutes of discussion, Greenspan agreed and left. He had promised Blinder a statement of some kind, and Blinder in turn gave the chairman his vote.

Greenspan knew that Blinder had essentially issued an ultimatum. Ultimatums were not useful around the Fed.

. . .

The second Clinton nominee to the Fed board was Janet Yellen, 47, a gray-haired Yale Ph.D. who had taught economics at Harvard and the University of California at Berkeley. She had worked at the Fed in the 1970s as an economist, written extensively and was currently a professor at Berkeley's business school. Yellen was a strong advocate for low unemployment, which she believed was good for the country and better than any possible government policy for the disadvantaged. She was sworn in several days before the August 16 FOMC meeting.

At the meeting, Greenspan, the old members and Blinder and Yellen gathered in the second-floor meeting room at the Fed. For more than an hour, Greenspan led a discussion on the state of the economy. Bank presidents and governors talked about the economic performance they saw, ranging from hot to middling to even somewhat cold—reflecting the sometimes wide variation of economic activity in different geographical areas. Blinder said that he thought they could allow unemployment to get lower without inflation. "I'd just like to say I don't think 6.3 percent unemployment should be the FOMC's aspiration level," he said. "I have a strong feeling that we ought to be shooting for a lower unemployment rate than that."

Yellen said she agreed and thought it possible to "even shave a few tenths more off the unemployment rate without risking significantly a pickup in inflation."

"Let me get started," Greenspan said after everybody had spoken. As he launched into his customary summation of the economy, the chairman again indicated his strong distrust of the economic growth numbers that the committee had before them. Recent numbers suggested that productivity—the number of goods a worker produces per hour—was down, and Greenspan still didn't believe it. "I find utterly noncredible the probability that, in the real world, productivity declined," he said. Profits were up, but prices weren't. Increased productivity was, in Greenspan's mind, the only mathematically possible way to account for the increased profits that the Fed district bank presidents were reporting.

"A statistic we don't talk about very often," Greenspan added, ". . . is the extraordinary rise in net business formation." New business formation had taken a "fairly sharp upswing," an event that is not consistent with an economy that is in its final and declining stages. A sharp upswing in business formation showed that the momentums in the economy were hardly slowing, as some had argued.

The situation as a whole made Greenspan nervous. "This stuff is really beginning to move," he said.

"I think one has to conclude, as far as policy is concerned, that another upward notch in rates is clearly called for at some point," he said. The voluminous staff report on the economy, prepared for each committee meeting, estimated that the Fed would eventually have to raise rates a full percentage point. Greenspan said that he didn't know if this was the right number, but ½ point "may be enough if we do it now." If they moved ½ percent now, the chairman said, the chances were better than 50–50 that they would not have to increase rates any further before the end of the year.

"I'm a little concerned that ¼ a point would merely raise the issue of when the other shoe is going to drop," Greenspan continued. He offered his personal assessment of the market reaction to a ½-point raise: "My own view—I'm being a little more detailed than I usually am, so I hope people will excuse me in this respect—is that it's very important if we were to do ½ a point, that we not give the impression that somehow we anticipate major accelerations and this is just the beginning of a long series of ½ percent increases. . . . I think we have to be very careful to avoid giving that impression. The only realistic way we can avoid that is to issue some type of statement." The statement could declare the Fed's "intention to hold for a while without tying our hands, which we cannot do."

Pleased that Greenspan was living up to his agreement, Blinder thought there was now a fighting chance that this might be the last needed rate increase.

"The more I think about that as a potential sort of policy package, the less I like all the other alternatives," the chairman concluded.

"I just want to take two minutes to emphasize that it really is a package," Blinder said shortly after the chairman had finished. "So with such a strong statement, I not only support but support enthusiastically the suggestion of the chairman." Just in case his point was missed, he added, "Without it, I would not."

Greenspan read a draft of a proposed statement, which stated vaguely that the Fed expected the rate hike to be sufficient "at least for a time." That could mean months or to the end of the year, but the chairman knew that it could also mean precisely 4 minutes and 37 seconds—or less. In other words, the statement meant almost nothing.

Greenspan called for the votes on the ½ percent increase, to be accompanied by the statement.

Yellen was quite surprised. Despite the on-one-hand, on-the-other-hand quality of some of the discussion and the apparent differences among some of the members, it was clearly a committee that was not going to live with higher inflation and had become incredibly aggressive in raising the fed funds rate. She had heard reliably that the rate increases did not make the president's day—and here she was, a new Clinton appointee at her first FOMC meeting, being asked to vote for a ½ percent increase. There were already 11 votes for the chairman's proposal. As the junior member, she was the last to cast her vote.

Yes, she said, making it unanimous. The increase might help them buy a longer expansion, she reasoned.

After the meeting, Greenspan complimented Blinder and told him that he had earned his pay.

The interest rate hike caused rallies in the stock and bond markets, where traders saw the Fed's half-point hike as a strong offensive against inflation. It angered some congressional Democrats and others who believed that the rate hike risked sending the economy into a severe downturn.

Nearly all of the coverage in the media focused on the ½ percent hike, with very little mention of the Fed's statement regarding its intention "at least for a time" to avoid any further moves.

A confrontation had been avoided. Blinder felt it was a good outcome, but he also realized that Greenspan was in total control.

Less than two weeks later, most of the FOMC members attended the Kansas City Federal Reserve's annual retreat in Jackson Hole, Wyoming. Held at the foot of the Grand Teton mountains, the conference offered much needed relief from Washington, D.C.'s August swamp weather. Central bankers from around the world, in addition to academic economists, policy makers and journalists, attended seminars in the morning and then enjoyed outdoor activities in the afternoon.

The overall theme of the gathering was "Reducing Unemployment," and Blinder was asked to give some concluding remarks at the end of the conference on Saturday, August 27.

He had spoken at the Jackson Hole conference before, as an academic unbound by the customs and responsibilities of working at the Fed. He made it clear at the outset of his 20-minute speech that he understood the difference: "It is quite clear that in my new job, my role is to say nothing—and certainly not to say anything interesting," he joked.

In a further attempt to be funny, Blinder quipped that he was happy to see the others in attendance were seriously talking about reducing unemployment, as opposed to increasing it. Fed-induced recessions to control economic growth and avoid inflation had traditionally sent unemployment skyrocketing. Not everybody laughed.

Blinder then argued that the Fed might be too focused on preserving price stability and fighting inflation. Shouldn't the Fed embrace with equal intensity the goal of maximum employment, a goal written explicitly into the most recent law governing the Fed? "The central bank *does* have a role in reducing unemployment," he said.

The next day, Blinder was dismayed to read the *New York Times* story on page 26, which stated that in his speech he "publicly broke ranks with most of his colleagues" and that his comments "revealed an intellectual split" within the Fed. On Monday, August 29, the *Times* pounced again with a business section front-page story headlined "A Split Over Fed's Role; Clashes Seen After Vice Chairman Says Job Creation Should Also Be a Policy Goal." The story drew a sharp contrast between Blinder and Greenspan, who had recently reaffirmed his view that inflation fighting was the primary goal of the Fed.

As Blinder saw it, he'd been asked to deliver the summation speech at a seminar called "Reducing Unemployment." What else was he supposed to talk about?

The Full Employment and Balanced Growth Act of 1978, called the Humphrey-Hawkins Act after its legislative sponsors, mandated that the Fed do its best to achieve maximum employment, and Blinder thought he had merely drawn attention to that responsibility. A *New York Times* story disagreed, noting that emphasizing jobs over inflation was like "sticking needles in the eyes of central bankers."

Greenspan went on vacation without commenting, leaving Blinder to twist in media winds, which eventually dubbed the situation "L'affaire Blinder." A three-inch stack of stories about a rift at the Fed followed. *Newsweek* columnist Robert J. Samuelson declared that Blinder was not only soft on inflation, a mortal sin in central banking, but that he also lacked "the moral or intellectual qualities needed to lead the Fed."

A simple word or sentence to key Fed reporters from the chairman, even off the record, noting that the whole matter was part of a standard policy debate could have ended the furor, Blinder believed. He interpreted Greenspan's silence as intentional. For one reason or another, Greenspan wanted to let him twist.

Yet Blinder did not raise the issue with him directly, realizing that Greenspan had not only plausible but perfect deniability. The chairman hadn't created the controversy, and surely he couldn't be held accountable for the media. Blinder didn't want to go begging. In his mind, the "chairman who wouldn't speak" took on a life of its own. Blinder believed that Greenspan was manipulating the press. His silence was just as damaging as, if not more so than, any negative comments that he might have made. Nobody, Blinder believed, knew how skillfully Greenspan played the Washington political inside game. He was witnessing its subtle but deadly sting firsthand.

Though he never said it publicly, Greenspan thought Blinder's speech was unnecessarily provocative and somewhat muddled intellectually.

Blinder was scheduled to give a speech in a downtown Washington hotel on September 8. Afterward, dozens of reporters and many cameras awaited him. Blinder realized he had a choice either to act like a football player or to stop like a civilized person to answer a few questions. He stopped and answered the questions, downplaying any philosophical rift between himself and the chairman.

The next day, *The New York Times* reported that Blinder had held an "unscheduled" press conference. Son of a bitch, he said to himself. It looked as if he were putting himself forward, showboating. Fed governors didn't have press conferences. If he hadn't been discussed as a possible contender for Greenspan's job in 1996, Blinder believed the press attention would have subsided. He consistently maintained that he had never spoken to the White House about the possibility, and he seemed hurt that his relationship with Greenspan had been damaged. Nonetheless, Blinder refused to close the door on the possibility that he might become the next Fed chairman.

He talked to *The Wall Street Journal* and was asked if he wanted to succeed Greenspan. "I don't spend a lot of time thinking about it," he said, suggesting that he spent at least some time on the subject. "It's a fantastic opportunity if it comes along. For the time being," he continued suggestively, "we have a very good chairman of the Fed. The job is not open."

At the next FOMC meeting six weeks later, September 27, Greenspan paid homage to their "at least for a time" statement and said they would have to have strong evidence to move now. He didn't think it existed, but at the next meeting they probably would have to raise rates another ½ percent.

In the days before that next meeting on November 15, Blinder thought the economy was looking stronger—too strong. A roar was coming up from the markets, saying that the Fed had goofed with its sideline statement and was behind the curve. Forecasters were beginning to predict that in the current rate-tightening cycle, the fed funds rate that was now at 4¾ would eventually reach 8 percent or higher. Blinder knew that the Fed had to act, but he thought that the predictions of an 8 percent fed funds rate were ludicrous.

Greenspan asked to see him again. When the chairman arrived, he said he wanted to make a dramatic gesture to show that the Fed was not behind the curve, to show the Fed's teeth in a big way.

Blinder agreed, saying that the economy was running hard and something had to be done. He told Greenspan that he would have no trouble with a ½ percent increase at the coming meeting, as Greenspan had suggested at the September meeting.

Greenspan wanted to move a full ¾ percent.

Blinder was a little bit surprised. He had concluded that they would eventually have to move a total of ¾ percent, but he thought that it might be wise to do it incrementally.

Greenspan wanted to get there right away. He didn't cite any specific data, focusing instead on his feeling that the pot was boiling and that ¾ percent was the only way for the Fed to get out ahead of the markets.

It was a major disagreement. Blinder was worried that a ¾-point raise all at once could shatter confidence in the markets and have a negative effect on the rest of the economy, particularly on the people who were out there trying to buy homes.

Greenspan stood firm.

Hmm-hmm, Blinder finally said noncommittally—a kind of unspoken "I don't know . . ." He did not indicate to the chairman that he would go along.

Blinder and Yellen conferred about the staff forecast that was circulated to the FOMC members before the meeting. It assumed the Fed would raise rates 1½ percent over the next several meetings. Given the 1¼ percent increase that year already, the total rate increase would be an astonishing 3¼ percent in one year. Both Blinder and Yellen thought this was way too much. Given the one-year lag in impact, that would mean much of the drag on the economy would occur in 1996—election year. They both decided to speak up at the November 15 FOMC meeting.

Blinder had the staff run a model on the impact interest rate changes might have on the overall economy. The strong doses of interest rate decreases put into the system by the Fed in 1991 and 1992 would have their maximum impact in 1993 and 1994 and then wither away, according to the complex mathematical model the staff used. In 1994, the stimulus provided by the easier policies of 1991–92 was causing the economy to grow an additional 1½ percent, the model said. By 1996, however, the effects of policy in 1991–92—and the additional 1½ percent growth that that policy brought with it—would have worked their way out of the system.

Further, if the Fed raised rates by 3¼ percent by early next year, the impact, according to the model, would be to take about 1 percent off the 1996 economic growth rate.

So the joint effects of the Fed's interest rate policy from 1994 to 1996 would be stunning. By 1996, they were looking at a total swing of 2½ percent off the national growth rate. That was a giant number. The economy had grown only 3¼ percent the previous year. If they did what the staff forecast, the Fed could grind the economy to a halt.

"Now, what concerns me the most," said Yellen at the November FOMC meeting, "is that the assumed further tightening of 1½ percent entails considerable downside risk to the economy that will be concentrated in 1996.

"There is a real risk of a hard landing, instead of a soft landing, if we are too impatient and overact." Though she supported some increase in rates, she said the 1½ percent over the next several months could be overkill. She said more than once that it would make itself felt with a hard landing in 1996.

Blinder pointed out that the staff projection of another 1½ percent fed funds rate increase in the next several months included a projection that this would have almost no impact on the long rates. An impact on the long-term rates couldn't be ruled out, he said. It was not impossible. "I think it takes a certain amount of guts to project that," he said sarcastically. "I commend the staff for having that much guts; it is more than I have." He took 10 minutes to present his model, showing how the amount of tightening described in the forecast would represent a swing of 2½ percent in national growth from 1994 to 1996. What they were contemplating was not trivial. "It is very strong medicine," he said, enough to stop even an econ-

omy with considerable momentum. "It is therefore not to be pre-
scribed lightly."

"I must say the discussion this morning has been one of the best
discussions I have heard around this table in quite a long while,"
Greenspan said when the others had finished. He said he would not
dismiss the comments of Blinder and Yellen.

"I think we are behind the curve," he added after offering a
brief assessment of the economy. "I think that creating a mild surprise would be of significant value."

The chairman then remarked that the markets had already fac-
tored in a rate increase above the ½ percent that some were arguing
for—and that they needed to be out ahead of those expectations.
"So, I think that we have to be very careful at this stage and be certain that we are ahead of general expectations. I think we can do that
with ¾ of a point."

To underscore his strong feelings, the chairman added, "I must
tell you that ½ percent makes me a little nervous. No, I take that
back: It makes me very nervous, and I would be disinclined to go in
that direction." Anyone voting against him, in other words, was in
favor of a very nervous chairman.

"I fear that doing ¾ of a point today rather than ½ of a point
may send us down an oversteering path," Blinder said. He reminded
the committee that "the Greenspan Fed has never once moved the
fed funds rate by ¾ of a point in either direction. Not once. When
this Fed has erred, it has been on the side of caution. . . . I always
thought that was a good idea.

"I think this will be like feeding red meat to the bond market
lions," Blinder went on. "They will chew it up and ask for more. A
Federal Reserve that did ¼, ¼, ¼, ½, ½, ¾ does not look to an outside
observer like it is about to stop. I think we will create what are already strong expectations that we are not about to stop.

"My personal preference is strongly for ½," Blinder concluded.
". . . I thought hard about whether I should dissent on this matter,
and I did not decide until last night. I finally decided that I won't.
. . . I think it is better to show a united Federal Reserve against the
criticism that we are surely going to get for this move." Blinder
would go along with the rate hike, but he made it clear that he
would stand strongly against raising rates again at the next meeting.

"Okay," Greenspan said, right on the tail of Blinder's long
speech about his struggle. "I propose that we move ¾ percent."

All 12 members voted yes.

Blinder had gone with the chairman because he didn't want to use the power of his dissent on what could be seen as a tactical dispute. The practical difference between ½ percent and ¼ percent, in terms of measurable effects on the economy, was quite small. Blinder's chief concern was where they might be heading in the months to come.

He also knew that there was a tradition at the Fed that members go along with the chairman unless they are really uncomfortable, terribly uncomfortable. This is especially true of the vice chairman. Nobody at the Fed, as far as Blinder knew, could remember the last time a vice chairman had dissented from the will of the chairman.

Finally, Blinder realized that there would be more arguments about when the Fed would stop raising rates, and that those arguments would be more important than this argument. If he shot his cannonball now, it would be wasted—because he wasn't going to change the decision. He would have fallen on his sword for no reason.

Blinder came from an academic environment, where he was used to following his conscience. It had become clear to him that voting solely on the basis of his convictions and economic conclusions wouldn't work at the Fed.

Greenspan made his speaking rounds to business groups, including the Business Council.

We cannot raise prices, CEO after CEO told him. Many had tried and been cut down by their competitors.

What do you mean, you're having problems? Greenspan pressed one group at his table. Profit margins are going up. Stop complaining.

The CEOs explained that their competition would invest in new technology, bring their costs down and then bring their prices down, grabbing market share.

Greenspan suspected that it was productivity growth again. In the real world, productivity, the measure of how much a worker produced in an hour, was obviously shooting up. But the methods of measuring it and the habits of economists who insisted on years and years of data before reaching even a tentative conclusion were keeping the world from learning of a potentially stunning change.

10

_____

On Christmas night, Sunday, December 25, Greenspan met with Guillermo Ortiz Martinez, the Mexican finance minister, and Lawrence H. Summers, the 40-year-old undersecretary of the treasury for international affairs. Summers, a Ph.D. economist who had won full tenured professorship at Harvard at the extraordinarily young age of 28, wanted to make sure the Fed and its chairman were involved in the major economic initiatives undertaken by the Clinton administration so they would have a stake in the outcomes.

Mexico was experiencing a significant crisis, and its leaders had decided to devalue the peso a few days earlier. The country had experienced a burst of economic growth by relying heavily on foreign investment, particularly from the United States. Confidence in the currency and investment potential in Mexico had now plummeted, and the country had just about run out of dollars. Mexico's basic solvency was in doubt.

The foreign investment surge in Mexico in the early 1990s was largely attributable to the high return investors found there. Investors could earn about 12 percent on short-term Mexican debt—several times what could be made on short-term U.S. debt. Both experienced Wall Street firms and U.S. mutual funds had poured money in. But in early 1994, political instability—an uprising in the province of Chiapas and a political assassination—caused investor momentum to shift away from Mexico, and money flowed out.

The Mexican authorities' response to the situation had reinforced Greenspan's faith in monetary gradualism and aggressive inflation fighting. Mexican authorities at first failed to raise interest rates, apparently loath to risk a recession—which then forced them to raise rates dramatically later, a drastic move that had helped create the current crisis.

Now, the Mexican government wanted a sizable financial support package of loans, and then everyone would live happily ever after.

Greenspan didn't like the idea. Loans or guarantees from the United States would risk "moral hazard," a term used by economists to refer to bailing out those who had made risky investments—creating an expectation that they would be bailed out the next time. He believed strongly that the government should not insulate free-market investors from risk. At the same time, he admired the way Mexico had over the previous decade shifted from an inflation-prone, highly unstable, rigid, government-controlled economy toward free markets. Mexico had become the world's poster child for emerging third world economies—a model dozens of other countries were following or being urged to follow. That was part of the problem. Mexico's ruin could mean, at least temporarily, the ruin of the cherished free-market model. Discrediting the model might have a larger impact on the world economy than whatever might happen to Mexico, pushing many other developing countries off the cliff. On top of that, new computers and communication had created the globalization of finance. Money flowed instantaneously across borders. Catastrophe in Mexico could trigger a worldwide contagion before they could calculate the full impact.

The Fed could have guaranteed U.S. bank liabilities or loans in Mexico, but Greenspan immediately dismissed such involvement as utterly inappropriate. U.S. investors should not be protected in such high-risk investments.

Over the first two years of the Clinton administration, Greenspan had worked with Bob Rubin, but he did not know him well. Now Rubin, about to take over from Bentsen as treasury secretary, initiated a running meeting over several days at Treasury about the Mexican crisis, which worsened as 1995 began. Rubin invited Greenspan and Ted Truman, 53, the outspoken, strong-willed head of the Fed's Division of International Finance since 1977.

Greenspan was immediately attracted to the nature of the debate at Treasury. Summers presented all the arguments for a financial assistance package to Mexico, then gave many of the reasons why not to assist.

Rubin's questions showed he was acutely aware of the uncertainties. As the group seemed to move toward a decision to assist, Rubin would insist on airing the 3 or 10 reasons why that course of action was a bad idea. Chief among them was the argument that U.S. assistance would be viewed as a bailout of U.S. investors in Mexico and revive arguments that Mexico was "too big to fail." As the others seemed then more comfortable with not providing direct assistance, Rubin would veer back to the arguments in favor of assistance. Vigorous dissent was appreciated and invited. Neither Rubin nor Summers seemed to be selling his own ideas; instead, each was trying to find a solution. It was the group decision making that Greenspan found very attractive as he floated in and out of the discussion.

Rubin pressed, insisting on systematic thinking about their choices and the relative probability of the various options working or not working.

Finally, the weight of evidence suggested that some sort of direct assistance from the United States was called for. The risk to the world and U.S. economies was real, and an aid package with tens of billions of dollars in loans, with strict terms and high interest rates, would be a minimal investment in international stability.

Greenspan said that some assistance package was what he called "the least-worst" of the alternatives. We have to do something. If they were going to provide loans, the basic rule, he said, should be to figure out how much might be needed and then to do more. It was the same principle that former chairman of the Joint Chiefs of Staff, General Colin Powell, had applied in the 1991 Gulf War. Powell's doctrine of overwhelming military force called for sending enough to guarantee success. There were no absolute guarantees in a foreign debt crisis, but Greenspan had a refinement of the principle: Send enough to reduce the probability of failure to below your point of tolerance. If they tried and failed, it would send an awful message to the world and U.S. financial markets about the inability of the U.S. government to affect outcomes in international financial crises.

To top it off, Mexico's Ortiz came to Washington and declared to Greenspan and Treasury officials that as finance minister he had no idea what he was going to do—saying, in effect, It's not our problem, it's your problem.

Rubin was convinced that there was a possibility of what he called "systemic impact," meaning that an economic meltdown in Mexico would trigger a cascading international financial crisis with no foreseeable stopping point. He wanted Greenspan behind him.

On January 11, 1995, Rubin took the oath of office as treasury secretary at the White House. He then proposed to the president that the administration request an aid package of some $25 billion from Congress to loan to Mexico. Some of Clinton's political advisers, including Chief of Staff Leon Panetta, noted that if, on Clinton's urging, the United States loaned $25 billion to Mexico and it didn't come back, the failure could cost the president reelection.

The president posed a number of questions. If Mexico was going to collapse financially, when would they know it was inevitable? Would they have days or weeks of warning?

Rubin and Summers said that the $25 billion would be given not at once, but in installments. The first installment would be only about $3 billion, and there would be some solace, but not a lot, that they would then be able to see if the financial markets found the package credible before they had actually to loan more from the $25 billion.

Rubin noted that markets were psychological animals, and if the world financial markets came to believe the package was sufficient to have a meaningful impact on Mexico, then international investment money would start to flow back into the country. Money alone would not necessarily solve Mexico's problem. The country had to regain the credibility of its people and the world investment community.

Rubin and Summers made it clear that the penalty for failure would far exceed any reward if they succeeded. Applying Greenspan's doctrine of sending more than they thought was needed, they upped the price tag. They proposed that the president ask Congress to appropriate $40 billion in loan guarantees to Mexico. To be relevant to the outcome, they had to be willing to put a massive amount of money on the table. Nobody had ever done anything quite like it before.

There was another factor. Ted Truman, the Fed's international chief, had authored a paper concluding that a collapse in Mexico would have such a severe impact, it would lead to a 2 percent *decline* in annual growth in the United States. That was a staggering number. No one had to remind Clinton that such a decline would have immense political repercussions in the year before he would be running for reelection.

"After all this chickenshit ethical stuff," Clinton said, referring to the continuing investigations of Independent Counsel Kenneth W. Starr, "I'm doing this because I think this is the right thing to do, even if we lose the election." He seemed to relish the decision. "I couldn't sleep at night if I didn't do this."

He added that he could do it only because Mexico is on the

U.S. border. If the problem were in India or some other country, he wouldn't be in a position to do it.

During his first year as president, Clinton had pushed through the controversial North American Free Trade Agreement (NAFTA), which opened the doors to trade with Mexico. He had invested much political capital in free trade, and he was not going to let Mexico fall into economic chaos. He approved the $40 billion request. He then called the congressional leaders, Senate Majority Leader Bob Dole and House Speaker Newt Gingrich, to the White House to brief them on the crisis and his $40 billion request. Both Republican leaders, Dole and Gingrich, gave their support.

Soon conservative Republicans in the Senate and House were in near rebellion. They didn't want to dump so much money into another country.

Gingrich asked Greenspan to call Rush Limbaugh, the popular conservative radio talk show host, and lobby him on the Mexican loan proposal and explain why it was essential. The ratings claimed that Limbaugh had 20 million listeners, and he was giving Gingrich a hard time, having great fun denouncing and ridiculing the Speaker's support of Clinton's plan to give away $40 billion of U.S. taxpayer money south of the border.

Greenspan took the position that if anyone wanted to know his views, he would offer them. He reached Limbaugh by phone, saying Newt had asked him to call, and laid out the arguments in about 10 minutes. He didn't want to push particularly hard, wanting only to make sure that Limbaugh was aware of the possible consequences.

On Thursday, January 12, Greenspan joined Rubin at the White House to give a background briefing to reporters on the $40 billion plan. The camera lights were turned off in the White House press room, and under the ground rules they could be identified only as "senior United States officials."

Greenspan was not used to the skeptical questioning of the White House press corps, and he seemed slightly flustered by the interrogation.

On January 13, Greenspan accompanied Rubin to Capitol Hill to lobby for the $40 billion. Included was a two-hour meeting with 100 legislators.

Despite the support of the Republican and Democratic leadership in the Congress, it soon was absolutely clear the $40 billion request would not pass. Mexico was really on the ropes now, and a dangerous impasse had developed.

• • •

One of the senators on the banking committee whom Greenspan had cultivated was Robert Bennett, a 6-foot-5-inch Utah Republican who had been elected in 1992. As a freshman senator initially in the minority, Bennett was generally ignored. But he went to banking committee hearings and did something unusual—he actually stayed after the opening statements, listening, questioning witnesses intently and absorbing. Greenspan invited him to periodic one-on-one breakfasts at the Fed. Bennett had been an entrepreneur millionaire, heading firms that made audio discs for talking toys and then another that produced calendar day planners and organizers.

Senate Majority Leader Dole appointed Bennett to come up with a way out of the Mexican crisis. Bennett spent that weekend studying. On Sunday he invited Wayne Angell, the former Fed governor who was a key informal economic adviser to Dole, over to his house. Angell, who was now chief economist for Bear Stearns, said that the only alternative was to use the Exchange Stabilization Fund (ESF), which had been set up 60 years earlier to permit Treasury to intervene to stabilize currencies in an emergency. There was some $30 billion in the fund, and Treasury had full control of it. Was Treasury willing to go out on a limb?

Bennett called Greenspan to explain.

"You can't do that," Greenspan said. "Wayne is wrong."

Bennett said it would require a little backbone, but Congress had authorized and provided money for the fund over the years. "Why do you need congressional approval?"

"Because if we do it without congressional approval," Greenspan explained patiently, "Congress will come down on us with their fury. We can't do that."

"What happens if you do it," Bennett replied, "and Congress is silent?"

There was a long pause. "That would work," Greenspan said, "if you could guarantee Congress's silence."

On Monday, January 16, Martin Luther King Jr.'s birthday holiday, Bennett reached Dole.

"We can solve this without a vote," Bennett said, explaining what the Exchange Stabilization Fund was. Congress would have to be silent—not literally, of course, because there would be the inevitable speeches and denunciations. But as majority leader, Dole could guarantee there would be no vote.

"Call Rubin," Dole said.

"Absolutely not," Rubin said when Bennett reached him. "No way, forget it, don't even talk about it. We can't go that route." It would be an end run around Congress—which, if angered, could cut off funding or change the law.

Bennett said that Greenspan thought it was possible if Congress did nothing.

"Well," Rubin said, "I'll talk to Alan."

Over the next several weeks, Dole and House Speaker Newt Gingrich had some of the governors from the states along the Mexican border to Gingrich's office. Texas's new governor, George W. Bush, was one of the strongest voices. The border economy would just go completely down the drain, he said. You guys got to do something.

Dole called Clinton, and the next day, January 31, the administration announced it was using $20 billion from the fund. Many congressional Republicans howled, claiming that the administration was circumventing Congress.

Rubin figured that the Republican opponents were most comfortable criticizing the administration, because they lacked the courage to act to prevent the assistance. The critics were obviously worried that if they blocked it and all hell broke loose, they would be blamed.

Rubin called Bennett.

"Senator," the treasury secretary said, "it took us two weeks to figure it out, but you were right."

Treasury eventually loaned the Mexican government $12.5 billion, and the Mexican economy improved and stabilized. The interest rate on the assistance loans was so high that Mexico paid the whole balance back early, in full. Greenspan considered it the first crisis of the new international financial order.

Prior to the February 1 FOMC meeting, Greenspan again made his private rounds with some of his committee members. He told Blinder he wanted a ½ percent rate increase.

Since November, Blinder had admitted to himself that the ¼ percent rate hike made that month had probably been a good idea. Based on the data now available, he had been wrong to oppose it. But he thought that yet another hike, particularly of ½ percent, was taking things way too far. In less than a year they had raised rates 2½ percent, and it was time to wait to see if that would be enough castor oil to do the job.

After a brief meeting, Greenspan left, without the assurance that Blinder would vote with him.

Greenspan also told Yellen that he was inclined to favor a ½ percent increase. Like Blinder, she didn't think it was a good idea. The economy seemed to be slowing, she thought, and she did not commit to support him.

Yellen had attended several FOMC meetings by now, and she thought that every time she walked into the meetings she heard the same arguments: The economy is hot, we have to raise rates. My God, she thought, it was a good thing they met only every six weeks and not every single week, or the rates would be through the roof. She half wanted to scream out, There's a lag here, folks! Rate increases take a year or more to have a real impact.

Yellen and Blinder conferred. Maybe they should dissent, oppose Greenspan, put a stop to this overkill. Before they knew it, they would be in a recession that their acquiescence might have caused. They talked to Governor Larry Lindsey, who was also very uncomfortable with the informally proposed ½ percent hike. Lindsey also considered dissenting, but Greenspan sounded Lindsey out and persuaded him not to dissent.

Blinder and Yellen continued to discuss it. Maybe it was time. It would be a real statement. As the two Clinton-nominated board members, they felt that a dissent from just the two of them would be widely viewed as political, especially a year before the presidential election—but they continued to flirt with the idea.

In the February 1, 1995, meeting, Greenspan pushed for the ½ percent increase. He didn't know for certain that it would be the last increase in the current tightening cycle, but he believed they were getting close. The bond market was signaling that it expected more inflation and more rate increases, and the FOMC was still behind the curve. When they were behind, they had to jump to try to close the gap if possible. Inflationary expectations fed on themselves. Raising rates might contain those expectations, so that they would gradually dissipate.

When it was their turn to vote, Blinder, Yellen and Lindsey all went with Greenspan's recommendation. The vote was unanimous. In one year, the fed funds rate had been doubled, from 3 to 6 percent.

Blinder didn't like being steamrollered. In a speech in Richmond, Virginia, two weeks later, he declared that the preemptive strategy of raising rates to cut off the top of a boom suggested that the Fed had to be prepared to lower rates preemptively even before the economy might slow. Policy speeches were typically the domain only of the chairman, and Blinder knew that his speaking openly about Fed policy would needle Greenspan. That was exactly what he wanted to do.

Word reached Blinder through the staff that Greenspan was unhappy. As usual, Greenspan said not a word about it.

In prepared testimony before the Senate Banking Committee a few days later on February 22, Greenspan noted that the Fed had acted "to head off inflation pressures not yet evident in the data." He continued, "Similarly, there may come a time when we hold our policy stance unchanged, *or even ease* despite adverse price data."

It was the first time the chairman had spoken of such a strategy in public. Blinder was delighted when some market analysts suggested that he had pushed these words into Greenspan's mouth, although it wasn't the first time Greenspan had raised the possibility of the need for preemptive easing. He had done so earlier in internal Fed meetings. Blinder viewed Greenspan's public discussion of the possibility of preemptive easing as a tacit admission that the Fed had gone too far in raising rates.

Blinder also thought that Greenspan's public remarks effectively took away the tightening effects of the ½ percent increase that Blinder had opposed. Immediately in the wake of Greenspan's remarks before Congress about possible preemptive easing, the long-term bond rates went down. Greenspan's speech had reassured the market that the Fed wouldn't clamp down too hard on the economy. Although Blinder had voted with the chairman for a rate increase, the net effect on the economy—after Greenspan's testimony—was almost as if the Fed hadn't raised rates at all.

For Greenspan, wringing inflation expectations out of the economy often required that the Fed increase rates an extra time, take one more turn of the screw to really make sure they'd gone far enough. This was not always necessary in a tightening cycle, but he believed that it was necessary now.

In the months after February, data began flowing into the Fed suggesting that the economy was slowing substantially. Blinder went to Greenspan a number of times and beseeched him to lower rates. Greenspan would sometimes give Buddha-like responses, listening, hardly saying a word; other times he would argue with Blinder. Overall, Blinder thought that the chairman showed a fair amount of sympathy to his desires to ease up on the economy, but Greenspan made it clear that he did not want to rush things.

For Greenspan, preemptive action was more important on the tightening side, in order to keep inflation in check. Failing to ease rates early enough could be corrected with little difficulty, but allowing inflationary pressures to build without preemptive action might mean the difference between continued economic prosperity and a relatively severe Fed-induced recession if they had to increase rates suddenly and sharply. He remembered too well the Volcker era, when the Fed had driven short-term rates to 19 percent in order to stomp out inflation.

By the summer of 1995, Greenspan was feeling quite pleased. Inflation was still in check, and overall economic growth was slowing. Perhaps the soft landing was working—a slowdown without a recession. Was it possible? He wasn't sure. In the past, economic slowdowns had often become recessions.

On Wednesday, June 7, 1995, in an unusual appearance, Greenspan answered reporters' questions at an international banking conference in Seattle. Threading his way carefully through his own doubts and the media's desire to know the future, he managed to present both good news and bad news.

On the good news front he said, "I don't see any problems that really disturb me."

As to possible bad news, he said, "As a consequence of the sluggish economic outlook, the probabilities, as some of my colleagues have indicated, of a recession have edged up, as indeed one would expect."

The result was contradictory headlines:

"Greenspan Sees Chance of Recession"—*The New York Times*.

"Recession Is Unlikely, Greenspan Concludes"—*The Washington Post*.

Greenspan laughed at the differing interpretations. He called it "constructive ambiguity." Since he didn't want to make inadvertent news, he deemed the press conference successful.

On Sunday, White House Chief of Staff Leon Panetta was on *Meet the Press* and was asked if the Fed should reduce interest rates.

"Well," Panetta said, "it would be nice to get whatever kind of cooperation we can get to get this economy going." Growth was hovering at an anemic 2 percent.

Asked if he was jawboning the Fed to get rates lower, Panetta replied with his overeager grin, "Is that what it's called?"

Treasury Secretary Bob Rubin was furious. The administration had been so disciplined, avoiding any public or even private effort to pressure Greenspan. The soft landing would occur because the administration and Greenspan didn't let the economy get out of control. It wasn't science, Rubin knew, but he believed Greenspan was making a series of highly informed judgments—the best they had. White House pressure to cut rates could have the opposite impact and actually prevent a rate cut.

In addition, Panetta, the former Clinton budget director, was too often acting as if he were the primary economic policy spokesman—to let people know he was the man. As treasury secretary, Rubin was the primary economic policy spokesman.

Rubin immediately went public with a rebuke for Panetta and an assurance, almost an apology, to Greenspan. Of Panetta, Rubin said in a public statement, "I can assure you that his comments were not intended to signal any shift. Our policy with regard to the Federal Reserve has been consistent from the beginning of the administration—and that is not to comment." He even added that Panetta had been "careless in how he responded."

President Clinton seemed to agree with Rubin. It appeared that Panetta was briefly put in the doghouse—an unusual place for the White House chief of staff, who was supposed to be managing the executive branch on behalf of the president. Rubin and others knew that a side of Clinton agreed with Panetta, but in terms of politics and public perception, Clinton's relationship with Greenspan and the Fed was more important than his relationship with his chief of staff.

Lay off, Rubin had said in effect to the president, remember the soft landing and long-term interest rates—those used by businesses to finance expansion and economic growth. The bond market was coming back, and long-term rates had dropped a sharp 1½ percent since the fall. They were getting the payoff.

Greenspan took Panetta's comments as a cheap and ineffective hit. Rubin had it right, not because of their growing friendship, but because Rubin saw it was in the president's self-interest to avoid political meddling with the Fed. What was interesting, Greenspan realized, was that his relations with the administration were so good that the White House was more concerned about the perception of Panetta's comments than Greenspan was himself.

Two weeks later, in a June 20 speech to the Economic Club of New York, Greenspan again left contradictory impressions.

"Doubts Voiced by Greenspan on a Rate Cut"—*The New York Times.*

"Greenspan Hints Fed May Cut Interest Rates"—*The Washington Post.*

Now Greenspan had a chance to practice some of his fine-tuning. Having doubled interest rates from 3 to 6 percent during 1994 and early 1995, he realized that he might have overshot, but only slightly. To bring the economy in for the soft landing now required a mild reversal—a slight easing. On Thursday, July 6, 1995, Greenspan proposed a rate cut of ¼ percent. It would be the first decrease in nearly three years and the first rate cut during the Clinton administration.

Yellen was sure that they had overshot. She noted that the data since the last meeting had been overwhelmingly negative. Growth was so slow that it could conceivably build into a recession. They would probably have to cut rates even more, she said.

There was only one formal dissent. Thomas H. Hoenig, president of the Kansas City Fed, wanted no rate cut because he believed the economy needed no help and would pick up on its own.

On news of the cut, the Dow jumped 48 points to a new record high of 4664.

Both Greenspan and Rubin were concerned about the extraordinary strength of the stock market. Over the summer, Rubin called a meeting of key Treasury and Fed personnel at the Treasury Department. The question he wanted addressed was why the stock market was going up so fast. Greenspan and several Fed experts attended. The initial conclusion was that the increase in corporate earnings and profits was attributable to the spread of capitalism abroad into Russia, Eastern Europe and Latin America.

Greenspan was skeptical and wanted to know how much U.S. corporations were making abroad. He asked Steven A. Sharpe, a Fed Ph.D. economist who tracked corporate profits, to go further and see if he could develop an economic model to track and attempt to account for the high stock prices.

"Knowing what's going on with profits is critical," the chairman said. Healthy profits generally meant a healthy economy. Early detection of a decline in profits was essential for locating turning points in the economy.

In New York, Felix Rohatyn, perhaps the city's best known investment banker, had been closely watching the first two and a half years of the Clinton era. An ardent Democrat and outspoken liberal who had been briefly considered as Clinton's treasury secretary, he believed that the president was not getting the full story on the economy. Rohatyn, 67, a managing partner at Lazard Frères Co., was the grandson of a member of the Vienna stock exchange. He had immigrated to the United States during World War II and had a European manner, polished and engaging behind a pair of thick glasses. He cultivated wide connections in the international investment banking community. In the 1970s, he was tapped by the governor of New York to head the Municipal Assistance Corporation, which had rescued New York City from near bankruptcy.

Rohatyn knew CEOs who had reengineered their businesses and were passionately convinced that the American economy could grow at a faster rate than the old model of 2½ percent a year without inflation. He had written articles sounding this theme for *The Wall Street Journal* and the *New York Review of Books*. He spoke with Erskine Bowles, the White House deputy chief of staff and a former North Carolina investment banker. A golfing buddy of the president's, Bowles urged Clinton to meet with Rohatyn and a group of CEOs before going on vacation that summer.

The group that assembled in the Oval Office included Rohatyn and five CEOs—Paul Allaire of Xerox, Dana Mead of Teneco, George David of United Technologies, Bernard Schwartz of Loral and Paul O'Neil of Alcoa.

Bowles, Laura Tyson, the new head of the National Economic Council in the White House, and Treasury Secretary Rubin also attended.

The president ran the meeting as one CEO after another described how they had restructured their businesses. They delivered a single message on the economy: Greenspan was going to slow it down, and he didn't need to. Higher growth without inflation was possible. The old perceived wisdom did not apply to a new emerging economy dominated by firms that were leaner and better organized.

Rohatyn said he was absolutely certain. He believed that markets at times did not work and government had to be more interventionist, more "can do." The low rate of economic growth was not enough to meet the social and public investment needs of the country. The opportunity for a new, pro-growth policy was at hand.

Rohatyn left the meeting feeling that the president, Bowles and Tyson were sympathetic.

Rubin had sat silently, listening, taking notes.

Rohatyn and his wife, Elizabeth, had two adjoining weekend houses in Southampton on Long Island, New York. Greenspan and his steady date, NBC television correspondent Andrea Mitchell, visited one weekend that summer.

"I hear you're not worried about inflation," Greenspan asked Rohatyn as the two strolled in the garden.

No, Rohatyn said emphatically, he just believed the economy could grow faster than 2½ percent a year without inflation.

Okay, Greenspan said noncommittally.

In the White House, Tyson could see that the president was taken with Rohatyn's approach. It was a theory of economics that was neither pessimistic nor dreary. So many economists were busy telling Clinton what he couldn't do that the president was happy finally to have someone tell him what he could do. It was as if he wanted to say, Get these economists out of my life.

Some political advisers were warning Clinton that Greenspan was a dangerous independent. Look what he did to Bush; he's going to do it to you, several warned him. And here comes Rohatyn saying, It's a new world. Tyson thought Clinton had found in Rohatyn the economic equivalent of his then chief political strategist, Dick Morris, someone bubbling with new ideas and plans, someone who could take the president's wishes and convert them to action. Someone who would not be constrained by old approaches or theories. The recessive liberal activist Democrat in Clinton seemed to be stirring.

On November 30, Rohatyn published an op-ed piece in *The Wall Street Journal* arguing that higher non-inflationary growth was within reach. He blasted both the Republican Congress and the Democratic president. "Their greatest sin is to accept, and implicitly condemn, the United States to our present growth rates."

Greenspan was still feeling confident. The economic expansion was five or six months longer than normal, a tentative indication that the soft landing might be working. It would take another six months to tell for sure. He still believed the soft landing was just theory, but at moments he was proud that they just might have carried it off. He quite extravagantly compared the theory to Albert Einstein's theory of relativity, which revolutionized the understanding of the universe, light, matter and energy. Einstein, for example, had hypothesized that light would bend, but it took years for physicists to prove he was right.

Once, Greenspan had read one of Einstein's original 1905

papers on relativity. Greenspan considered himself a somewhat accomplished mathematician, capable of working advanced calculus problems—integral and differential equations—which he sometimes tackled for fun and relaxation. He got some 10 to 15 pages into the paper before realizing it would take much more study, perhaps reading as many as four books, to understand the next step.

He continued to find fascination in Einstein's work as a model for discovery—careful, scrupulous observation and picking apart the measurements in the economic data to determine what was changing.

The chairman had another problem. He had been telling himself that he should not expect reappointment to another four-year term. After all, he had been appointed to the job twice by Republican presidents—by Reagan in 1987 and by Bush in 1991. A Democratic president would want to choose his own chairman. If Greenspan were president, he would want to choose his own person. It wasn't plausible that he was going to get another chance.

By November 1995, no one at the White House or in the administration had brought up his reappointment in their frequent conversations with him. And, of course, Greenspan had not brought it up. His term was over in five months. He was wearing fashionable double-breasted suits at times and eating only vegetables for lunch, generally looking fit and ready. He was also waiting.

In the meantime, as he had from the start, the chairman worked the Washington network—parties, private lunches and dinners, tennis matches, a steady stream of private, off-the-record gossip, chat and court intrigue. To some it was an ugly and to others an appealing feature of the nation's capital. Greenspan found elements of both. Nonetheless it was a useful channel for political intelligence. When the subject of his future came up, he would adopt a stance of studied nonchalance. He would have had eight good years. If Clinton reappointed him, he would accept. If not, that too would be okay. He worked at showing neither anxiety nor pain. He wanted that to be clear. He shrugged. He smiled. He was a man comfortable and at the top of his game. But the message was clear that he was available. He spoke admiringly of presidents who did the politically unexpected.

Greenspan recalled to several people a story about the importance of independence, making it clear he valued his. About 25 years earlier, when his consulting business, Townsend-Greenspan, was going strong, a CEO of one of the large brokerage houses tried to buy the firm. He was reluctant to sell. The CEO wrote a price on a piece of paper, placed it in an envelope, handed it to Greenspan and said, Take it home, open it and think about it over the weekend. At home, Greenspan opened the envelope. It was a wonderful price, very high and tempting. Later that day Greenspan got a pain in his stomach, and it would not go away. The next day he had the same pain. It would not leave him. He concluded that it was a signal— the body knowing something before the head. He realized that with the sale of his business, he would be selling his independence. He declined the offer.

The FOMC met December 19, 1995, for the last time of the year. Greenspan proposed another ¼ percent cut, taking the fed funds rate down to 5½ percent. Blinder and Yellen were strongly in favor. Though some of the bank presidents were very reluctant, the ¼ percent cut passed unanimously. Many market analysts called the cut a surprise. Others called it another Fed Christmas present.

What a year for Greenspan. In most respects, he had the economy right where he wanted it. Inflation was low, at less than 3 percent for the year. Unemployment was also low, steady in the 5½ percent range, with the addition of 1.8 million jobs for the year. After 3½ percent growth the previous year, the annual growth was down in the range of 1½ percent. There had been no recession. Greenspan had delivered. The economic analysis he had given Clinton in December 1992 was working. The payoffs he had anticipated were evident. By keeping inflation low and cutting the federal deficit, the intermediate- and long-term interest rates—the key rates for businesses, home buyers and consumers—were 2 to 2½ percent below their levels at the beginning of 1995. Bond prices, which move in the opposite direction as interest rates, were up substantially, and the stock market was up about 35 percent with the Dow at 5117—its best year in two decades.

He was available.

11

ALAN BLINDER and his wife, Madeline, flew to Acapulco, Mexico, after Christmas to vacation on the beach, so he could stare at the water and decide whether he should seek reappointment as vice chairman when his term expired in early 1996. It was a hard decision. After less than two years at the Fed, he was profoundly frustrated.

Blinder believed he had figured out what was so disconcerting. Greenspan didn't allow any risk. If there was a 2 percent or a 4 percent probability that something might happen—such as Blinder succeeding him or Blinder's star rising—Greenspan worked to bring the probability down to zero. Most people would tolerate low chances. Greenspan wanted to stomp out the slightest probability. That's why Greenspan had stuck the knife in him, Blinder believed, in so many ways and so skillfully. And there were no fingerprints.

Blinder decided he should leave. He wanted to be a lame duck for as short a time as possible, so he cut it tight and told the White House only two weeks before the expiration of his term. As a little piece of revenge, he decided not to tell Greenspan. Blinder figured the chairman could read about his departure in the newspapers. After all, Greenspan had never really told him anything, never really let him in the way Blinder had hoped. He realized it was childish on his part. The news of his departure hit the papers on January 17.

Greenspan said nothing to Blinder, but he presided at a little going-away party for him.

You know, Greenspan said graciously at the ceremony, it seems like you just got here, it's been wonderful to have you.

Ha, ha, Blinder thought as he stood nearby in deep discomfort.

How much, Greenspan continued, he had enjoyed having Blinder as a colleague, how valuable he had been to the FOMC and the board, what a shame he was leaving so soon.

Ha, Blinder thought again. He concluded that Greenspan was not a straight person, not open and direct in the way that Blinder expected of colleagues.

He had just wanted to be part of the interest rate game, and Greenspan had not permitted it.

From the White House, Laura Tyson sounded out a number of people to see if they could help her draw up a list of possible successors to Blinder.

She spoke with Felix Rohatyn, Clinton's favorite New York investment banker.

I might be interested in the job myself, Rohatyn said.

Tyson was surprised. She admired Rohatyn and had some sympathy with his higher-growth goals, but she knew that Blinder had felt squeezed at the Fed.

Felix, Tyson said, the vice chairman of the Fed doesn't really do that much, especially with Greenspan—a long-term, very effective chairman—at the helm. The vice chairman goes to the boring meetings that the chairman doesn't want to go to and gets the least interesting assignments.

No, Rohatyn said, the vice chairmanship would give him a platform for his views. He and Greenspan went back decades. "We're friends," Rohatyn said. "We've known each other for a long time. It would be different because we're friends. I would be able to have more influence." He knew New York and the financial markets cold, and the international scene as well. It would be a perfect fit with Greenspan's Washington knowledge and vast technical understanding of the economy.

Tyson didn't think that it was a good idea. Still, she reported what Rohatyn had said to the president.

"What a great . . . what an interesting idea!" the president said. One of the key issues for Clinton was how much the economy could grow without inflation. He didn't like the conservative model of 2½ percent annual growth. "We'll have a really interesting debate, a national debate about this issue between the Fed chair and the vice chair," he said. Clinton was loving the idea. He could reappoint Greenspan—an issue still unsettled at that time—and also have someone pressuring the chairman from within the Fed to allow more economic growth.

Tyson had a sinking feeling. Just what the financial markets needed—open debate and perhaps even warfare within the Fed. She tried to discourage the president.

The more they talked about it, the more Clinton loved the prospect.

Tyson figured her job was to give advice, but if it was being rejected, then she had to try to accomplish what the president wanted. She informed Rohatyn of the president's enthusiasm.

Rohatyn was even more interested but said that before the idea got too far or became public, he wanted to see Greenspan and Bob Rubin to make sure they were comfortable with it.

Rohatyn and Blinder spoke by phone. Blinder had decided that he owed Rohatyn a warning.

"Why are you doing it?" Blinder asked. "I'm leaving because I can't stand it." He explained that only one person counted at the Fed, and it was Greenspan. After Greenspan, probably the most important force at the Fed was the staff, which had the real power and squelched dissident thoughts or alternative thinking unless Greenspan agreed, Blinder said. He told Rohatyn that Greenspan and the staff would join forces against him.

"I think you're wrong," Rohatyn replied. "I'm going to try to change it."

"But you'll never do that," Blinder said. Rohatyn had no idea what he was up against.

Rohatyn was not going to back off. He believed that the Fed mattered more to the economy than Treasury and almost as much as the president. The Fed—and its chairman or representative—would be America's messenger to the dawning global economy. Speaking to that new world was critical, and he wanted to be a part of the message. Pressing on, Rohatyn set up meetings with Rubin and then Greenspan, to make sure they would support his candidacy. He went to see Rubin at Treasury.

Over the years, Rohatyn had come to understand that Rubin was cautious, not one to jump at a new suggestion. But he was also a Democrat who shared some of Rohatyn's views.

Rubin said he would be happy to see Rohatyn over at the Fed, that it would be a plus.

Privately, Rubin thought it was a terrible idea. His own relationship with Greenspan worked well. If they had the slightest disagreement, instead of shouting opinions at each other, they calmly compared their analyses. There were always identifiable reasons for differing judgments. It rarely got emotional.

In contrast, Rohatyn was proselytizing about more growth. True believers could upset the balance within an institution. Rohatyn had sounded too much like a crusader.

Rohatyn, by the same token, believed that few people understood the closeness of his relationship with Greenspan. Decades earlier, he had hired Greenspan's consulting firm, and he had remained one of Greenspan's clients for years. In the 1970s, when Greenspan had been at the White House as Ford's chairman of the Council of Economic Advisers, he and Rohatyn had been walking together on West Executive Drive, on the White House grounds.

"One of these days," Rohatyn had said, "wouldn't it be nice if I were secretary of the treasury and you were chairman of the Fed?"

In 1992 after Clinton's election, when Rohatyn had been mentioned as a possible treasury secretary (the job Bentsen got), he had lunch with Greenspan. They were halfway toward the goal Rohatyn had suggested in the 1970s.

"This is a town that is full of evil people," Greenspan had said. "If you can't deal with every day having people trying to destroy you, you shouldn't even think of coming down here." Normal human beings could look you straight in the face and lie about things they had done, Greenspan warned. It had happened to him, and it was obviously designed to gain advantage. Greenspan maintained that it was morally evil to lie outright. Rohatyn had been struck by his friend's observation and believed instinctively he was right.

Now, Rohatyn told Greenspan about the prospect that they would be working together at the Fed, that he would be nominated to be the vice chairman.

Greenspan was uncomfortable, but he told Rohatyn that he could do the overseas travel, which Greenspan didn't like. He would welcome someone who could do that.

It was a tepid endorsement to say the least, but Rohatyn took it as positive.

On January 19, 1996, *The Wall Street Journal* broke the story that Clinton was considering Rohatyn for the vice chairmanship. The story noted that Rohatyn had criticized the goal of achieving only 2½ percent economic growth each year. Rohatyn was described as perhaps "Wall Street's best-known investment banker" and Lazard's "top dealmaker." The story also noted, "Unlike some previous Fed vice chairmen, Mr. Rohatyn probably would be seen as Mr. Greenspan's likely successor—if the Fed chairman were to leave office while a Democrat was president."

Greenspan flew off to Paris that weekend for the January 20–21 meeting of the Group of Seven (G-7) major economic powers. Whatever might happen with Rohatyn, he was still unsure about his own status. His term expired in six weeks. It was unsettling. He was effectively a Republican lame duck chairman—a position of weakness, with a Democrat in the White House. The main positive sign was that he had seen or heard of very few trial balloons floated in the media suggesting alternatives. From his experience in Washington he knew that was an important signal, but it was not conclusive. Some news stories were treating his reappointment as inevitable, but he had no assurances.

Since nothing was certain, Greenspan had to consider what he might do if Clinton appointed someone else as chairman. Under the law, if no replacement was named and confirmed, he would remain chairman. One possible scenario was that Clinton would wait until after the presidential election and then, if reelected, pick his own chairman.

According to the arcane procedures of the Fed, Greenspan had an appointment to the Board of Governors that did not expire until the year 2006. His term as chairman expired on March 2, 1996. If he was not reappointed as chairman, he could remain on the board. It would be very unusual, but he decided that it was almost certainly what he wanted to do. If he had to move down the table out of the chairman's seat, he felt that there was enough respect for his views that he could still have some influence.

The calculation also had to do with the lack of attractive alternatives. Greenspan was not interested in making more money; he had millions already. He would be 70. He didn't want to go back to New York City, and he loved Washington. But most of all, he loved the Fed. He had access to the best economic data in the world, and there was an intellectual purity to the work that was done there. He had found his place. The title and seat at the table were less important.

Staying at the table in a less exalted position would somewhat resemble the career path of John Quincy Adams, the sixth president of the United States. After a term as president, Adams served 17 years in the U.S. House of Representatives, where his vast knowledge and gloomy high-mindedness made their mark until he died in office at the age of 81.

Rubin never considered it a real question. Reappointing Greenspan was a no-brainer. He had attended one meeting in the White House residence to discuss a possible successor to Greenspan. It would have been irresponsible not to have seriously considered alternatives. Fresh, new thinking was essential in all matters, Rubin believed, even the seemingly obvious. It was one of the reasons some of his colleagues at Treasury found him cold, too businesslike at times.

A few names were tossed around—the current and past New York Fed bank presidents McDonough and Corrigan, the previous board vice chairman David Mullins. Rubin didn't think any was a serious alternative. Here Greenspan, an experienced, known chairman, and a Republican, was delivering the exact interest rate policy the economy—and administration—needed. In addition, if they nominated someone else, the administration would get a real fight, if not a bloody defeat, from the Republican-controlled Senate. It was important to have a Clinton nominee confirmed. It was easy to make Greenspan theirs, because in all important respects he already was.

Rubin and Tyson essentially said to Clinton, Look, there's no list, but if you ever were going to consider it, this is the kind of list you'd get.

Tyson's main point was that they had all come to view Greenspan almost as a member of their team. They didn't think of him as a Republican. He wasn't running the Fed as a Republican.

For Tyson, there was an element of luck in the performance of the economy. She knew that it all could have turned out differently. If the economy and the markets had tanked, Greenspan would be the nation's and the world's great villain.

Everyone at the meeting, including Clinton and Gore, agreed the president should reappoint Greenspan.

Rubin was also at the G-7 meeting in Paris, where he and Greenspan had a chance to speak privately. Taking advantage of a quiet moment, they walked together toward a series of large plate-glass windows at one end of the room, with a view of Paris before them. The two men had established a feeling of trust, perhaps as much as two adult males in high government posts might find possible. For Greenspan, such friendship, closeness and agreement gave him a sense that they were working for the same firm. Greenspan had once remarked privately, and only half-jokingly, that he considered Rubin the best *Republican* secretary of the treasury ever, though he was a Democrat.

"When you get back," Rubin said, "the president's going to want to talk to you."

Greenspan could tell by the body language that it was all favorable.

"The president's quite pleased with what you've been doing," Rubin said.

The implausible had become plausible. Greenspan realized it was the soft landing that made his reappointment possible. Without it, his future would likely be different. It had taken years—saving the banks, Clinton's 1993 economic plan, the rebirth of the overall economy and the building of consumer confidence. Greenspan knew he had helped hand Clinton what he called "a pro-incumbent-type economy."

In many respects, it was more than that. Inflation was about 3 percent—for the fifth year in a row, which was the best economic performance since the Kennedy administration. At the end of January, unemployment was at 5.6 percent, lower than most economists thought possible without triggering inflation. The Dow Jones was at 5381, up almost 40 percent from the previous January. Overall economic growth was between 2 and 3 percent. But most important, there had been no recession.

Clinton understood the power of the economy in a presidential election. The 1990–91 recession—and the economic doldrums and pessimism of 1992—had been the foundation of his first presidential campaign. The campaign's memorable slogan "It's the economy, stupid," devised by political strategist James Carville, contained a pledge that Clinton would be engaged and in touch with the forces that affected people's daily lives. The last three presidents to lose—Ford, Carter and Bush—had failed in part because they had mismanaged the economy, or had been perceived to have mismanaged the economy.

Ten days later, at the January 31, 1996, FOMC meeting, the bank presidents and governors presented some evidence that the economy was slowing. Business investment in computers was slowing. Motor vehicle inventories were up, meaning sales were down. The forecast was that the economy most likely would pick up over the year, but Greenspan said that the risk of a drop in growth was significant. Given the low amount of inflation, he saw only a limited risk in a slight easing. He proposed another ¼ percent cut in rates.

Some noted that postponing the rate cut could be defended, given the uncertainty of the situation and the possibility that the weakness in the economy was quite temporary. If this were so, an interest rate cut could help create inflationary pressures. Still others remarked that the sluggishness could be read as a call for a more significant rate cut.

Greenspan had found the middle course, and his ¼ percent cut was approved unanimously.

Meanwhile, Tyson spoke with Greenspan by phone about the Rohatyn nomination. This was the way the president wished to proceed.

Greenspan sent a simple message: He could live with it. It would be okay, he was not going to block it.

Several key Republicans on the Senate Banking Committee, which would have to vote to confirm him, soon voiced public opposition to Rohatyn. Fed governors each had to come from different Federal Reserve districts, and the New York slot was filled by Greenspan. Rohaytn was trying to figure out a way to use the residence he was building in Wyoming as a way to serve from another district, but the whole issue posed a technical obstacle that critics could use to derail the nomination.

Tyson warned Rohatyn that trouble was brewing. It looked as if he didn't have a single Republican vote on the Senate Banking Committee, and Republicans controlled the Senate.

"I know a lot of Republicans," Rohatyn responded. Many were his friends.

"Good," Tyson said. "Then use them."

Rohatyn had served on the board of directors for Universal MCA, the giant film and music conglomerate, with Howard Baker, Reagan's chief of staff and a former Senate Republican leader. He asked Baker, who was now in private law practice in Washington, to make some calls.

Baker made a bunch of calls to Republican senators to tell them how Felix had saved the credit of New York City, that he wanted the Fed vice chairmanship and that they would be lucky to have him. But Baker couldn't get a handle on it. It was pretty clear to him that someone was poisoning the well, but he couldn't tell who.

When Tyson spoke with Rubin, she could see he was uncomfortable.

It is not the right thing, he said. It wouldn't be good for the Fed, and he didn't think it would be good for the president to stake out a firm position on Rohatyn, because they could lose.

Next, Tyson heard from a senior member of the White House staff in charge of liaison with the Senate about a likely Rohatyn nomination. "Do you know what Alan Greenspan is doing?" the senior staffer asked.

No, she did not.

He's setting up all the chips so that it won't happen, the staffer said. Republicans were frustrated with Clinton, and the Republican attack machine was always poised to strike at his nominees. Republican Senate Banking Committee members took their cues from Greenspan, and though the chairman wasn't opposing Rohatyn, he wasn't saying that he wanted him, either. It was subtle, but it was happening.

Tyson couldn't find any hard evidence of Greenspan's direct involvement, but clearly the negatives were building.

Senator Connie Mack, Florida Republican and a key member of the banking committee, went after Rohatyn—publicly declaring him a dangerous, big-government, liberal interventionist.

Rubin learned from some Democratic senators that he could get a confidential reality check about Rohatyn from Senator Bennett, the Republican on the banking committee.

"What will happen if we send you Greenspan as chairman and Rohatyn as vice chairman?" Rubin asked Bennett.

"We will confirm Greenspan in a heartbeat," Bennett said, "and Rohatyn will not get out of committee." If for some reason Rohatyn got approved by the banking committee, his nomination would be filibustered on the floor of the Senate, Bennett added.

"Yeah, but they go together," Rubin said, not tipping his hand. "We'll send them up together."

"It will take a nanosecond to separate them," Bennett said, "and Greenspan will be confirmed . . . and Rohatyn will be filibustered until Connie Mack doesn't have a breath left in his body."

"Senator," Rubin said, "thank you for your candor." It was what he had been telling the White House, and they wouldn't believe him. Now maybe they would.

On Monday, January 29, *The Washington Post* ran a front-page story reporting that most economists, including Greenspan, did not believe higher sustained economic growth over many years was possible. The next week, on February 4, Stanford University economist Paul R. Krugman weighed in in *The New York Times Magazine* declaring that higher-growth proponents like "financier-pundit Felix Rohatyn" were living with a "delightful fairy tale." Krugman wrote, "In fact, the so-called revolutions in management, information technology and globalization are vastly overrated by their acolytes."

It was now clear to Rohatyn that neither the White House nor Greenspan was going to make the required effort. He calculated that he might spend three months fighting to win the post, and it would be a big nuisance for all—Clinton, the Fed and himself—with no assurance he could win it. The low level of enthusiasm was so evident that he felt he could almost touch it. After all, he had powerful forces on his side—much of the business community, the president and even the conservative editorial page of *The Wall Street Journal.* But they all seemed not to matter. On February 12, Rohatyn faxed a withdrawal letter to the White House. White House Chief of Staff Leon Panetta urged him to hold off for a day. Rohatyn said no.

He exchanged perfunctory phone calls with Rubin and Greenspan.

Yeah, it was too bad, they all agreed. After all, it was an election year, and the Republicans were playing politics.

Clinton needed a new candidate. Tyson walked over to the office of Alice Rivlin, 64, the petite, intellectually powerful budget director. In the first 18 months of the Clinton administration, Rivlin had been the deputy budget director to Leon Panetta, who had been the high-profile, outspoken director. Now that Panetta was White House chief of staff and Rivlin the budget director, Panetta still tended to act as if Rivlin were his deputy. Tyson thought that it was time for her to get out.

"Alice," Tyson said, "I have a really good job for you."

"Let me think about it," Rivlin said.

Rivlin, a Ph.D. economist, had perhaps the most impressive policy credentials of anyone in the Clinton administration. She had written or coauthored books on education, socioeconomics, social action, economic choices, the Swedish economy, the elderly and the American dream. She had been founding director of the nonpartisan Congressional Budget Office, which gave Congress its first real handle on the complex federal budget, from 1975 to 1983.

Moving in and out of the Brookings Institution, a leading moderate-to-liberal Washington think tank, Rivlin was a premier deficit hawk, arguing aggressively and sometimes in an impolitic manner that cutting the federal deficit was central for Clinton's credibility and an improving economy. She was a charter member of the Smart Women's Club, an informal luncheon group that included Donna Shalala, Clinton's secretary of health and human services, and Meg Greenfield, longtime editor of the editorial page of *The Washington Post*. She went to see the president.

Clinton said he was worried that 1996 would turn out to be like 1994, with the Fed raising interest rates. He wanted to reappoint Greenspan, but he wanted Democrats in the two other openings to fill Blinder's seat and that of John LaWare, who was also leaving. Clinton said he sought to balance Greenspan with people who would be more pro-growth. He wanted credible economists. Rivlin was enough of a deficit hawk that the Republican Senate should easily confirm her. How about it?

No, Rivlin told the president. She loved working as the budget director, being a cabinet member. She wanted to stay on.

Privately, however, Rivlin found the White House endlessly difficult. In some ways, she was exhausted by the confusion she encountered there. She would come in early in the morning, confident of the six things she was going to do that day, and by 8:30 a.m. they would have her doing six other or additional things.

Clinton asked for a second meeting. He was up for reelection, he said, a year not to be taken lightly. He indicated that what would happen at the Fed with interest rates could be as important as anything. He needed a package—Greenspan and two Democrats. The loss of the Congress in the 1994 elections had been devastating. The party could not afford to lose the presidency in 1996. The Republican Senate would be reluctant to approve his nominations in the presidential election year, but the pairing of Greenspan and Rivlin might carry it.

Rivlin felt there were some strong arguments for getting back to a more normal life. But if she accepted the offer, she knew it would be more to solve a problem for the president than because she really wanted to be at the Fed. She finally said yes.

Tyson called Blinder to inform him that Rivlin would be his replacement.

Blinder was astonished. He hadn't thought that Rivlin would have any interest at all. As budget director, she had what Blinder saw as a "real position," a cabinet post that wasn't worth leaving to be the Fed's vice chairman. Why would someone voluntarily move from A list to B list?

With Rivlin's acceptance, Clinton finally had his package:

Greenspan, Rivlin as vice chair and Laurence H. Meyer, a Democrat with impeccable academic credentials, who would fill the other vacancy on the Fed board. Meyer, 51, was an economics professor in St. Louis, and he also headed one of the most successful economic forecasting firms in the country. He had worked extensively with the Reagan and Bush White House economic advisers and had credibility in Republican circles.

The president wanted a team that would be confirmed quickly so that they would affect the upcoming decisions on interest rates.

At a fund-raising dinner at the Sheraton Hotel in New York City on February 15, Clinton took the podium. He was in full campaign mode, even though the Republicans were chewing each other up in the presidential primaries and he was unopposed. Too many people were playing politics, he said.

"An example of what should not be done that most people in this room are familiar with was the outrageous political treatment of my intention to nominate Felix Rohatyn to be the vice chairman of the Federal Reserve," Clinton said. He asked Rohatyn, who was in the audience, to take a bow. Clinton said they ought to have the debate about how fast the economy could grow.

"That's why I wanted to put Felix Rohatyn on the Federal Reserve. But the politics of Washington said, No, we insist on the conventional wisdom; we insist on holding people down; we don't think it's worth debating—over and out." He went on to denounce the cynicism of the age.

Erskine Bowles, the deputy chief of staff, knew of Rubin's quiet but strong opposition to Rohatyn's nomination. Yet Rubin hadn't left any fingerprints. Even the president didn't know. Bowles realized that even presidents didn't always get their way, especially when the forces they were pushing against were both powerful and concealed.

A week later, just before 5 p.m. on February 22, Clinton stepped into a press conference in the Oval Office.

"Today I am pleased to announce my decision," Clinton said after a brief introduction, ". . . to reappoint Alan Greenspan as the chairman of the Federal Reserve. He brings his years of experience as a prominent economist and, I might add, a leading Republican."

He announced the nominations of Rivlin and Meyer.

"Mr. President, do you think these three people will be able to engage in the kind of debate you were talking about last week?" a reporter asked.

"I do," Clinton said, adding, "I think that the truth is that we're entering a new economy and it's a subject that ought to be open to honest debate."

After the announcement, the president and Greenspan chatted for a few minutes. The back-and-forth, the challenging discussion that the president wanted at the Fed, was already taking place, Greenspan assured Clinton. He seemed put off that anyone would suggest otherwise. "The FOMC *is* a debating forum," he said.

After Clinton's press conference, Tyson held a press conference in the White House briefing room to describe the process involved in picking the three nominees.

"A number of people on the Street today," a reporter said, referring to Wall Street, "are concluding that after ginning up this big debate about—or saying that he wanted to gin up a debate about—the growth rate and how fast the economy could grow without raising the risk of inflation, that in the end, after pressure from the banking committee, the president has backed off that, chosen two economists who are not known for making statements that look anything like the sort of statements that Felix Rohatyn has made. And that essentially has put forward nominees which are safe, right in the middle of the road, very sort of mainstream.

"Any reason why we shouldn't regard this as a sort of chickening out by the administration?" the reporter asked.

Tyson ducked the question.

"Knowing what's going on with profits is critical," Greenspan again reminded Steve Sharpe, the meticulous, mild-mannered Ph.D. economist on the Fed staff. Sharpe's job as a staff economist was to track corporate profits for the Fed, and Greenspan wanted regular reports and memos with data. The chairman knew that profits were absolutely central to businesses, and he wanted the information mined as much as possible. If there was any indicator of the health of the economy, it was profits.

Greenspan looked regularly at a monthly report from a firm called I/B/E/S, which provided a comprehensive estimate of earnings for the next three to five years for the main Standard & Poor's 500 companies. For a year he had been surprised at the extraordinary growth in expected profits. The companies anticipated average profit growth in the lofty range of 14 percent a year, and Greenspan was skeptical. The estimates were biased, because I/B/E/S compiled them from Wall Street securities analysts. Such analysts, Greenspan knew, had to be optimists. Pessimistic or bearish analysts generally didn't work on Wall Street, because they couldn't sell stocks. But the bias of the analysts was constant, because the same people—or people from the same bullish culture—provided the estimates year after year. What concerned Greenspan more was that the I/B/E/S reports were weighted by the total stock value of the firms. In an era of heightened stock prices, the result might contribute to an exaggeration of expectations. Greenspan asked Sharpe if it were possible to take the data and reweight it by earnings—the amounts the firms were actually making.

Sharpe wrote a computer program that showed that earnings per stock share were expected to grow above 11 percent annually over the next several years—still quite a large number.

Greenspan knew the importance of profits from his years of working for businesses. Profits drove businesses. It was simple and basic, but the new generation of economists that had come out of the universities over the last 20 to 30 years was heavily focused on econometrics, the branch of the profession that relied on sophisticated mathematical modeling. As Greenspan knew, for somebody with mathematical capability, econometrics was like a drug. He would have been sucked in himself, but such study was not available when he was a student at New York University and Columbia in the late 1940s and early 1950s. He was a generation too early. So he had focused on the nuts and bolts of standard businesses, examining, among other things, their profits and how those profits related to the overall health of each company. His work on building forecasting models for the rolled steel strip used for appliances and the heat-treatable aluminum plate used for F-4 U.S. Navy Phantom jets had demonstrated to him that expectations for soaring profits didn't occur in a vacuum. Something else had to be going on.

Greenspan went through the basic algebra using fairly reasonable assumptions. He saw little or no increase in prices, no real increases in labor costs, but simultaneous giant profit increases. Again, the only explanation was rising labor efficiency, more productivity. Workers were making more goods per hour. Mathematically, it was the only answer. He couldn't prove it, but he was certain. There was no way, he realized, that without his business experience he could have looked at those numbers and reached these conclusions. At 70, Greenspan realized it was a blessing not just of experience, but also simply of age.

The I/B/E/S writers were confident that productivity was increasing. "What are corporations doing with their enormous cash flows?" Richard Pucci, an I/B/E/S analyst, had asked in a commentary several months earlier. "Certainly not paying dividends!" Corporations were investing in modern technology. "These immense investments in modern technology are another piece of the 1996 earnings puzzle. . . . Its ability to effect productivity improvements is being sorely underestimated by most social and economic observers."

Greenspan realized that his arguments amounted to little more than back-of-the-envelope calculations to the Ph.D.'s on the FOMC and the staff. Only vast models and years of statistics would convince them—a kind of care he appreciated, on the one hand. On the other hand, he was pretty certain he was right.

How to convince the others?

The Republican Senate, which was increasingly hostile to Clinton, was giving Rivlin a hard time, dragging out both her confirmation and Greenspan's as well. He stayed on as chairman in the absence of a successor, but Rivlin dangled. Greenspan ran into her at a social event.

"I hope they do it quickly, because I may really need you at the next meeting," he confided.

The pressure from other FOMC members to raise rates was mounting substantially. The old economic models that most economists held sacred included the NAIRU, the non-accelerating inflation rate of unemployment. If unemployment dipped below the NAIRU, which was then commonly thought to be around 6 percent, economic theory held that inflation would start up. But unemployment was in the 5½ percent range. Why was there no burst of inflation?

The old belief held that with such a low unemployment rate, workers would have the upper hand and demand higher wages. Yet the data showed that wages weren't rising that much. It was one of the central economic mysteries of the time.

Greenspan hypothesized at one point to colleagues within the Fed about the "traumatized worker"—someone who felt job insecurity in the changing economy and so was accepting smaller wage increases. He had talked with business leaders who said their workers were not agitating and were fearful that their skills might not be marketable if they were forced to change jobs.

Janet Yellen was sympathetic to Greenspan's hypothesis, and she was deeply bothered that the Fed staff seemed too set in their ways to engage alternative views of how the economy was functioning. Each staff forecast before the FOMC meetings insisted that inflation was about to take off unless interest rates increased substantially. Greenspan appeared to be going it alone.

Yellen went to work. She knew that a single year of anomalous data didn't necessarily mean anything. The same held for a two-year period. The deviations of 1994 and 1995, when unemployment had dropped and inflation remained essentially stable, were not enough. But now, halfway through 1996, the deviation was continuing and becoming what she termed "increasingly deviant."

Yellen thought Greenspan spoke a language different from what was taught in graduate school. Outsiders and non-economists thought his Fedspeak was the language of economics, but the chairman's language was highly idiosyncratic, often not fully grounded in the data. He was prone to take leaps. At the FOMC, Yellen noticed that the Ph.D.'s on the committee, or some members of the staff, would be nearly rolling their eyes as the chairman voiced his views about how the economy might be changing. Nobody challenged him or dared say anything, but it weakened his hold on the committee.

Yellen told Greenspan that she might be able to find a theoretical underpinning for his job insecurity thesis. For most of her career, she had worked on labor markets. She had developed a standard model that went back about a decade, based on the theory of wages and efficiency. Working with data, graphs and some 14 complex equations, she drafted a 13-page memo that she sent Greenspan on June 10, 1996. It concluded that since workers had been paid more in the earlier years of the 1990s, the higher pay had induced them to feel greater attachment to their jobs and to be more productive—both in terms of quitting less and in terms of working harder to keep the jobs they had.

"Following our recent discussion concerning labor market issues," Yellen's cover letter began, "I thought I would try to codify my own thinking about the theoretical links among job insecurity, the pressure of wages, prices and profit margins, and the natural rate of unemployment. The attached note outlines the theory that I consider relevant. It shows why an increase in job insecurity due to changing technology or other factors could induce a permanent decline in the natural rate of unemployment. . . ."

Greenspan thanked Yellen. The memo was an economically conventional way of saying what he wanted to say. He had it circulated to the FOMC.

. . .

On June 20, the Senate confirmed Greenspan to another four-year term as chairman by a vote of 91 to 7. Republicans tried to defeat Rivlin, but she was confirmed 57 to 41. Laurence Meyer was confirmed without dissent, 98 to 0.

During the FOMC's two-day meeting July 2–3, the members drifted into a long discussion of what price stability actually meant. Was the current 3 percent annual inflation sufficient price stability? Yellen felt that 3 percent was probably acceptable but was surprised to see that many, perhaps most, members felt that 3 percent was not price stability. They wanted to bring inflation down, say, to 2 percent. She knew that meant the FOMC would tolerate more unemployment. The standard rule of thumb was that to drop inflation by 1 percent, they would have to go through two years of 1 percent higher unemployment. Since unemployment was roughly in the 5½ percent range, the discussion suggested that the committee might permit unemployment to go up to roughly 6½ percent to drive inflation down further.

Yellen's husband, the economist George Akerlof, had just published a paper that argued that driving inflation too low might create higher permanent unemployment. The committee engaged in a lengthy but inconclusive discussion of the issue. Yellen was surprised that the committee almost never talked about its overall strategy or its ultimate goal for acceptable rates of inflation. How can you operate if you don't know what your goal is?

Of course, the answer was that the flexibility and lack of clearly stated goals gave the FOMC, and Greenspan in particular, much more maneuvering room. It also demonstrated how inexact economics and interest rate policy were. Greenspan had come to believe that inflation numbers for the past were basically irrelevant. Their job was to deal with the future—with inflation expectations. They wanted stable prices in the next six months, not the past six months, so targeting an inflation number would be meaningless. He wanted inflation expectations to be benign, so consumers and businesses did *not* factor inflation into purchasing or investing decisions.

At the meeting, Greenspan was able to convince the FOMC not to raise rates. Only Gary Stern, the Minneapolis Fed bank president, dissented, because he thought a modest rate increase was called for. Even with only a single dissent, Greenspan could hear the hoofbeats. He was running into increasing resistance to the committee's interest rate restraint. He couldn't rely on his back-of-the-envelope calculations about prices and profits, even though he considered his computations about 95 percent accurate. He needed validation.

. . .

At the chairman's weekly breakfasts with Rubin and his deputy Larry Summers, Greenspan had been floating his ideas about productivity growth.

"Yeah, but Alan," Summers said once, "maybe there's a constant error, and it should've been plus 1 percent for the last 40 years. How do you know it's accelerated?"

Greenspan wasn't sure, but he kept coming back, week after week, with more ideas. Summers tried them out on Treasury's top economists, who thought the notions incoherent, if not idiotic. Greenspan's theories simply did not fit into the rigorous, well-tested economic models and concepts that had been developed over decades.

During the coffee break of the FOMC's next meeting, on Tuesday, August 20, Greenspan collared Larry Slifman, the associate director of the Fed's Division of Research and Statistics. Slifman, a small-framed, intense Ph.D. economist of considerable caution, had been on staff going back to the Volcker era.

"Look at these numbers," Greenspan said, pointing to a special monthly report of charts and tables that Slifman's division had prepared for him. It was a crude attempt to refine the pricing and profit data by types of businesses. Greenspan pointed to data on prices, which were relatively stable, and then to profits, which were still going up, and then to productivity—the output per hour of a worker. The charts showed productivity going down.

"Does this make sense to you?" Greenspan asked him.

Slifman at first thought they might have made a mistake with the data. But Greenspan said once again and more pointedly that he thought there was something wrong with the incoming data from the Commerce and Labor Departments.

For years Greenspan had had Research and Statistics work on special studies that "disaggregated" data, broke it into finer pieces. Government statistics tended to come in overall total numbers that lumped together quite different segments of the economy—industrial and non-industrial production, for example—eradicating some important distinctions in the process. He had wanted them separated. He then had asked for more refinements, including a breakdown on the unit costs for the production of goods or supplying of services.

Greenspan wanted the numbers so he could get his hands around different kinds of businesses. There was not just one economy but many, and individual parts and types performed differently. How were the service businesses such as auto repair doing compared to retailers or manufacturers? National numbers with everything lumped together didn't tell them enough.

In Slifman's division, the economists sometimes called Greenspan's requests the "embellishments and enhancements," or they'd say that the chairman wanted more "slicing and dicing." Greenspan had kept one research assistant busy much of that summer on special projects.

When Greenspan had come to the Fed nearly a decade earlier, Slifman had been dismissive of his research requests, certain they would be dry holes. But over the years, he had discovered that many yielded several barrels a day—and some occasionally produced a gusher of new, useful ways to look at information.

Greenspan had been questioning the official productivity numbers for almost three years. The numbers could not be right. The problem in part was that disputing them was almost like arguing with the reports of yesterday's temperature range in the newspaper. Someone had assembled the data from all over the city. If your backyard thermometer registered something different, it was hardly convincing.

How to find the flaw? Where were the errors most likely to be?

Greenspan continued his own calculations. He wanted to start with some basic data that he knew were more accurate than the official government reports. First, the government provided another series of reports on the general price level of manufactured and other goods. These were very reliable because businesses knew what they were charging and customers knew what they were paying.

Second, the government reported domestic operating profit margins. Again, these were incredibly reliable because businesses had to know how much they were making. Various reporting requirements to stockholders and relatively rigid accounting practices also made these numbers accurate.

Next, it was a matter of basic economics. The price of producing something was algebraically equal to the unit labor costs plus the unit non-labor costs (depreciation, interest and taxes) plus unit profits.

It was generally accepted that about 70 percent of production costs were labor. The other costs—depreciation, interest and taxes—didn't change much over the short run and could safely be assumed to be constant. Greenspan knew what average labor costs per hour were, within a reasonable range, from the reliable labor cost statistics. In the end, he had one of those tight, perfect formulas. The only variable was productivity, output per hour. With profits rising but prices staying the same, the laws of mathematics dictated that productivity had to be going up and unit labor costs had to be going down.

Put it more simply. Take some item with a market price of $10—say, roughly $6 in labor costs, $2 in other costs and $2 in profit. Suppose the price stays at $10 in a low-inflation environment, other costs remain at $2, and profits go up to $3. That would mean labor costs had to be lower, at about $5. Since wages had not gone down, the only way for this to be possible was for the output per hour to have gone up. Productivity had to be rising.

Greenspan wondered how he could prove it to the satisfaction of the economists.

"Do you have a few minutes?" Greenspan said on the phone to Larry Slifman right after Labor Day. The chairman suggested Slifman bring with him someone expert in national income.

Slifman and Carol Corrado, another Ph.D. in economics and the chief of the industrial output section, went to Greenspan's office. He had the formula written out:

Price = labor costs + non-labor costs + profits

They agreed.

Greenspan sketched out a massive research project. He wanted them to take all of the aggregate data on productivity and break them into their component parts by business sector—the legal forms of business organization. Find some way to separate out the farms and corporations, the manufacturers and the financial firms, he told them. He suggested a way it could be done. They would have to make their own calculations and a few careful assumptions.

Corrado could see that the chairman almost saw the forensics as he laid out a detailed research agenda.

After about 45 minutes, Slifman and Corrado left, feeling they had been assigned the economist's equivalent of a Manhattan Project.

The chairman was also developing a parallel track. He delved deeper into the ranks of the Research and Statistics Division. "I would like for someone to produce numbers for me on output per hour—productivity—by industry," he requested. There were dozens of different industries—farming, mining, public utilities, finance, health service, education and even motion pictures. He wanted productivity calculations for each.

Slifman and Corrado merged the legal breakdown with the breakdown by industry. On Thursday, September 19, Corrado wrote a computer program that looked back to 1960, producing 155 categories.

When they looked at the results, the stunner was that the service businesses, from the gas stations to the sole proprietorships and partnerships—roughly one-third of the businesses in the country—showed a ½ percent *decline* in productivity over the last two decades.

Slifman's wife was a lawyer in that service category. He knew it was totally impossible that productivity had declined in that profession over the 1980s and 1990s. Something was wrong with these numbers. But more important, those numbers were dragging down the overall productivity statistics for the corporations that were the other two-thirds of the businesses.

It was a double discovery of immense significance. The service productivity numbers, which were negative, had to be wrong. These wrong numbers were dragging down the aggregate productivity numbers for the economy as a whole. Therefore, productivity was higher across the board.

Greenspan was delighted. It was, at this preliminary point, a hypothesis that could readily dissolve. But it was a possible explanation. He had the economists up to his office before the next week's FOMC meeting to express his appreciation.

In the weeks before the next FOMC meeting, the pressure to raise rates had ratcheted up another notch. A story had leaked to Reuters news service that 8 of the 12 Federal Reserve Banks had requested at least a ¼ percent increase in the discount rate; 3 of these 8 wanted a ½ percent increase.

BusinessWeek magazine was reporting discord. "A Tug-of-War Inside the Fed," read one of their stories that month. Another was headlined "Political Hardball Inside the Fed: Using the Press, Regional Banks May Force Greenspan's Hand."

As the FOMC gathered in their cavernous meeting room on Tuesday, September 24, tension was unusually high.

Greenspan finally had some hard evidence. For three years almost to the day, he had been insisting that something was seriously wrong with their data. He quoted from the Slifman and Corrado study and dwelled on their double discovery. Using the tables they had compiled, he showed that disaggregating demonstrated that productivity in the service businesses had declined for years. This was just flat-out implausible.

Greenspan related this with the deepest conviction. Those numbers were dragging down the productivity growth numbers for the corporations and manufacturers, raising the obvious point that those numbers were too low for productivity growth. Productivity growth numbers were the hardest to capture—it had taken economists up until the late 1970s to determine that productivity growth had begun to decrease in the late 1960s. On top of this, Greenspan noted that the consumer price index was overstating inflation by approximately 1 percent, because the CPI didn't accurately measure new products, rent and other consumer goods. Nonetheless, the core inflation rate as reported by the government was only 2.6 percent over the last 12 months—*the smallest increase in three decades.*

He put it bluntly. There was a real world out there, and they were not measuring it properly. The dominant feature of the outlook was uncertainty. Since higher inflation was not a foregone conclusion, it would be best to do nothing. Because several of the committee members wanted to raise rates now, Greenspan proposed that they maintain the directive that would give him the power to raise rates between meetings if any alarming new data arrived. The prudent course would be to hold steady, no increase.

Bill McDonough, the 62-year-old New York Fed president and FOMC vice chairman, was ready to speak next. In the time since he had succeeded Gerry Corrigan three years earlier, he had forged a close relationship with Greenspan. He realized that being the Fed's man in the New York financial markets was one of the best jobs imaginable with that relationship. He suspected the job would be a goddamn nightmare without it.

McDonough's role as the speaker after the chairman was first to say, I support the chairman, and second to give his reasons. Because he was the contact person with the financial markets and the chief players in New York, no one would challenge or debate him on his analysis of the market perceptions of their various actions. McDonough, a suave, gracious, well-dressed man with bushy eyebrows that dance when he talks, was a Democrat who had been with the First National Bank of Chicago for 22 years before joining the New York Fed. He had previously discussed the productivity issues with Greenspan and agreed with his analysis. It was difficult but necessary to discard the old orthodoxy, because the economy was creating jobs for those who needed them most. Though that didn't solve the problems of the inner city, it helped. McDonough was convinced it was the single most important thing they could do—provide jobs for minorities and the urban and rural poor. Keeping unemployment low and getting it lower if possible was the chief task at hand as long as inflation could be kept down. The Fed could not operate as if the most dangerous thing in America was the last poor guy who found a job.

The other critical factor was the anti-inflation credibility that the Fed had established with its preemptive rate hikes in 1994–95, when rates went from 3 to 6 percent. The New York financial markets, McDonough knew, had been very impressed with the dramatic moves to keep on top of inflation, even when no inflation was in sight. The willingness to take bold preemptive action back then had given the Greenspan Fed an anti-inflation medal of honor in the eyes of the markets, McDonough believed. The markets would trust the decision not to raise rates.

McDonough, eyebrows in motion, gave a passionate summary of his views. It was critical they stick together and stick with the chairman. They had to be united. It was a version of the speech that Greenspan had given back in February 1994 when they had started to raise rates. McDonough said he would vote to support Greenspan, as he always had.

Rivlin also said she supported the chairman and would vote for no rate increase. She was delighted to see herself anchoring the dovish faction with the chairman and the FOMC vice chairman.

Yellen was torn. Despite her conviction that something different was going on with worker insecurity and productivity increases, she wished that Greenspan had proposed a rate hike. It would have been smart to go up ¼ percent, she felt, and it was becoming difficult to be intellectually honest and not admit they needed to raise rates. The economy was likely growing too fast. Though sympathetic to Greenspan, she thought they were beginning to take too great a risk by not going up.

She finally said that if she had her druthers, she would vote to increase, but she added that she could support the chairman's proposal to hold steady. The force of Greenspan's personality and his strong desire carried her. She also realized that he was not asking them to never raise rates. He was saying only, Let's hold off for now and then revisit the question in light of more information in six weeks. She felt enormous pressure not to oppose him, and as the votes were taken she realized the others felt it, too.

There was frequently a sharp contrast between the hawkish

statements of some of the members and their dovish votes to go along with the chairman. If there had been a secret ballot, Yellen mused to herself, Greenspan almost certainly would have lost. If the members could write their votes on little pieces of paper and anonymously throw them in a hat, she calculated that there would probably be nine votes against the chairman. He would receive as few as three votes—his own, McDonough's and Rivlin's. Yellen, who considered herself a dove, realized she would have voted to raise rates in a secret ballot. But out in the open, she voted with Greenspan. That disturbed her.

The sense of urgency for an immediate rate increase dissipated as all but Gary Stern, president of the Minneapolis bank, voted with the chairman to hold steady. Stern believed the low unemployment rate of 5.1 percent would eventually be associated with rising inflation.

"Fed Avoids Rate Hike," ran the headline in an unusual front-page story in *The Washington Post* the next morning, reporting on a decision not to act. *The New York Times* ran a front-page story headlined "Federal Reserve Makes No Change in Interest Rates." The stories contained no real details about why the Fed had not moved or about any of the internal tension.

"With the economic outlook unusually uncertain and a presidential election around the corner," the *Post* story read, "Chairman Alan Greenspan and other Fed policymakers chose to leave rates alone." The story noted accurately that "the decision on rates was a close call for the Fed" and quoted analysts who believed that "the nearness of Election Day may have tipped the balance in favor of leaving them unchanged."

In October, Slifman and Corrado invited some key economists from the Commerce Department and the Bureau of Labor Statistics over to the Fed for a working session on their productivity findings.

Rivlin got word of the meeting and decided to attend, but she had to hunt for the small conference room in the nether regions of the Fed building, where the meeting was being held. When she arrived, she was surprised to see the chairman himself—coat off, sleeves rolled up—in heated debate with about 10 government productivity experts. She sat down.

"Well, no, Alan," Bob Parker, now chief statistician at the Bureau of Economic Analysis at Commerce, was saying, "you're not right about that." Nobody at the Fed called him "Alan" in meetings. Rivlin realized that these were Greenspan's people and that position in the hierarchy meant nothing. Information and analysis alone counted. Memories and relationships seemed deeply embedded— Greenspan's equivalent of the playing fields of early adulthood and labor statistics debates from the 1970s and 1980s. Greenspan had known Parker for 25 years.

Again calling the chairman "Alan," Parker insisted that it was hard to measure productivity in non-manufacturing businesses. Coming at the issue from the profitability of businesses, as Greenspan wanted to, was insufficient, Parker said. What about the discrepancies in translating the statistics of income into wage, salary and profit components?

Later in the meeting, Rivlin called Greenspan "Mr. Chairman" after she had made a point to the group. Parker was embarrassed and wanted to crawl under his chair.

The group reached no conclusion, but it was clear that the economy was growing, unemployment was down, inflation and wages weren't going up much and profits were up. They all seemed to agree that productivity had to be going up, but they weren't measuring it. Why? No one had a clear answer as they shared their puzzlement.

For Greenspan, the issue was serious but the process great fun.

In November, Clinton won reelection with 49 percent of the vote. Former Senate Majority Leader Bob Dole, the Kansas Republican, received 41 percent, and Ross Perot received 8 percent.

Republican Greenspan was not unhappy.

In the course of their regular breakfasts and almost daily phone conversations, the firm of Greenspan & Rubin continued their discussions of the skyrocketing stock market. Over the last five years, the Dow had advanced from about 2500 to over 6000 that fall— more than doubling. The increase by December of 1996 was a lofty 26 percent for the year.

Rubin couldn't believe how high the market had gone. Never in his lifetime had he seen anything like it, and he was deeply worried. People had lost their discipline in making financial decisions. The market was dramatically and perhaps dangerously overvalued.

Did Treasury and the Fed have an obligation to do or at least say something? It was the one element in the economy that was out of balance. The Japanese had provided a telling lesson: After a meteoric rise, their stock market had plummeted and their economy was in the doldrums.

Rubin was aware that nobody could know for sure. Anything

that was obvious would already be reflected in the market, he believed. But was there something that wasn't obvious that they should try to figure out?

Both Rubin and Greenspan knew that the treasury secretary could hardly speak out against the stock market and issue a warning. The White House would have to be involved, and the president's political advisers considered the bull market a badge of honor. Several times, somebody at the White House had proposed that the president should ring the bell at the New York Stock Exchange, and Rubin had to go to battle station to stop it. He told the president that he would live with that film clip forever if the market went down. From the beginning of the administration, Rubin had told Clinton, If the economy does well, you ought to talk about it—but if the markets do well, don't use that as your credential because markets go up and markets go down. Since pride in the stock market run-up was part of the psychology at the White House for at least some, Rubin could hardly try to unring the bell.

Greenspan decided to give it a try.

He had agreed to accept the Francis Boyer Award at the American Enterprise Institute, a conservative think tank in Washington, in early December and to speak at the black-tie dinner ceremony.

He began work on his speech while taking his ritual early morning soak in the bathtub. His tub was deep and narrow, with armrests so he could comfortably read and write. He decided to voice his concerns about the stock market in a long historical discussion of the notion of prices. He would carefully pose those concerns in the form of a question. How do we know, he wrote, when—and the phrase just popped into his head—"irrational exuberance" has unduly escalated the value of stocks?

He knew the phrase "irrational exuberance" would have market consequences. The market *was* overvalued. But on another level, by phrasing it as a question, he was giving himself cover. He would just be professing his uncertainty, because who could know for sure?

He circulated the draft speech to others at the Fed.

It was a typical makes-my-eyes-glaze-over Greenspan speech, but at the end Rivlin saw a cloaked but clear warning about "irrational exuberance" in the stock market. It seemed like an offhand remark, not necessarily related to the rest of the speech. All the same, Rivlin feared that it might be taken too seriously. She walked next door to Greenspan's office, a marked-up copy in hand.

"Do you really want to say that?" she inquired.

"I think I do," he replied.

After delivering the speech, Greenspan returned to his table, where his girlfriend, Andrea Mitchell, was also seated.

"So what was the most important thing I said?" he asked her.

She looked perplexed, not at all sure. He was sure.

After the speech, the markets in Japan, which were still open, began to drop sharply. The Dow fell 145 points in the first half hour of trading the next day but rebounded, ending the day off only 55 points at 6381.

In his office four days later, Greenspan said to a trusted senior Fed staffer, "Every business cycle is the same with the exception of some fundamental difference that characterizes that particular cycle, and rarely, if ever, is in evidence in other cycles. The crucial issue is to identify what that particular phenomenon is."

Perhaps it was the stock market, perhaps not. Was it a bubble or not? He was sure that job insecurity was part of the mystery, keeping inflation down. Clearly productivity growth was another factor. But how much, he didn't know.

Earlier that month, *The Washington Post* had published a story stripped across the top of page one by John M. Berry, the paper's respected Fed watcher. Headlined "U.S. Sails on Tranquil Economic Seas, Recessions No Longer Seem Inevitable," the story quoted many prominent economists saying they didn't expect a recession in the next five years.

Greenspan also didn't see a recession coming. It would take six months for it to build, he thought. Yet he had said that before, only to find three months later that he was eating crow.

Greenspan had been virtually living with Mitchell, who was 20 years younger, for nearly 12 years. Their first connection had been through music: she played the violin quite well as a child. Greenspan, a devotee of baroque music, and Mitchell went to classical concerts at the Kennedy Center, often using the presidential box.

At the end of 1996, Greenspan began to think about proposing. At a birthday dinner for Mitchell with a dozen close friends at Galileo, one of Washington's best Italian restaurants, Greenspan gave a glowing toast to her. A number of guests felt it was as near to a proposal of marriage as possible, with the expected next sentence to be a request that she marry him. But it never came.

He later confided to one person that he actually proposed to Mitchell twice before she accepted, but either she had not understood what he was saying or it had failed to register. His verbal obscurity and caution were so ingrained that Mitchell didn't even know that he had asked her to marry him. She found it difficult to understand the depth of his emotional commitment to her.

On Christmas Day, Greenspan finally asked, flat out, "Do you want a big wedding or a small wedding?" It was a message no one could miss.

Mitchell was taken by surprise but accepted at once.

They announced their engagement at a going-away party they threw for Laura Tyson, who was leaving as director of Clinton's National Economic Council.

Four months later, they were married in a private seven-minute civil ceremony at a plush country inn in the Virginia hunt country outside Washington, the Inn at Little Washington. Supreme Court Justice Ruth Bader Ginsburg, Clinton's first appointee to the High Court, performed the ceremony. About 75 guests attended, including former chairman of the Joint Chiefs of Staff Colin Powell, Democratic lawyers Bob Strauss and Lloyd Cutler, Henry Kissinger, Alice Rivlin, Mike Kelley of the Fed, media figures Katharine Graham, Ben Bradlee, Sally Quinn, Jim Lehrer, Barbara Walters, Tim Russert (Mitchell's bureau chief), David Brinkley, Al Hunt and Judy Woodruff and Senators John Warner, Virginia Republican, and Daniel P. Moynihan.

Several days after his wedding, Greenspan told an associate, "I should have done it sooner."

12

As 1997 began, Greenspan reminded himself of his maxim "If you're not nervous, you shouldn't be here."

On February 26, he testified before the Senate Banking Committee and hit the stock market again. "Caution seems especially warranted with regard to the sharp rise in equity prices during the last two years," he said. "These gains have obviously raised questions of sustainability." Since the beginning of 1995, the Dow had jumped a staggering 80 percent.

A week later, at the House Banking Committee, the chairman attempted to deny that he was trying to "jawbone" the stock market.

"That's not what I was intending to do," he said. "It can't be done."

Greenspan was claiming impotence about the stock market while trying doggedly to influence it. He was attempting a subtle distinction. The suggestions about "irrational exuberance" and "sustainability" indicated that the stock market might be relevant to the Fed as they evaluated their monetary policy. It was a fact that the market was very, very high. He was not necessarily saying that it was *too* high or that the Fed would try to bring it down. If the Fed did try to bring the market down, their problems would only grow worse. Congress and others would want to know when the stock market was too low and at what point the Fed might be expected to boost stock prices. Greenspan didn't want to get close to setting a trading range—the maximum permissible high and the maximum permissible low. It was not the Fed's job. He didn't think they could do it if they tried.

Nonetheless, he wanted to issue a clear warning: The stock

market was unusually high, the Fed was watching vigilantly, and they had to consider the possible impact on the economy and consumer spending. It made him nervous.

At the end of March, Dr. Laurence H. Meyer had been a governor at the Fed for nine months. Appointed by Clinton the previous year, Meyer would never forget the day he came to Washington to be interviewed by President Clinton in the White House residence. They met for about 45 minutes, and the president did nearly all of the talking, trying to relax Meyer, speaking about the history of various White House rooms and his overall economic goals. If the president had asked the basic question—Do you think the economy can grow faster without inflation?—Meyer was prepared to say no, that there was a lot of loose economic talk going on that was contrary to his understanding of how the economy worked. Meyer believed that if unemployment were too low, it would spark inflation—and in his view, the economy was already in the danger zone, quite close to the NAIRU. But Clinton never asked the question, and Meyer was nominated and confirmed.

With a Ph.D. from MIT, he had founded Laurence H. Meyer and Associates, a successful economic forecasting business in St. Louis, in the early 1980s. Working with economic advisers in the Reagan, Bush and Clinton administrations, he had been known for the accuracy of his economic forecasts. For a single three-year period in the 1990s, his forecast for the growth of the consumer price index was off by only $\frac{1}{10}$ percent. He had received many national awards, including the Annual Forecast Award from a panel of blue chip economists as the nation's most accurate forecaster in 1993 and 1996. For Meyer, a data-driven intellectual, forecasting was all sophisticated, rigorous economic modeling.

At his first FOMC meeting, Meyer had come to the realization that the committee meetings were mostly prepackaged. During his first presentation, he found himself speaking at 100 miles an hour, almost out of control, and he burst out saying, "This is even more fun than I thought it was going to be."

The room broke into laughter.

But Meyer was struggling now in the spring of 1997. All of his training, all of the models and concepts that had worked with such precision, told him that higher economic growth and lower unemployment would soon trigger a rapid increase of dangerous inflation. He wasn't buying Greenspan's argument about productivity growth. He thought it bordered on fantasy. But he had not dissented thus far.

At the FOMC meeting on Tuesday, March 25, 1997, the staff report provided mounting evidence that the economy was more than robust. Consumer spending, business capital expenditures and housing construction were all up. Though there was no sign of inflation, Meyer and some of the others wondered whether it was time to increase rates, perhaps by a large amount, a preemptive move similar to what the Fed had done in 1994.

Speaking first, Greenspan had proposed a ¼ percent increase, arguing that such a move would be the other side of the prudence that had led them *not* to raise rates the previous fall.

Brilliant, Meyer thought. Here Greenspan, the poster boy for the New Economy, was playing the old economy, inflation hawk card. The chairman was keeping a foot in both camps, both the New Economy/higher productivity school and the old economy/inflation-fighting school. It was a masterly management of the process, Meyer concluded. He voted with the chairman.

From the dovish side, Alice Rivlin believed that the economy was beginning to heat up. The stock market was feeding economic growth and perhaps getting the economy into inflationary trouble. Maybe they should at least *look* vigilant. The Fed hadn't acted in more than a year. A ¼ percent hike wouldn't make any real difference one way or the other. It wouldn't hurt, she figured, aware of the irony of the situation—which was that inflation was actually going down. But she voted with the chairman. So did all the other committee members.

The ¼ percent increase, which put the fed funds rate at 5½ percent, was again front-page news. The Greenspan Fed had never made just a single move up or down, so the expectation was that more increases were around the corner. *The Wall Street Journal* said that Fed watchers bet on one, two or even three additional increases over the rest of the year. *The Washington Post* said only one or two more ¼ percent hikes were expected.

In one of his first discussions with Greenspan, Meyer had asked if there were any guidelines for giving public speeches. No formal rules, Greenspan said, but there were informal rules. Rule one: Don't do speeches. The chairman noted that no one followed rule one. So rule two: Don't say anything that will move markets.

Meyer had agreed to give a speech April 24 at a luncheon at the Forecasters Club in New York City. He carefully typed out his 25-page speech and had an advance text released to the press.

"I am a strong and unapologetic proponent of the Phillips

Curve and the NAIRU concept," he declared. These economic concepts held that low unemployment would eventually lead to high inflation. If there weren't enough unemployed workers, wages would shoot up.

Meyer said also that the economy was growing at an "unsustainable" rate, and that the previous month's ¼ percent interest rate hike was "small, prudent, and preemptive." The tone suggested that more rate increases were coming.

About 1:30 p.m., the wire service headlines read, "Fed Poised to Raise Interest Rates in May" and "Fed Gov. Meyer Signals More U.S. Interest Rate Increases Likely." The Dow fell 20 points and the bond market dropped, with 30-year Treasuries losing $2.50 for every $1,000 of face value.

The next morning Meyer read a front-page story in *The Wall Street Journal*. The headline read, in part: "How Hard Mr. Meyer Tries Not to Move the Markets; Why He Failed Yesterday." He was slightly sick, but no one at the Fed said much to him.

Shortly thereafter Greenspan invited Meyer down to his office. Let's just talk about the economy, the chairman proposed, and the Fed's interest rate decisions.

They talked about the forces on the economy and the data they had. Meyer confessed that he was on the edge and was struggling. His own forecast and those of many other private forecasters showed repeatedly that the economy should slow down, and it hadn't. All the forecasts expected inflation to pick up, and it hadn't. The models he had grown up on and had used for so long in his own forecasting business dictated that growth was too high and unemployment was too low. He particularly choked on the idea that unemployment could go this low and stay there at a sustainable rate without inflation. The unemployment rate for April had dropped to 4.9 percent—the lowest since 1973.

Let me tell you what I'm thinking about, Greenspan said. This is why I'm not concerned. He went over the disaggregated data on productivity in more detail. The world and the economy were changing. It was their job to figure out how and why.

They were two of the best economists in the country, and they could talk, and they did—for a long time.

Meyer was impressed. It had been a wonderful discussion. The chairman wasn't asking for his vote or even his support. He realized that Greenspan had a particular vulnerability. Tradition dictated that the chairman couldn't be on the losing side of a vote. Meyer thought that the chairman was entitled to know, in advance, where members were when they walked into the FOMC meetings. If he himself were going to vote against the chairman, he would warn him. When he walked into the meetings, Meyer felt he had already made a commitment. He didn't care how convincing anybody else was. He might say, You've changed my mind, but you haven't changed my vote. If so, then he'd walk out of the room and tell the chairman, Sorry, next meeting you don't have me anymore.

Because of the deference shown the chairman, Meyer realized that Greenspan went into FOMC meetings with a bunch of votes stuffed in his pocket. If Meyer wanted to change interest rate policy, he would have to change the chairman's mind first.

Greenspan had a subtle but firm hold on him. The chairman was an agnostic on the notion that unemployment could go only so low before triggering inflation. What was the number? It was amorphous, non-observable. It all depended on economic conditions, and rigid adherence to a specific level made little sense.

Some others on the FOMC were unhappy that Meyer was running around declaring that too many people were employed. Ed Boehne, the longest-serving member of the committee, thought Meyer was a public relations disaster. How could the Fed justify or explain itself to the public when one of its governors made such declarations? For Boehne, the lowest possible unemployment rate without inflation was not a fixed number—perhaps it floated between 3.5 percent and 6.5 percent. It might be a useful analytical tool for economists, but it was not good for interest rate policy makers to fixate on it.

Greenspan thought Meyer was a bit tone-deaf politically, but as usual he didn't say anything.

On Tuesday, May 20, 1997, Meyer came to his office well before the 9 a.m. FOMC meeting scheduled for that day. Normally he didn't have time to read the newspapers, but he picked up *The Wall Street Journal* and made his way to the editorial page, which didn't like interest rate hikes that seemed designed to stifle growth.

"The Meyer Fed?" blared the headline. "The bond market has since recovered from its Meyer shock," he read. The editorial ridiculed him and his ancient thinking, especially the concepts that low unemployment causes inflation. "The notion, in other words, is that inflation is caused by too many people working." Though praising Greenspan in general, the editorial read, "Trouble is, Mr. Greenspan today sounds a lot like Mr. Meyer."

When Meyer arrived at the meeting, some members ribbed

him, laughing at the idea that he had hijacked the Fed. Perhaps he should give the Fed back to the chairman, one joked.

Greenspan again said nothing. His task was to sound just enough like Meyer but not too much, keep a foot in the camp of the anti-inflation hawks like Meyer as well as the pro-growth New Economy apostles. If *The Wall Street Journal* thought Meyer had unusual influence, all the better.

After a long discussion of the economy, Greenspan recommended no immediate interest rate move but an asymmetric directive, with a tilt toward raising rates. Meyer voted with him. The sole exception was J. Alfred Broaddus Jr., a vehement anti-inflation hawk who headed the Richmond bank. Broaddus, 57, a Ph.D. economist who had spent almost his entire career in the Richmond bank, wanted to raise rates immediately.

That month the Dow was up over 7000.

At the White House, Gene Sperling, who had succeeded Laura Tyson as head of the National Economic Council, had been interviewing candidates to fill Lawrence Lindsey's seat at the Fed. He believed he had found the perfect person, so he called Greenspan. Sperling liked to let Greenspan know in advance, so if he absolutely went crazy, they had a chance to reconsider.

We're going to put up Roger Ferguson, Sperling reported.

Who is he? Greenspan asked. I've never heard of him.

A B.A. in economics, a law degree and a Ph.D. in economics—all three from Harvard. A partner at McKinsey, the premier international management consulting firm, and currently their director of research. And he's African American.

I understand you have many goals, Greenspan said.

The Clinton administration had made diversity a prominent priority. It's a difficult time, the chairman added, and the Fed needed technical expertise. Ferguson's career path was somewhat unusual for a Fed appointee, and Greenspan wanted someone who could come in and hit the ground running on some of the regulatory and technical banking issues.

Sperling said Ferguson had given one of the best interviews he had ever seen. Summers also thought Ferguson was terrific.

What we do here day in and day out can be very technical, Greenspan repeated. The board was shorthanded.

Sperling said Ferguson was the man for the job.

It's the president's decision, Greenspan replied. It's very nice of you to call and give me a heads-up.

The White House had come up with too many unqualified candidates. Greenspan had wanted them to nominate Ted Truman, the Fed's controversial, brilliant and bombastic international chief, as a governor, but they had refused.

Ferguson was nominated and soon confirmed.

About a month later, Greenspan called Sperling.

"I just want you to know Roger Ferguson is terrific," he said. "You were right. This guy is outstanding." Ferguson knew a great deal about the check payment system, technology, computers, productivity.

On July 22, Chairman Greenspan provided his own dose of exuberance. "We have as close to stable prices as I have seen, certainly since the 1960s," he told the House Banking Committee. Though cautioning that the fed funds rate of 5½ percent "will need to be changed at some point to foster sustainable growth and low inflation," he attributed much of the boom to increased productivity. "We do not now know, nor do I suspect can anyone know, whether current developments are part of a once- or twice-in-a-century phenomenon that will carry productivity trends nationally and globally to a new higher track." The Dow jumped 155 points, closing over 8000.

But the March ¼ percent rate increase had had an unintended impact on the global financial markets. Many global investors were borrowing money in Japan, which had interest rates in the range of 1 percent, and then using the money to invest billions of dollars in Thailand. Because of the risk in Thailand's booming but shaky economy, investors were receiving returns on bonds and other debt in the range of 15 percent. Borrowing low in Japan and investing with high returns in Thailand was creating a profit bonanza on the interest rate spread somewhere in the range of 14 percent.

The Fed increase of ¼ percent in March and the presumption that more increases might follow seemed to suggest that long-term interest rates in the United States would soon be going up, perhaps way up. Though the U.S. long-term rates would never approach Thailand's 15 percent, the much safer U.S. bonds were suddenly much more appealing. New York Fed officials who watched the international markets closely believed this contributed at least in part to a sell-off in Thailand by foreign speculators.

That summer, Thailand went into economic crisis. Though it was not yet widely known, the central bank of Thailand was effectively bust.

Rubin consulted with Greenspan. Some at Treasury wanted to use the Exchange Stabilization Fund, which had been used to rescue Mexico, to prop up Thailand. Rubin said this wasn't Mexico and that the Republican Congress would be skittish about use of the ESF.

"Look," Rubin said at one meeting with Greenspan, "we don't know what's going to happen, but it may be we're going to need that ESF, and if we use it now, and Congress actually takes our ability to use it away, then what would happen when we *really* need it?"

Greenspan thought there were forces at work in the Asian economies that they didn't fully understand. Several questions had to be raised: What might be the impact on the United States economy? What was the degree of interconnectedness? What could the United States do to affect the outcome? Should the United States try to assist whenever a country was in economic distress or turmoil? As they had worried vis-à-vis Mexico, suppose the United States tried to help and failed? Would that send an awful message to the financial markets about U.S. impotence? Rubin wanted to leave Thailand to the International Monetary Fund (IMF) and support their efforts. Greenspan agreed. Unpredictability in the global financial markets was putting everyone's teeth on edge.

In the fall, Greenspan sent out contradictory public messages about interest rates, the economy and the stock market, reflecting some of his own uncertainty. On October 8, in testimony to the House Budget Committee, he declared, "The economy has been on an unsustainable track," adding, "It clearly would be unrealistic to look for a continuation of stock market gains of anything like the magnitude of those recorded in the past couple years." Three weeks later, on Monday, October 27, the Dow plunged 554 points—the largest point drop in history. This sent Rubin out to declare publicly on the Treasury steps: "Remember that the fundamentals of the U.S. economy are strong."

But the economic fundamentals of a number of other countries were growing increasingly unsound. Businessmen abroad were playing dangerous investing games.

The day before Thanksgiving, the Fed and Treasury learned that South Korea was in real trouble. Its central bank reserves were pouring out of the country at about $1 billion a day. They had only several days of reserves left, and the South Korean economy was on the verge of collapse.

Rubin, his deputy Larry Summers, other Treasury experts and Greenspan went into crisis mode. Korea was the eleventh largest economy in the world. It had graduated into an investment-grade country, meaning that it was considered a solid place to invest. This wasn't Thailand or Indonesia. Could Korea go into default? What would be the consequences?

The exposure of Japanese and European banks in Korea was greater than that of the U.S. banks. Given the weakness of the Japanese economy and its shaky financial markets, Korean default could trigger a catastrophic chain reaction.

Greenspan understood that new technology, which had created the global economy in which capital flowed quite freely, had a punishing downside. The shock of a financial disturbance in one large country could be transmitted swiftly and decisively around the world. Generally, markets worked best if they were allowed to suffer on their own. But in this case, while the probability of a disaster might be small, the outcome could not be left merely to chance, Greenspan believed. A vicious cycle of growing and self-reinforcing fear could destroy the underpinning of any financial market—confidence.

Greenspan felt the threat could resemble the 1987 stock market crash. Even 10 years later, he could still find no credible explanation for the abrupt one-day decline in stock values that had built up over years. The shock of uncertainty could lead to withdrawal and then denial and even panic or paralysis. On the other hand, uncertainty could also lead to wishful thinking, which was just as dangerous.

By mid-December, the Korean crisis had reached extremis, and on Thursday, December 18, Rubin invited his Treasury team and Greenspan to dinner in a private room at the Jefferson Hotel, where Rubin lived. They went round and round. Nobody seemed to have a good idea how to avoid default or manage default.

"Some problems have no solutions," Rubin remarked. He mentioned again the danger of acting and then failing, which would provide the world with evidence of U.S. powerlessness.

Was there some way to get the United States and other world banks to extend the terms of their outstanding loans in Korea? That might give Korea time. Could they stop the bleeding? That would mean seeking voluntary restraint on the part of the banks. Who could speak with the banks?

Greenspan was not sure that the treasury secretary should do it. Treasury had no direct regulatory control over the banks, but that power belonged in part to the independent comptroller of the currency, who technically reported back to the treasury secretary. And the Fed, Greenspan believed, had a substantial conflict of interest because of its direct regulatory role. The banks could conceivably decline Rubin's request, but they could not resist the chairman of the Federal Reserve, who could retaliate. "They can say no to him," Greenspan said. "They could not say no to me."

Rubin called John Reed, the veteran chief of Citicorp bank. Citi had for decades been the lead bank for Rubin's old firm, Goldman Sachs. When Rubin was Goldman's chairman, he had visited Reed each year to share Goldman's confidential numbers on its extraordinary profits.

They agreed that Korea had the possibility of turning into a classic run on the system, as banks all over the world were pulling out. Rubin had been trying to see if the U.S. government could put up $10 billion and U.S. banks raise another $10 billion, hoping that that would stabilize the situation.

No, Reed said. He believed that no one in his right mind would lend money to Korea with reserves going down $1 billion a day. He thought it possible that the banks could agree to a standstill to extend the terms of outstanding loans in Korea. Billions in loans were coming due on January 1, and banks everywhere didn't want to see a collapse. "Why don't you let us try to solve the problem without any money?" Reed asked.

Rubin said fine.

It took several days for Reed and other private bankers to get an informal standstill agreement.

Rubin also worked out an agreement with the finance ministers of the major economic powers, to try to persuade the banks in their countries to extend the terms of Korean loans.

Now it fell to Rubin to make the calls to the U.S. banks, to make sure everyone was on board for the standstill. He had to make it clear that it was voluntary. He also had to make sure it happened. He had a compelling case: The United States was not going to put any money in. There would be no bailout. Without a standstill it would come to an end, to default.

Rubin found that the main New York banks were sophisticated enough to know the benefits of collective action. Those calls weren't difficult. One Chicago bank was reluctant. The CEO asked, Why should we do it? Rubin spent some time in conversation, and the CEO agreed to go along.

Some bankers felt they were being coerced. Summers felt it was as if the best cancer specialist in the world were recommending an amputation and saying, It's your choice, your decision, but there is no alternative. The choice was rolling over a loan versus losing the money or a large portion of the money if Korea collapsed.

On Christmas Eve, Rubin was out of touch, and one of the bank CEOs reached Summers. Summers explained the choice.

"This is a hell of a Christmas present," the banker said angrily, knowing he would have to go along.

The loan delays saved Korea from defaulting.

As Greenspan was coming more and more to the center of the American and world economic story, he nonetheless had taken a backseat on Korea. He was central to the enforcement decision made by the firm, but Rubin and Summers were the front-line enforcers.

Over the holidays, Greenspan and Andrea invited a number of the Fed governors, bank presidents and other friends to their home in Northwest Washington for a party. Philadelphia Fed president Boehne wound up next to the chairman, looking out over the pleasant, deep-wooded area at the back of the house. For 10 years, Boehne had watched with amusement how Greenspan, who constantly attended parties, still seemed uncomfortable in social settings—even in his own home.

"Andrea thinks she wants a dog," Greenspan said, attempting small talk. He apparently took Boehne's background—raised and educated in Indiana—as an indicator that he would know about animals.

"Tell me about a dog?" Greenspan asked, as if he wanted the full story.

Taking him literally, Boehne explained that a dog needed to be let out every 8 to 10 hours, had to be fed daily, that a puppy would have to be house-trained—sometimes a frustrating task.

Greenspan had already decided that a dog would definitely be too disruptive to their lives, and they were not going to get one. Period. But with meditative nods, he permitted Boehne to continue.

A dog owner couldn't go out of town on the weekends, Boehne said, unless someone came in regularly to walk and feed it. The other alternative was expensive boarding at a kennel. A male would go out in the back and spray all over, he noted, and a female would be a problem because she would be chased by the other dogs.

"Well," Greenspan asked, "how do you tell your wife you don't want a dog?"

13

On Friday, January 30, 1998, Greenspan, Rubin and Summers appeared before the House Banking Committee to defend their efforts in the Asian crises. Greenspan was supporting the Clinton administration's request for increased U.S. funding for the International Monetary Fund, which was providing money and loans to the Asian countries.

"I will just cut this short by saying a few months ago, I would have been an unequivocal no in opposition," said Maxine Waters, a Democrat from Los Angeles, during her opening statement. Waters, 59, represented South Central Los Angeles and Watts. Like many liberals in Congress, she objected to providing huge amounts of money to the IMF while a number of American inner-city areas remained underdeveloped.

"Today," she went on, "I have an open mind, and one of the reasons I have an open mind is because of something as simple and fundamental as Chairman Greenspan being willing to listen to what I am concerned about, and taking that trip to South Central Los Angeles and walking along a block that can be redeveloped, that can be invested in."

Waters had asked Greenspan to accompany her on a visit to South Central Los Angeles several weeks earlier. She didn't think that Greenspan would want to go with her. This was the same man, after all, who as CEA chairman in 1974 had testified to Congress that "percentage-wise," the people who were most hurt by recession were Wall Street brokers. In a room filled with consumers and minorities, Greenspan had literally been booed, and following a public outcry, Greenspan later qualified his statement, saying, "Obviously the poor are suffering more."

But the Greenspan of 1998 had accepted Waters's invitation, taking a walking tour of some of her district's hardest hit areas. After they returned, Waters told a number of people that the chairman had been absolutely terrific on the trip—curious, caring.

"And because of that," Waters concluded, "my mind is open, and I hope we can fashion a solution that works."

Privately, Greenspan felt that throwing government money into underprivileged areas was largely a waste. Nurturing capitalism and property ownership were the only long-term solutions.

Rubin, Greenspan and Summers presented a one-two-three punch in support of the administration's policies. They represented a broad center section of the political spectrum, spanning the moderate Democratic to the moderate Republican. They were a phalanx, and no one could breach their ranks. One of them alone—let alone all together—could overwhelm almost any member of Congress with economic facts, history, analysis and technical detail.

At one point in his testimony, Rubin said that Deutsche Bank AG, the largest bank in Europe, had set aside $777 million in reserves for its losses in Asia.

"$773," Greenspan interjected.

"$773," Rubin corrected. "I apologize." After a moment's reconsideration, he added, "Well, I'm not so sure. I bet you a nickel."

"You're on," Greenspan said.

"We have got a nickel, even-odds bet," Rubin said playfully. "There is a slight side bet between the chairman and me, which he will probably win."

An aide soon whispered in Greenspan's ear. Rubin had been right. Greenspan pulled out a $20 bill from his wallet and handed it to Rubin.

Later, when he was asked about the possible creation of an international bank regulator, Greenspan replied, "I would be very concerned if we were looking at some major superregulator. Superregulators tend to overregulate and make unbelievable mistakes.

"I would suspect that I would know most of the people who would be in charge of making the types of judgments that would be required for that, and I will tell you that they don't have a clue as to what to do. I would much prefer to allow very complex market forces to tell us."

In other words, leave the deciphering—and, ultimately, the regulation—of that complexity to the firm of Greenspan, Rubin and Summers.

No one challenged the presumption.

On Tuesday, May 5, Greenspan went to the Oval Office to see the president. It was the fourth month of Whitewater Independent Counsel Kenneth Starr's investigation of Clinton's relationship with former White House intern Monica Lewinsky. There was a sense that the investigations were closing in.

Greenspan had not visited the president formally for 16 months, and Clinton's economic team wanted Clinton to bask a little in the positive domestic economic news. In any case, an hour with Greenspan was always educational and worthwhile, and on this occasion it would be a momentary diversion from the president's mounting personal and legal troubles. Rubin, Summers and Sperling also attended.

"This is the best economy I've ever seen in 50 years of studying it every day," Greenspan told Clinton. There had been a boom in productive capital. Money that businesses were spending was yielding an extraordinary return because of increased worker productivity. The computer and high-technology investments were paying off. And those payoffs had to be real, because the higher profits and economic growth had continued for several years now.

The president asked whether Greenspan had seen an article in *The Economist* comparing the United States and Japan.

Greenspan said that Japan had failed to attack the consequences of its stock market decline, a mistake the United States had avoided by dealing relatively quickly with the banking crisis and the savings and loan collapse.

He said that the stock market was very high by historical standards, but it could stay high. Despite his statements about "irrational exuberance," the chairman said, it's basically an illusion to think that the Fed could tinker with the stock market. At the same time, the huge stock market run-up had made people feel wealthy, and he was concerned that the spillover would have an impact on the real economy. Spending would go up and possibly drive inflation up as well.

Overall, the growth and spread of technology had been vital, Greenspan said. Computerization ensured that there were few shortages or bottlenecks in the economy, allowing for quick replacement and quick refurnishing. The only constraint on the economy was labor. There was a limited supply of workers, and there were starting to be more shortages. The reserve army of workers was shrinking, which had the positive effect of bringing less educated people, and people from the welfare rolls, into the workplace, but there might also be a negative effect. Normally, with so few people unemployed, wages should begin to rise. History tells us that there should be more inflation than there is, Greenspan said. At the same time, he noted that the economy was experiencing its lowest rate of inflation since 1970.

Sometimes, the chairman told the president, you learn a lot when things don't turn out as they're supposed to.

The way astronomers discovered the planet Pluto, Greenspan said, was that Neptune was not strictly following the law of gravity. Some force, then unseen, had to be operating on it. Astronomers figured out where to look and discovered the new planet.

In a similar way, the economy was not following the laws of economics. He did not have any hard evidence why this was happening—hard in the sense of being provable to economists. He really had only anecdotal evidence. Technology, global competition from our own open markets and the competitive environment within the United States were all keeping prices down.

Greenspan added that there were so many more people with money in the stock market than there used to be. The millions who used to follow the Brooklyn Dodgers baseball team years ago were now following their 401(k) retirement and pension accounts.

In a rare television interview that August, former President Bush said that Greenspan had been responsible for his 1992 defeat. "I think that if the interest rates had been lowered more dramatically that I would have been reelected president, because the recovery that we were in would have been more visible," Bush said, adding a zinger, "I reappointed him, and he disappointed me."

Greenspan found it sad. In 1992, Bush and Brady had been urging him to lower rates more and faster. Greenspan knew that the economy had actually been in an economic recovery in 1992, and that it was President Bush who had failed to explain that politically. But he chose not to challenge the former president. He still felt a deference toward anyone who had served as president, and he didn't feel the issue was one for him to raise with Bush.

On Monday, August 17, 1998, President Clinton appeared before independent counsel Starr's grand jury to testify under oath. He acknowledged his relationship with former intern Monica Lewinsky. That evening, in a speech to the nation, he said that he had misled everyone—the public, his wife.

That day, the Russian government devalued the ruble and declared a moratorium on debts, sending another shock around the world—but one that was overshadowed by Clinton's troubles.

At the New York Fed, Bill McDonough saw Russia as an accident waiting to happen. The markets had been acting as if the worldwide contagion from Thailand to Korea were over. It wasn't. The Russian debacle's initial impact was chiefly on bonds, a market inadequately covered by the financial press. McDonough watched it more closely than any other market, because it was the most important.

With bonds, investors act like a bank, loaning money to businesses and governments in exchange for a fixed interest rate of return and the eventual repayment of the principal amount of the loan. The total value of outstanding bonds or loans to businesses and governments internationally was about $35 trillion—four times the total annual U.S. gross domestic product. The Russian default sent bond interest rates way up. Since the price moves in the opposite direction of the interest rate, the values of most foreign and corporate bond portfolios dropped dramatically.

With public attention focused on Clinton and on the stock market—the ups and downs of both—the public and media paid scant attention to the bond market. In certain respects, it was the hidden market.

The size of the bond market had grown astronomically over the last two decades. Borrowing in the bond market was four to five times that of bank lending, making it the main source of credit in the United States.

There had been only one bear bond market—a sustained falling in price—in the last two decades, and that had been in 1994. Since then, the largest financial institutions in the United States—Goldman Sachs, Merrill Lynch and some of the other firms—had calculated that they had comparatively small risks in their bond market investments. In general, the firms calculated their risk assessments on the largest measurable interest rate variations of the past two decades. After the Russian collapse, some bond interest rates varied 5 to 6 percent—dramatically more than even the most sophisticated investors had calculated to be the maximum risk. This continued to drive prices and the value of many bond holdings down substantially.

Within a week of the Russian default, there was little to no bond market trading. Prices were being quoted, but few would buy or sell. Selling could mean losing as much as half of an investment in a bond. And no one really wanted the bonds, because their value could drop further. Investors ran to quality bonds, especially U.S. Treasuries. It was becoming difficult, if not impossible, for people or businesses to borrow money. The markets had seized up. None of the big investment firms could gauge their possible losses, because with all the turbulence the value of their bond portfolios was unclear. Though there were some news stories about volatility and instability in the bond market, the magnitude of the problem was largely unreported.

Over at the Treasury Department, Deputy Secretary Larry Summers was getting reports from staff who talked to key people in the markets. Some were frank about their inability to trade, which meant that bonds, though still certainly valuable in the long run, were not liquid. Summers realized it was not hugely in anybody's interest to advertise this degree of illiquidity, so it wasn't being reflected in the media coverage.

Over the weekend of August 29–30, Greenspan attended the Kansas City Fed's annual Jackson Hole conference. After dinner one night, he gathered small groups of FOMC members in attendance and quietly moved from one group to the next, hoping to avoid attention. He told his colleagues that he wanted to send a public signal. They had not moved interest rates in nearly 18 months, and they still had an asymmetric directive with an upward bias. He explained that he wanted at least to signal that they would be getting rid of the upward bias. The others assured him they agreed.

On August 31, the Dow plunged 513 points, a 6 percent drop that erased the gains of the entire year. The trouble in the bond market was spilling over into the stock market.

Greenspan talked by phone with McDonough. McDonough, who had not been at the conference, agreed that a senior Fed official needed to say something fast, and not at a press conference. That would be a little too dramatic.

Greenspan was scheduled to give a speech at the business school at Berkeley on September 4. Reporters had been alerted to keep an eye out. Greenspan included some comments about the problems abroad. Speaking obliquely, as usual, he said, "It is just not credible that the United States can remain an oasis of prosperity unaffected by a world that is experiencing greatly increased stress." What was happening abroad fed back in the U.S. financial markets.

Earlier in the year, he said, the FOMC was worried mainly about inflation—but at the August meeting, a day after the Russian collapse, there had been little concern. Now, he said, "The committee will need to consider carefully the potential ramifications of ongoing developments since that meeting." Front-page news stories reported accurately that the chairman was hinting at an interest rate cut.

At the Greenwich, Connecticut, headquarters of Long Term Capital Management (LTCM), a secretive and powerful speculative partnership of very wealthy investors, the Russian collapse had triggered an earthquake. Founded in 1994 by John Meriwether, the former vice chairman of the Salomon Brothers investment bank, and former Fed Vice Chairman David Mullins, LTCM included two Nobel Prize winners and dozens of Ph.D.'s. LTCM was a hedge fund. Hedge funds aggressively play both the expected ups and downs in the market, essentially doubling their bet by investing heavily in the stocks expected to rise and short selling those expected to decline. LTCM was also highly leveraged, meaning it borrowed 95 percent or more of the money it invested.

LTCM's overall investing theory, based on complicated mathematical formulas, was to identify temporary price discrepancies in various world markets and to bet that those discrepancies would converge toward historical norms. Many trading numbers or rates operate around a norm. Notice the variations, invest assuming that the numbers will return to the norm and most of the time an investor will be right. On one level, it was an important discovery, to capitalize on small variations that seemingly made no sense.

As an example, in an early investment LTCM's data showed that 29½-year U.S. Treasury bonds were less expensive than the 30-year Treasury. The partners in the firm figured that the values of the two bonds would converge over time, so they bought $2 billion of the 29½-year bonds and sold short another $2 billion of the 30-year bonds. By putting up only $12 million of their own capital, LTCM took a $25 million profit on the transaction just six months later.

In 1994 and 1995, LTCM made more than 40 percent profit each year for its partners and investors, who had put billions into the firm. Another $100 billion was borrowed from banks and various large investment banking firms such as Goldman Sachs. Competition from other firms who started to use the same methods soon increased, and LTCM began to buy into various leveraged stock market investments and foreign currency transactions—not just bonds.

The Russian default had started a stampede. Instead of converging, bond prices moved away from the norms that LTCM was counting on. In early September, LTCM notified its investors that it had lost $1.8 billion, or nearly half the investors' own capital that had been put in the firm. It was a staggering loss. A large number of their current investments couldn't be sold, because the worldwide bond market was nearly frozen. But this information was not getting out to the public, largely because Ken Starr had published his lurid 452-page report of Clinton's sexual relationship with Monica Lewinsky.

On Friday, September 18, New York Fed President Bill McDonough was in his lush, old-world paneled office when he received a call from LTCM's Meriwether and Mullins. He was well aware their high-flying firm was in trouble.

Their message was simple: LTCM had suffered some quite large losses, and they were having difficulty finding banks or investment firms that would loan them money to avoid defaulting. There was no panic in their voices.

McDonough knew Meriwether was a cool customer who probably would never sound panicky, and Mullins was a real market pro. Nonetheless, they were blowing the whistle on themselves. They were nearly out of capital. All this was sufficiently significant, they said, that they would like representatives from the Fed and Treasury to come to Connecticut. "We'd like you guys to take a good look at our books so you know what's going on."

McDonough realized that this request meant they had really lost their asses. Meriwether and Mullins would not let outsiders into one of the most secretive financial concerns in the world unless the trouble was big. McDonough considered himself the battlefield commander, so it was for him to decide whether representatives of the Fed should go up there. This was also partly a policy question, so the Fed chairman had at least to know and give his approval.

McDonough knew he was more of an activist than Greenspan, who would obviously prefer a free-market solution. As the president of the New York Fed in the tradition of Corrigan, McDonough understood that he was supposed to be in charge of activism. He had better play his role. In some respects, he was Greenspan's ambassador in New York. That's what ambassadors are for, he thought. On occasion they get shot.

He called Greenspan, explained the situation and said he wanted to send a team to LTCM. They would be better off if they knew more, and they weren't going to know more unless they went to Connecticut. Nobody had the picture of how big this thing was. They had to get it.

Greenspan gave his approval.

McDonough spoke with the heads of about 10 major banks and securities firms. "What's going on, what are you hearing?" he asked. Everyone volunteered concern about the losses at LTCM and whether it could have an impact on world markets. They were indirectly expressing worry about the impact on their own businesses.

McDonough called Rubin. The treasury secretary wondered aloud what would happen if it leaked that Federal Reserve and Treasury officials were looking at LTCM's books, but he agreed it was worth the risk. Ignorance was not something that would be to their benefit. At the same time, Rubin thought LTCM was a relatively minor problem by itself but was a symptom of the breakdown in discipline. In his opinion, it was not going to cause major problems.

McDonough had a speech scheduled in London. If he canceled, and that cancellation were linked to a possible leak about a Fed-Treasury team visit to LTCM, they could set off a real panic. He went to London.

McDonough dispatched Peter Fisher, his number two at the New York Fed, to Connecticut on Sunday, September 20. About 10 a.m. that morning, Fisher, a tall, curly-haired Harvard Law graduate, arrived at LTCM, which was housed in a plain brick building that could have been dentists' offices.

For about six hours, Fisher reviewed the books. There were a number of huge surprises. First, LTCM had large positions in stock options, and perhaps, according to one estimate, their buying and selling was responsible for 30 percent of one speculative market, where they bet stocks would be less volatile. Second, LTCM had cross-default terms on all their loans. This meant that if they defaulted to a single lender, that default would automatically trigger defaults to all their lenders. A single default would mean all of their assets, their investments, would be dumped back to the lenders.

Fisher could imagine the fax machines at LTCM running nonstop with close-out orders to their lenders as word of any initial default spread. Up to 16 big banks and Wall Street firms, including Goldman, Merrill and the other big Wall Street investment houses, had money in LTCM. The collapse of LTCM would ricochet through the United States and the world financial system. A fire-sale liquidation, an abrupt and chaotic close-out, could start a chain reaction of more selling. Investor confidence would plummet. People would rush out of the bond market, leading to a further widening of the interest rate spread between private bond debt and U.S. Treasuries. The vicious cycle would lead to higher credit costs to U.S. businesses and a giant impact on the American economy. And all of this would occur at a time when markets were not functioning well to begin with.

This is for the history books, Fisher thought, a potential once-in-a-century meltdown. He called McDonough.

There is a 1 in 10 probability of wiping out the U.S. bond market for a week or a month, he said. After that, no one could know what might happen next.

On Monday, September 21, a big Asia sell-off occurred. The early news reports said that it was because the videotape of President Clinton's grand jury testimony in the Lewinsky investigation was being played on television. Fisher laughed at the notion. Savvy investors were anticipating LTCM's failure and were dumping.

Greenspan set up a conference call of the FOMC that day to make sure everyone was on board for testimony he was planning to give on the Hill. He wanted to hint more directly that a rate decrease was coming without formally committing himself or the FOMC. No one objected.

McDonough returned from London about midnight Tuesday. The details were terrifying. An abrupt and disorderly close-out of LTCM's investments could pose a real risk to the American economy, he concluded. By Wednesday morning, it was clear that LTCM was going to have to be bought by somebody, or it had to have a capital infusion of several billion dollars. Unless one of these things happened that day, LTCM would collapse the next.

McDonough and Fisher realized that the large Wall Street investment banking firms like Goldman were as highly leveraged in some respects as LTCM. The consequences of a run were unimaginable.

Fisher had arranged for representatives, mostly the CEOs, of 16 banks and brokerage firms to meet at the New York Fed at 10 a.m. Wednesday morning. Jon Corzine, the head of Goldman, told McDonough that it was possible that billionaire investor Warren Buffett, the head of Berkshire Hathaway and the second richest man in the world, might head a team that would buy LTCM.

I want to talk to Warren, McDonough said, to make sure this is for real. He knew Buffett well enough to know that if Buffett were going to invest $4 billion, it would not be a lighthearted decision.

Buffett was in Montana with Bill Gates, head of Microsoft and the richest man in the world, on a bus touring Yellowstone National Park with four other couples. Buffett was willing to buy LTCM. He had calculated that if he put up $4 billion for the firm, the purchase would stabilize the worldwide markets and he could liquidate with a profit of several billion dollars. With all his money, he realized he could wait for the fat, easy pitches and swing. This was an opportunity to do just that.

McDonough called Buffett's private unlisted number. The line was one that Buffett regularly answered himself. At first he would try to disguise his voice until he confirmed he wanted to talk to the caller.

A nice, soft midwestern voice answered.

It's Bill McDonough, may I speak with Mr. Buffett?

Hi, Bill, Buffett said. The offer is real and he had put it in writing, he said. He would not let it fail. But his offer was good only for about an hour, given the bond market's volatility. He would need an answer from LTCM by about noon.

McDonough expressed relief and went into his boardroom, where the CEOs and representatives of the 16 firms waited.

Fellas, he said, there is another proposal available. I think that many of you would find that more attractive than anything else that could come along, in that it would completely solve the problem. And therefore with appropriate apologies I'd like you all to go back home or do whatever you want to do and come back at one o'clock.

That same Wednesday morning, Greenspan received a call from a familiar voice from the past—Gerald Corrigan, the former New York Fed president and old enforcer from the 1987 stock market crash. Corrigan was now a senior partner and managing director at Goldman Sachs and co-chairman of the firm's risk committee.

Alan, Corrigan said in his deep, friendly baritone, I want to pass along some information to you. I neither expect nor want any reaction or comment from you.

Greenspan listened.

The liquidity in the marketplace had just evaporated across the board, as the chairman surely knew. There were payments of hundreds of millions of dollars due that evening, Corrigan said, and if those weren't made . . . Of course, Greenspan was aware of the various meetings at the New York Fed. It was very dangerous, not quite as high up on the Richter scale as the 1987 thing, but it was close.

Thank you very much, Dr. Corrigan, the chairman said as he hung up.

. . .

About 12:30 p.m., LTCM rejected the Buffett offer, saying that they did not have the authority under their agreement with their shareholders to sell to Buffett.

In Montana, Buffett joked with Gates that the national park outing had cost him several billion dollars. Had he been in New York, he was convinced he would have closed the deal.

McDonough now realized that this was very convenient for Meriwether and Mullins, because they would have been kicked out at once had Buffett taken over. Now they had a chance to leave with more money.

The only rescue possible at this point would have to come from the 16 banks, securities and investment banking firms that had money in LTCM, and their leaders were waiting in McDonough's conference room.

In the 1950s, McDonough had served in the U.S. Navy as the damage control officer on a small destroyer escort. Damage control meant making the best of a bad situation. It was often obvious what to do to limit damage, such as sealing men in a compartment that was flooding and losing them in order to save the ship and the rest of the crew. But the question was whether you had the courage to do it.

In most respects, he found his next step an easy call. Although the Fed should not technically intervene in any way, McDonough thought that the consequences of inaction were grave enough to justify his involvement. Calling a meeting to get the major firms together was, in some ways, like a fire truck driving the wrong way down a one-way street to put out a raging fire. The normal rules didn't apply when the potential for damage was this large. It was time to be the Fed's enforcer, and he was in charge of fixing the mess.

He believed there were times to go into such a meeting and breathe heavily and say you have to do this—be a big shot, knock heads together, force a resolution. This time, he believed, it was different. He knew some of their secrets. These firms had enough of the picture to realize the danger to themselves. Some of them could go out of business if the markets went out of control. Several of the firms were operating as highly leveraged speculative hedge funds themselves and were in precarious positions. He decided it was better to play it low-key. He believed that it was almost a no-brainer for the firms, because the alternative was terrible. They had to find some way to rescue LTCM.

He also realized that the firms were scared, because no one was in charge. Normally, the markets were king and in charge, but the markets were not functioning.

Around the table were the current masters of the universe—fierce, secretive and competitive men. Distrust and suspicion ran deep. Some were angry. Speaking one at a time, they expressed very different views about how serious the problem was. They could speak for their banks or firms, but each would have to get approval from their boards of directors for any commitment of money.

McDonough offered sandwiches and coffee. He informed them that Buffett's offer had been rejected. It is much better in the public interest, he said, that these positions not be dumped on the market—that LTCM not fail. We all agree that it will fail tomorrow unless you do something today.

Herbert Allison, the president and number two at Merrill, took the floor. Small framed, balding, with ramrod-straight posture, Allison read from notes. The capital losses for all of those represented in the room could total $20 billion, he said, many times the $4 billion that was needed by LTCM to survive. The $20 billion loss would be a catastrophe. That might only be the beginning. They either found the $4 billion LTCM needed or it would be dead tomorrow. After an LTCM failure, they would then have very large holdings with no one to trade with, period. A fire sale of unimaginable proportions could begin, with prices crashing and everyone rushing to the door at once. The entire system was at risk. "Don't we have an obligation to the public," he said, not just to ourselves or our clients? "We're all in this together."

Allison proposed a crude solution—each of the 16 firms would contribute $250 million. One, Lehman Brothers, said it had problems and could put up only $100 million. Two others offered less. The major firms upped their contributions to $300 million. After five tense hours, agreement was reached at about 6 p.m. In all, $3.6 billion would be contributed. They would take over LTCM, and if the markets stabilized, they might get their money back with a small profit.

Everyone applauded.

Uptown at Citicorp, John Reed received a detailed report. Citi didn't have any direct exposure, but all of the bank's best customers—Goldman, Merrill Lynch and Salomon Smith Barney—were up to their eyeballs. Don't laugh, he told his credit managers, we have big bucks outstanding to them all. Citi loans to those at the table at the New York Fed totaled tens of billions of dollars, Reed estimated. If any one of those were to get in trouble, we're going to be in trouble. We are just one step away.

The agreement on LTCM, which had stabilized the markets somewhat, fell apart about five times over the next weekend. One bank tried to pull out but finally agreed to stay, and the deal was formally sealed on Monday, September 28.

McDonough explained to Greenspan that he and the New York Fed had just played the role of catalyst and honest broker. No public money had been offered or spent. He didn't have to pressure anyone to participate, but he believed that only the Fed could have called all of the players together into one room.

Greenspan wasn't happy. McDonough had lent the good name of the Fed to the resolution. The meeting could have been held in any other boardroom in New York. The Fed didn't have to play matchmaker. Greenspan thought that McDonough had exercised bad judgment, rushed in a little too fast. The probability that LTCM's collapse would unravel the entire world financial system was significantly less than 50 percent, but that was still enough to be worrisome. And so, to a certain extent, Greenspan was of two minds. But now it was over, and Greenspan felt it was his job to rally around the Federal Reserve System, and the best way to do that was to back McDonough.

The question now was what to do with interest rates. The fed funds rate had been kept steady at 5½ percent for 18 months.

On Tuesday, September 29, at 9 a.m., Greenspan gathered the FOMC. The focus of the discussion was global financial turmoil and its growing impact on the United States. The Russian debacle and LTCM had created new economic conditions.

Greenspan proposed a ¼-point cut in rates as a cushion and as insurance against erosion. The cut had little to do with inflation, or even with the U.S. economy in general. The need to send a signal was strong, and a rate cut was their only meaningful signal. Reports of market volatility and an increasing appetite for risk reduction by buying U.S. Treasuries abounded. If everybody fled to U.S. Treasuries, it would further drive down the prices of other business and non–U.S. government bonds. This would make borrowing costs for businesses that much higher.

Alice Rivlin, surprised to learn what a house of cards the international bond market had become, judged that the Fed was in a sense acting as the central bank of the world.

McDonough agreed. As the only superpower, and with the

world's largest economy, they had little choice, he said. If they didn't raise their hands and take charge, who would? Neither the president nor the secretary of the treasury nor the Congress could do much. Only the Fed.

After a long discussion, the FOMC agreed unanimously on a ¼ percent cut and included a bias toward another rate cut in its directive.

McDonough received disappointed reports from Wall Street. Some had hoped that the Fed would send a louder, clearer message with a bigger rate cut. Was the Fed awake? Did Greenspan understand what was happening?

Two days later, on Thursday morning, October 1, the House Banking Committee called Greenspan and McDonough to testify about LTCM and the Fed's role in what had occurred.

Greenspan was slightly uncomfortable. Congress's tacit acceptance of the Fed's interest rate decisions was critical, and he was reluctant to expend any of his capital on a side issue. But when the House committee had tried to haul McDonough up alone in the immediate aftermath of the LTCM rescue, Greenspan said he thought it would be appropriate to invite him also.

When Greenspan and McDonough took their assigned seats at the witness table, there was an empty chair between them. Sit here, Greenspan said quietly, pointing to the empty chair and motioning McDonough over to sit by his side.

McDonough was touched by Greenspan's show of solidarity. He was convinced that an LTCM collapse would have triggered a severe world financial crisis that could have turned into a world economic crisis, possibly even a recession in the United States. Greenspan seemed less certain of that, but the chairman was making it clear publicly that there was not a sliver of difference between him and McDonough.

Greenspan's concern was fear in the marketplace—a delicate psychological condition, whether rational or not. Fear or uncertainty caused people to withdraw or disengage. They could dump good and bad investments unthinkingly and wildly. Risk taking was necessary for the making of money in the investment world. Leverage had enhanced the growth of the economy and raised the standard of living in the United States. He didn't think it possible to regulate human folly or stupidity, especially in the environment of investment opportunity that had so many payoffs. He realized he was more laissez-faire than most and might tolerate a freer market;

he also realized that these hedge funds could almost as easily operate outside the United States, and that any effort to regulate them would drive them overseas.

The session began with Representative James A. Leach, the Iowa Republican and committee chairman, criticizing hedge funds such as LTCM. "They are seen by some to be run-amok, casinolike enterprises, driven by greed," Leach said. Some congressmen then voiced suspicions that the Fed had bailed out their Wall Street friends—"high-flying dude billionaires," Paul Kanjorski, a Democrat from Pennsylvania, called them.

Later in the hearing, Kanjorski noted the absence of television and other media at the public hearing. The world was obsessed with the unfolding Lewinsky scandal, as Clinton seemed on the road to impeachment. "I am just wondering, is there any way you can inject sex into this so we can get a little more national attention? . . . We are talking about the potential meltdown of the world's economic system instead of a fling at the White House, and yet nobody in the world seems to understand what may have transpired or may have been at risk in the last two weeks." Kanjorski then asked a number of questions about why the government shouldn't regulate hedge funds more closely.

"I am scarcely defending hedge funds," Greenspan responded. "But many of the things which they do in order to obtain profit are largely arbitrage-type activities"—buying in one market in order to sell in another—"which tend to refine the pricing system in the United States and elsewhere, and it is that really exceptionally and increasingly sophisticated pricing system which is one of the reasons why the use of capital in this country is so efficient. It is why productivity is the highest in the world, why our standards of living, without question, are the highest in the world." He was giving them a dose of his militant free-market capitalism. Keeping the government's hands off the market allowed people to develop ingenious ways to make money. As long as it was legal, he supported it because of the pure market efficiency.

"I am not saying that the cause of all of this great prosperity is the consequence of hedge funds," he went on. "Obviously not. What I am saying is that there is an economic value here which we should not merely dismiss."

Representative Bernie Sanders, a Socialist from Vermont who is treated as a Democrat in the House, pressed Greenspan. "According to the United Nations, Mr. Chairman, the world's 225 richest individuals have a combined wealth of over $1 trillion, equal to the bottom 47 percent of the world's population—225 people have as much wealth as almost half the world's population.

"Does that concern you? Do you think that that is just? . . . Does that concern you, Mr. Greenspan?"

Greenspan said that he generally would prefer less concentration of wealth. He also said, "It is not by any means clear to me that if you were somehow to take these 225 individuals and merely indicate to them that they no longer have any wealth, and you put them away on a desert island, that the state of the rest of the world would be improved in the slightest." Throughout history, Greenspan said, the mistakes of powerful and wealthy individuals have always created consequences for others.

Greenspan did not believe in short-term compassion. Redistributing $1 trillion from the 225 richest to the 3 billion poorest would not achieve much in the long run. In reality, those 3 billion people live on an average of less than $2 a day; the $1 trillion could provide them an additional $1 a day for a year. But Greenspan believed that only structural change, capitalism, the rule of law and the creation of private property ownership would lift up the world's poor. Endeavors to help those living at the Malthusian levels of survival were often counterproductive, creating longer-term problems. He did not share all his thoughts with the committee.

"I think we ought to, instead of looking at what we have now as some incredibly corrupt, unequal, unethical system, try to look at what the United States has become relative to what used to exist 100, 200, 300 years ago." The bottom line, Greenspan said, was, "The average American is far better off than at any time in our history."

Leach called the hearing to a close after four and a half hours. "I sense the chairman of the Federal Reserve Board is losing his voice but not his mind," he said.

McDonough thought that the shelling was probably the most unpleasant experience Greenspan had ever had before Congress. Thank you for your support, he told Greenspan later. Greenspan could have easily left him high and dry.

The markets got worse. Uncertainty and illiquidity continued. The interest rate yields on new 30-year Treasuries were nearly ¼ percent below those with maturities just a couple of months earlier. If the markets were functioning properly, there would be only a slight interest rate spread. It made no sense. The market was dysfunctional.

McDonough called Greenspan to recommend that the chairman exercise his authority and lower rates another ¼ percent before the next FOMC meeting. It would hammer home two points—the Fed was concerned, and the Fed was in charge. It would be very deliberate showboating, McDonough admitted. It was time to bang the gong, declare: Look at us, pay attention. The psychological message would be immensely important.

Greenspan did not commit himself.

Laurence Meyer strongly opposed interest rate moves between meetings. They shifted more power to the chairman, who already had plenty. He felt that meetings every six weeks, when the members had time to have their say and vote formally, were sufficient. But he, too, was getting calls from friends and associates.

One said, I called my broker to see if I could unload some positions in the bond market, and he told me they would give me prices but they wouldn't buy or sell at those prices.

A former client phoned Meyer to say, "You know, I don't ever call you, but I'm doing you a favor here because I want to just tell you what's going on." He described torment in the market. He could not buy or sell positions of any size.

What the hell did interest rates mean, Meyer thought, if you couldn't buy or sell at those rates? Were the very foundations of the financial markets and capitalism—prices—in some kind of jeopardy?

Ed Boehne, whom Greenspan considered one of the most balanced members of the FOMC, reported that he had been traveling all over his district of Delaware, southern New Jersey and Pennsylvania. Clearly, the FOMC had not cut rates enough. On his tour, Boehne said, he had checked into a hotel in State College, Pennsylvania. When the check-in clerk noticed he was from the Fed, he said, "Oh, you're from the Fed. You didn't do enough." Boehne told Greenspan, "When hotel clerks in central Pennsylvania tell you that you didn't do enough, it's time to do more."

On Monday, October 12, McDonough was in Washington to give three speeches. He briefed Rivlin about the dire market conditions. The FOMC vice chairman and the board vice chairman decided to go to Greenspan together.

In his office, they pressed for a rate cut. If they waited for the next FOMC meeting in November, it would look like business as usual—¼ percent in September, ¼ percent in November.

McDonough argued that the conditions were anything but

business as usual. Market business was as shaky as he had seen it. The Fed had to deliver an attention-getting surprise. Rivlin agreed.

After about a half hour, Greenspan finally said that he thought they were right, but then he added ambiguously that he wasn't sure it was time to make a big splash. Maybe we ought to wait. They didn't want to be seen as panicky. Business as usual had its benefits. But he agreed to a conference call of the FOMC. McDonough and Rivlin could present their view to the others.

Rivlin left believing that Greenspan was prepared to cut rates again, but that he was not moving as fast as she and McDonough thought necessary. McDonough was not sure how to read Greenspan. Was he just appearing to be reluctant? Was he perhaps thinking the whole time, Thank God these people are pushing me, so he could cite his two vice chairmen to bring along reluctant FOMC members? How Machiavellian was Greenspan? Or was he playing Socrates, perhaps trying to lead them, by questions and doubts, to what was really his own conclusion? McDonough didn't have an answer.

On October 15, Greenspan convened a telephone conference call of the FOMC. Risk aversion in the financial markets had increased, volatility was increasing and borrowing and lending were increasingly constrained. He was considering lowering rates another ¼ percent, he said, in accordance with the directive that had included the bias toward further easing. What did the others think? He turned it over to McDonough.

The international financial markets are simply not functioning, McDonough said. They had begun the necessary remedial work with the first ¼ percent easing two weeks earlier. They had to move again now. They couldn't afford to wait until the next meeting, because the wait was too long and would appear to be business as usual. Drama was necessary.

Rivlin, in a calm voice, then chimed in. She fully supported the move.

Even Meyer supported the rate cut. The believer in the old economic models, the opponent of chairman-directed rate moves between FOMC meetings, said he believed the cut was necessary.

McDonough thought that if they didn't have Meyer, they would have to invent him. Having Meyer on board underscored the seriousness of what they were confronting and what they were doing.

None of the others voiced any real objection.

Without taking a vote, Greenspan said that he had decided and would order a ¼ percent rate cut. It was announced at 3:15 p.m. The bond market soared, and the Dow, already up, registered a 330-point increase for the day—the third largest point increase in history.

Meyer believed the rate cut was simply a declaration, a way of telling people to relax: We at the Fed understand that the markets are not functioning, we take it upon ourselves to help restore smooth functioning of the markets, we will get the job done, whatever it takes.

For the Fed to be saying that, as the power over the sovereign currency, was saying a lot. Soon Meyer was getting reports from people in the markets near the epicenter of the crisis. One of the most important moves the Federal Reserve ever made, said one. Another went so far as to say that it was the greatest thing that had ever happened in modern times to help the markets.

On Tuesday, November 17, 1998, the FOMC convened for its regular meeting. Conditions in the financial markets had settled down, but Greenspan proposed another ¼ percent rate cut as a kind of insurance policy. Maybe another cut was not necessary, he said, but it was important to get the situation in the markets behind them. A financial collapse would envelop the United States. That was the risk. A ¼ percent cut could be taken back later. He feared the appearance of a larger credit crunch. He noted that there was no international structure of finance, no United Nations central bank, to oversee the crisis. They had to take action ad hoc. The financial markets had one feature: no buyers, only sellers. Another ¼ percent cut would send a message that the Fed was prepared to backstop the system.

Several said they thought it was a close call, but only Jerry Jordan, the Cleveland bank president, dissented from the chairman's recommendation. In a press release, the Fed announced the rate cut and said that it planned no more rate cuts to help stabilize the global financial markets.

The cut put the fed funds rate down to 4¾ percent, the lowest it had been in more than four years.

14

On January 14, 1999, Mike Prell, the veteran director of research and statistics for the Fed, spoke at the Charlotte Economics Club in North Carolina. For a dozen years he had been in charge of presenting the staff forecast to the FOMC. He acknowledged that his forecasts were frequently wrong, and at the end of his talk, he posed an unusual question: "Might people—business managers, consumers, investors—be taking risks that they would not have taken were it not for an exaggerated confidence in the ability of the Fed to cushion the economy and financial markets against any and all shocks? If so, there conceivably could be greater potential instability in the system than is readily apparent at this time."

Greenspan himself was concerned about a potential "exaggerated confidence" in the Fed's ability. But he figured there was nothing he could do about it other than to go about his job.

Alice Rivlin, who attended a lot of international financial meetings as vice chairman, had discovered that Greenspan was even more a mythic figure abroad—an Olympian symbol of financial stability in a booming economy that was the envy of the world. Central banks around the world were attempting to model themselves on Greenspan's, each interpreting differently how to apply the model. What could Greenspanism mean without Greenspan?

Since Rivlin had been at the Fed, articles praising the chairman had flowed off the presses as if he were the latest rock star. *Fortune*: "In Greenspan We Trust." *BusinessWeek*: "Alan Greenspan's Brave New World." She raised the downside of all this with the chairman. Alan, she said, it is important for you to reinforce the notion that you do *not* run the world. He had to demonstrate that the FOMC was a collective body. The more some of the rest of them were out making speeches and explaining policy, the better it would be for him.

He said he agreed, but soon enough he was not acting as if he did. The chairman kept himself out front, giving frequent speeches and serving as the face of the Fed before Congress and the rest of the world, a constant presence that fostered an identification between Greenspan and the excellent economy.

Rivlin was concerned that if something were to happen to Greenspan, the entire world would think something terrible had happened to the U.S. economy. He was becoming a cult figure.

When Clinton's Lewinsky troubles led to his impeachment in the House and trial in the Senate, Rivlin and Greenspan discussed it on several occasions. They shared their sorrow. Greenspan acted more like a mourner than a critic.

What a shame, he said, wagging his head in disbelief. Here was this very smart man, clearly head and shoulders above most of the presidents of the United States in terms of intellect, grasp of policy, seriousness, political skill and charm—yet he didn't have self-discipline. To risk so much for apparently so little. Neither Greenspan nor Rivlin could comprehend it.

In early February 1999, *Time* magazine featured Greenspan, Rubin and Summers on the cover as "The Committee to Save the World." The feature story described the role the three had played in preventing global economic meltdown from Thailand to Korea to Russia. Greenspan realized that if there had been a meltdown, the headline would have read, "The Committee That Destroyed the World."

On March 4, a *New York Times* editorial was headlined "Who Needs Gold When We Have Greenspan?"

By May, it was clear to Greenspan that the economy was growing very rapidly again, up to about 4½ percent annually—more than expected. He saw no real signs of inflation, but long-term bond rates were going up: the yield on the 30-year Treasury was up from about 5 percent to 5.9 percent over the past half year, signaling that investors feared inflation would soon increase. Consumer prices had increased .7 percent the previous month—the biggest monthly increase in six years. Despite his efforts to send a public signal back in 1994 when they had started to raise rates, the increases had come as a shock to the markets, driving long-term interest rates up significantly. If a rate increase became necessary soon, and it increasingly looked as if it would be, he wanted the public signal to be loud and clear.

At the May 18 FOMC meeting, Greenspan emphasized the uncertainty of the outlook. Productivity growth for businesses was in the 4 to 5 percent range each quarter, making believers of even the biggest skeptics like Meyer. These numbers were still helping to contain wage and price increases. But for how long? Overall uncertainty about the economic outlook was the dominant feature of what they were looking at. The chairman proposed that they not raise rates at once but adopt an asymmetric directive tilted toward a future increase. To make the message clear, they agreed to announce the tilt toward an increase that same day—the first such public declaration in the Fed's history.

The vote was once again unanimous.

"Fed Won't Hike Rates—For Now," announced the headline on the front page of *The Washington Post* the next morning. The tilt or bias toward future rate increases was big news. Other than the lone ¼-point rate hike in 1997, the Fed had not significantly raised rates in a full stair-step tightening cycle since 1994 and early 1995—more than four years before.

Like all the vice chairmen during Greenspan's tenure, Rivlin decided to resign. Her husband had prostate cancer. She had been at the Fed three years, and she enjoyed the work immensely, but it was certainly Greenspan's show. For the last year, she had also served as head of the financial control board that was attempting to restore financial health to the ailing District of Columbia government—virtually a full-time job in itself. And that was her show.

When she told Greenspan that she was leaving, he was unhappy to lose an important ally.

At the June 30 FOMC meeting, the economic forecast continued to suggest vigorous economic growth but subdued inflation. Greenspan felt that the three rate cuts of the previous year had put them in an unnatural stance. With the improvement of conditions abroad, it was time to take back one of those cuts and raise rates ¼ percent.

In addition, it looked as though the general price declines in oil, imports and health care that had helped tame inflation could be over or were even reversing themselves and going up.

Several members noted that since 1996, many businesspeople had said they couldn't raise prices without being crushed by their competitors. Now some were saying they were going to try to raise prices. That was a significant change, foreshadowing future inflation.

The main objection to a rate increase came from Robert D. McTeer Jr., president of the Dallas bank. He didn't believe they were in an inflationary environment and said he wanted to continue to test the growth limits of the new economy.

The others seemed to agree on a ¼ percent increase, but a substantial debate developed over whether to maintain the asymmetric directive with a tilt toward another increase.

The compromise was to raise rates ¼ percent but return to a symmetric directive, meaning no bias toward either an increase or a decrease. All but McTeer voted in favor.

The press release announcing the increase presented the move as a slight, cautious preemptive action and suggested no additional increases. The markets were startled and delighted, with the Dow hitting nearly 11,000. The hike was widely seen as market friendly and much less hawkish than anticipated. "The Fed smiled," said the lead to *The Wall Street Journal* story on the markets.

Greenspan had passed word to Rubin that the rate increase was coming—not that anyone reading the newspapers the previous month couldn't have anticipated it. Rubin had no real problem.

The president was not as confident.

Did this have to happen? Clinton asked his economic team. I don't see any signs of inflation, he added, asking the same questions he had posed in 1994 when Greenspan was raising rates. Was this another preemptive stranglehold on the economy? he asked, echoing some liberal Democratic senators who had been his most vocal defenders during his impeachment trial, in which he had been acquitted.

Rubin, Summers and Sperling defended Greenspan's decision.

Mr. President, Sperling said, he is just putting his foot on the brake a little. This is good. It will keep the expansion going longer. The risk of inflation with unemployment at 4.2 percent was too great.

Frankly, the president's advisers explained, Greenspan was on the softer side of the FOMC, a little to the left even of the people that the president had relied on his advisers to pick as his nominees, like Meyer. Clinton's objections were muted, not as intense or as deep as they had been in 1994.

A kind of greening of Alan Greenspan had taken place over the recent years. In a commencement speech at Harvard that month, Greenspan had not by any means called for income redistribution, but he had sounded more like Bill Clinton. "Expansion of incomes and wealth has been truly impressive," Greenspan said, "though regrettably the gains have not been as widely spread across households as I would like." Militant laissez-faire capitalists were not usually concerned about the distribution of wealth.

Janet Yellen, who had moved from the Fed to the White House as chairman of the Council of Economic Advisers, agreed that her former Fed colleagues had done the right thing. The economy had such a head of steam that the unemployment rate of about 4.2 percent was going to go even lower. That would certainly increase the risks of future inflation.

Yellen went to the president several times to underscore her main fear for the economy. The stock market was likely going to take a tumble, she said. A 10 to 20 percent drop would leave the economy just fine, if it didn't trigger a larger crisis in the financial markets. In fact, she told Clinton, they needed a stock market decline to get the economy to calm down so that growth and the unemployment rate could stabilize.

Rubin and Summers agreed.

The real world of the stock market continued to intrude on Greenspan's thinking. The stock market had been a central feature of his business life in New York, and he had meant it when he'd said that more people were following it than baseball. Well over 70 million Americans had investments directly or indirectly in stocks listed just on the New York Stock Exchange.

For several years, Greenspan had had the Fed economists attempt to construct mathematical, computerized models that might offer some insights into the stock market. It had become clear that two propositions were true. First, there was no rational way to determine that you were in a bubble when you were in it. The bubble was perceivable only after it had burst—which, for Greenspan, meant a drop of roughly 40 percent over a short period of time.

To forecast such a drop, someone would have to pit his analysis against the broad wisdom of the millions who thought they understood the economy and the businesses they had invested in. To do so involved a certain hubris.

Second, there was no doubt that the Fed could withdraw liquidity and raise rates so high that the whole thing would cave. But the crucial issue, which Greenspan felt was unspoken, was how to defuse the bubble—how to let the air out slowly, tightening enough to put pressure on the bubble, but not so much that it would break the economy. It could be a kind of soft landing for the stock market.

In Greenspan's view, the big 1987 crash had probably raised the Dow several thousand points. Investors saw the sharp decline of 22 percent in a single day, and then nothing serious had happened. They concluded that the outlook for stocks and the economy was better than they had presumed, so stocks went up even higher. Since 1987, whenever the Fed had raised rates the stock market invariably faltered, stabilized, recovered and then took off again.

There was the extreme case in which they could knock the stock market down completely with big rate increases, but as they moved away from the extreme case, their actions would merely try to diffuse, and not dangerously deflate, the bubble. The net result was that the tightening would get an upside response—stabilization and another takeoff—and not the downside.

Was there a precise point of tightening that could achieve a modest degree of stock market decline, that would *keep* the market down? In theory there must be *some* point at which this would occur, a point economists call a "saddle." But Greenspan concluded it was not predictable, and certainly it was not capable of being judged in any meaningful way. For practical purposes, there was no such point. The magic moment to suppress stock prices existed, perhaps in a fraction of a second out in the markets, but Greenspan determined that he could not find it.

This abstract reasoning made it seem, even to Greenspan sometimes, that he was backing off "irrational exuberance." But it was really just a wider analysis. He was still grappling.

In a speech on August 27, 1999, at the annual Jackson Hole retreat, Greenspan attempted to lay out some of his conclusions. He was even more elliptical than usual, saying that to anticipate a bubble accurately would be to pit one's own assessment against millions of investors, many of whom were highly knowledgeable.

It was a sufficiently obscure dose of Greenspanspeak that his colleagues and aides felt the need to interpret it. Several passed word to the press that the chairman had officially declared the end of "irrational exuberance." He had not. The New York Stock Exchange stocks were worth about $16 trillion. The growth in value—and the potential volatility—of the market was just that much more important to the economy than it had been in the past, so he was watching more closely than ever.

Greenspan had invited Sperling to attend the conference, and the top White House economics official was fascinated as Greenspan delivered his 20-minute speech and then answered questions. Wire service reporters hovered, watched, took notes, grabbed their cellular phones and at one point sprinted out of the room as the chairman seemed to be saying something new, especially about the stock market. It was as if Greenspan were the national tuning fork that might sound a clue, or even a final answer, about the disorderly music of the markets. Poor guy, Sperling thought, he can't be a regular person for even a minute.

Greenspan and Andrea discussed what he should do if he was offered a fourth term. What would it be like if he retired? Wouldn't it be nice to sleep past 5:30 a.m., travel, go to the beach, read novels, not have to leave the opera early to prepare for congressional testimony? Andrea worried about the stress of the job.

In all their years together, they had really had only one extended holiday—their four-day delayed honeymoon in Venice. They had found musicians playing Vivaldi in the churches, and the city's ancient power had enveloped them. At least he didn't hate it, Andrea thought. They took only one vacation a year, five days at a tennis camp in California after the Jackson Hole conference. This was a man who refused to stand in line for a movie because he thought it was a waste of time. At night, at times, the curtain would come down and he would turn to his business statistics or his small hand calculator. His idea of relaxation was doing calculus problems.

Years earlier, they had spent weekends looking for a country house before they realized that they loved Washington on the weekends. And Andrea was thinking about retirement and travel? She realized it was silly.

He would accept the offer if it came.

15

———————

"I bet he'll stay there until they carry him out," President Clinton joked to his economic advisers as they discussed a fourth term. Summers, who had taken over as treasury secretary from Rubin the previous summer, recommended reappointing Greenspan. He and Sperling had already sounded Rubin out as a courtesy, to see if he wanted the Fed job. But Rubin had declined, saying, "Alan's perfect for this."

White House Chief of Staff John Podesta got permission from Clinton to call Greenspan and offer the reappointment on behalf of the president. Podesta made the call one evening just before Christmas, reaching the chairman at his office.

Greenspan was formal. He said thank you. He seemed to say yes.

Podesta was on the way to the airport when he got Summers and Sperling on the phone for a conference call.

You guys follow up with Greenspan, he suggested. Just to make sure he understood clearly that he got an offer. There had been something vague about their conversation.

Summers and Sperling followed up. Yes, Greenspan said, it was a firm yes. He told Sperling to keep it quiet.

Greenspan was in a state of sober rapture. At 73, he found that his mind still functioned well. He figured he would know he was losing it when he started to have difficulty with mathematical relationships, and he was aware of no diminution of that mental capacity. He was fully engaged. His only problem was that occasionally he couldn't remember people's names.

The White House set Tuesday morning, January 4, 2000, for the announcement, wanting to make the timing of the announcement a surprise before Congress returned from recess. That way, Clinton could give his annual State of the Union address later in January and fully embrace the good economy and Greenspan, leaving no doubt about the chairman's future role. In February, the American economy would officially have enjoyed the longest expansion in its history. The White House wanted the Clinton-Greenspan team to be part of the celebration.

Only a handful of senior officials knew about the announcement. It had not leaked, and Sperling in particular was very proud that they had all kept their mouths shut.

The White House press office put out word that the president would have a "personnel" announcement, but it had come out garbled as a "personal" announcement. It was also the day Hillary Clinton was packing to move to the home the Clintons had bought in Chappaqua, New York, a Westchester County hamlet, in preparation for her run for the Senate seat. The suggestion that something "personal" was about to drop in the Clinton soap opera sent some reporters racing to the White House. Could it be a separation or a divorce? Many were disappointed to learn it was only Greenspan, who already seemed as if he had the Fed chairmanship for life.

Greenspan arrived at the executive mansion carrying the front section of the *Financial Times*, the world's business newspaper, on its signature light orange paper.

Sperling joked that the *Financial Times* would love to run an advertisement of Greenspan coming to see the president with no notes, no files, only their paper.

Clinton, Summers, Sperling and Council of Economic Advisers Chairman Martin N. Baily gathered around the dining room table next to the Oval Office with Greenspan. White House Chief of Staff John Podesta sat in a chair off to the side.

Clinton and Greenspan were almost glowing at each other, odd partners sitting there around the polished wood table, linked surprisingly to each other's greatest successes, wrapping themselves in each other's legacies.

"You know," the president said, addressing Greenspan to his immediate left, "I have to congratulate you. You've done a great job in a period when there was no rulebook to look to."

"Mr. President," Greenspan replied, "I couldn't have done it without what you did on deficit reduction. If you had not turned the fiscal situation around, we couldn't have had the kind of monetary policy we've had."

"After doing so well," Clinton said, "no one would blame you for wanting to go out now on top."

"Oh, no," Greenspan said, "this is the greatest job in the world. It's like eating peanuts. You keep doing it, keep doing it, and you never get tired."

Clinton folded his arms, tightened his body over his crossed legs and glanced over as if to say, I know what you mean. He seemed wistful.

The irony was palpable. Greenspan, at 73, had already served 12 years and would get to be chairman for another 4 years. Clinton, 53, had served 7 years as president and had only another year. The Constitution barred him from seeking a third term. The man 20 years older could go on, while the younger man would have to leave office and re-create himself.

Since the rate increase of the previous June, Greenspan had raised rates twice more, each by ¼ percent, and it didn't look as if he were going to stop. But the subject of interest rates didn't even come up directly. There was this intangible trust, almost a bond, between Clinton and Greenspan.

Who would have thought, seven years before at their first meeting in Little Rock, that such economic conditions were even possible—steady economic growth, low inflation, unemployment hovering at an unheard-of 4 percent and the Dow above 11,000. More than 20 million new jobs had been created since Clinton took office. Some economists would have put the odds at 1 in 1 million. Greenspan, ever a stickler about probability, couldn't even calculate it.

Of all the important people in Clinton's life, nearly all—including himself—had let him down or not lived up to their full promise. Hillary had failed to deliver health care, although she had stood by him during the Lewinsky scandal. Vice President Gore, though loyal, had not yet emerged as a vibrant successor. Dick Morris, the chief political strategist for the successful 1996 reelection campaign, had been forced out in a scandal and then turned on Clinton and written an informative but tattletale book. George Stephanopoulos, Clinton's young and trusted adviser, had also written a book full of inside stories of anguished decision making and private fury. Democratic leaders in the Senate and House had come and gone. Staff had come and gone. Rubin, the shining light of the cabinet, was gone. Clinton's vaunted campaign fund-raisers had brought scandal and doubt on the presidency. Clinton himself had not lived up to his own grand governing vision.

Greenspan alone had stood and improved his ground.

Clinton began questioning Greenspan about the economy and the impact of new technology. Greenspan found that, as usual, Clinton was asking the important and correct questions, formulated with a lawyerlike precision. It was such a good show that yet again Greenspan didn't believe it was a show.

Information technology, Greenspan said, defined the current period. Something profoundly different had occurred. Computers and the Internet were at the root of the extraordinary productivity improvement. Computers allowed vastly better inventory management in a way that had been unimaginable only years before. What was truly remarkable, however, was the vast dissemination throughout society of the new technology and the speed of the dissemination. All of this dissemination added productivity growth throughout the economy. There was little question that further major advances lay ahead. They were truly in a capital equipment investment boom.

Greenspan complimented Clinton on his efforts to use the budget surpluses to reduce the federal debt.

It's a very powerful idea for the public, the president said, the idea of being debt free.

If the federal government were debt free, Greenspan said, that would not take away its ability to do expansive things. Without debt, the government could eventually reborrow trillions of dollars if necessary in a crisis or an emergency. It would be available for the right moment. The surpluses and absence of deficits would also help keep long-term interest rates down, because the federal government would not be borrowing, making more money available for business borrowing.

As they left the dining room, Clinton and Greenspan waited for the others to assemble in the Oval Office for the announcement before going in themselves. On the wall, the president had a set of old presidential campaign buttons going way back, a small history of the country as seen through the prism of these campaigns. He began talking about them with knowledge and passion. It was clearly the way Clinton viewed history. Clinton would miss the campaigns, Greenspan thought, miss the way he had best defined himself. There was something sad and lost about him. His big fights were perhaps over.

In the Oval Office, the president did not, of course, mention his doubts about Greenspan's rate increases in 1994 and 1999. Instead, he noted that the economic success was due to many factors. "It seems clear that it is the result of the convergence of a number of forces: a great entrepreneurial spirit; stunning technological innovations; well-managed businesses; hardworking and productive men and women in our workforce; expanding markets for our goods and services; a complete commitment to fiscal discipline; and of course, a Federal Reserve that has made independent, professional and provably wise judgments."

Of Greenspan, Clinton added, "He was also, I think it's worth noting, one of the very first in his profession to recognize the power and the impact of new technologies on the new economy, how they changed all the rules and all the possibilities. In fact, his devotion to new technologies has been so significant, I've been thinking of taking Alan.com public; then, we can pay the debt off even before 2015." Greenspan's willingness to stay in the job should be "a cause of celebration in this country and around the world."

"Mr. President," Greenspan responded, "I first wish to express my deep appreciation to you for the confidence you've shown me over the years." He had loved every minute of being chairman, especially working with Clinton's treasury secretaries—Bentsen, Rubin and Summers. Turning to Clinton, he said, "And I must say you have been a good friend to America's central bank. Thank you, sir."

"Is the market irrational?" asked Helen Thomas, the veteran reporter from United Press International. "Do you stick by your previous statements on the stock market?"

"You surely don't want me to answer that," Greenspan replied.

"Yes, I do."

"You do?" he asked. "Well, I don't think I will."

Why stay? inquired another reporter.

"There is a certain, really quite unimaginable intellectual interest," Greenspan said, "that one gets from working in the context where you have to put broad theoretical and fairly complex conceptual issues to a test in the marketplace.

"It's a type of activity which forces economists like ourselves to be acutely aware of the fact that our actions have consequences."

The stock market continued to soar in the months after Greenspan's reappointment, but in the spring the Nasdaq exchange—almost entirely comprising New Economy high-technology stocks—plunged 30 percent. Many dot.com stocks dropped

80 or 90 percent, and the Dow seemed to stabilize between 10,000 and 11,000.

Greenspan and his FOMC continued the push to raise rates, with the fed funds rate reaching 6½ percent on May 16, but then they paused at the June meeting. Productivity growth was running in the range of 4 percent a year and was keeping down both labor costs and inflation. But Greenspan was worried, almost as if he had been playing a winning hand for too long. No one was more aware of the remote chances of such an unprecedented winning streak.

The 6½ percent fed funds rate was ½ percent higher than the 6 percent rate at the height of the 1994–95 tightening cycle. It was the highest the rate had been since early 1991. Was he on his way to achieving a second soft landing, as the economy continued its record expansion into a tenth year? He was holding his breath. It was a question no one, including Greenspan, could answer. When would the boom end? When would he goof? What was the hidden factor or brewing crisis that no one was anticipating? Stock market, banks, oil prices, Asia, Russia, hedge funds, an environmental crisis, a health catastrophe, drought, famine, scandal, war?

EPILOGUE

In Greenspan's December 5, 1996, speech, when he deliberately slipped in his highly quotable "irrational exuberance" remark about the high stock market, he also said, "The Fed must be as transparent as any agency of government. It cannot be acceptable in a democratic society that a group of unelected individuals are vested with important responsibilities, without being open to full public scrutiny and accountability."

Greenspan's policy of expanding openness and transparency has done more than merely increase the Fed's accountability. It has focused attention on the Fed and himself. If specific interest rate decisions were basically secret and front-page news only in the financial sections of the newspapers, as they were before 1994, they would be like trees falling in the forest that no one hears. Now the announcement of the FOMC interest rate decisions is a media event. "Only eleven days until the Fed meeting," declare the cable television financial channels. CNBC runs a countdown clock on the screen on the day of the meeting, anticipating a 2:15 p.m. announcement and treating it like a space shuttle blastoff or the New Year.

When the portion of the Humphrey-Hawkins Act that requires the chairman to testify twice a year before Congress lapsed in early 2000, Greenspan volunteered to continue his appearances. He can speak out twice a year in his cryptic code to make sure his tree is heard when it falls. He cannot help but know that such appearances only further cement the sense of his preeminence.

So much of his life is interior—inside his mind, with its private calculations and thoughts. Greenspan considers himself an introvert. His demeanor suggests that he hates expediency, prefers detachment and rigor. Yet he has a tendency also toward the political calculation and manipulation that have become necessary for longevity in Washington. He plays the game skillfully.

Greenspan's mastery of process, both inside the Fed and in Washington, has brought about a subtle transfer of political power to the Fed chairman. His 13-year stint is a textbook case of consolidation of power in an institution where others have equal votes. Outside the Fed, hardly anybody can muster the courage to criticize him anymore. No presidential candidate would think of saying anything negative about him. Success shields him not only from criticism, but also from the obvious question: Who elected you?

America's fixation on the economy and the historic and continuing expansion has come to reside in Greenspan. He has become both a symbol and a means of explaining and understanding the economy.

Unlike many economists, he has never been rule driven or theory driven. The data drive. Some of his most significant decisions may lie in what he has not done, the times he has stayed his hand. His is an unusual intellectual journey, from the cautious and nervous beginner during the 1987 stock market crash to the innovative technician who spotted productivity growth in the 1990s and refused to raise interest rates when the traditional economic models and theories cried out for it.

Greenspan can subtly confound his audience. His congressional testimony is now televised on cable channels and his statements combed for meaning, but almost never does he surrender a sound bite. He does not provide a clear declaration about the condition of the economy or the likely direction of interest rates. His long, convoluted sentences seem to take away at the end what they have given at the beginning, as they flow to new levels of incomprehensibility. He uses what he calls "constructive ambiguity."

He never appears on talk or interview shows where he might be subjected to journalistic interrogation. In the first months of his tenure, Greenspan made one such appearance, Sunday, October 4, 1987, on ABC television's *This Week with David Brinkley*. During the course of the interview, he projected his conflict. He said that there were no signs that inflation was picking up but also that those signs might be around the corner. The Fed might have to raise rates, but they might not. He has not done a television talk show since. His public words are carefully filtered and weighed. When someone at a party once asked Greenspan how he was, he jokingly replied, "I'm not allowed to say."

Several years ago, when it looked as if President Clinton had said something that contradicted Greenspan's view, Gene Sperling phoned Greenspan to give him a heads-up that the press would be making inquiries.

"I'll just say a little bit this way," Greenspan told Sperling, "and a little bit that way, and I'll completely confuse them so there'll be no story." There was not.

In this culture, politicians, actors and nearly all public figures are produced and handled. Greenspan emerges as one of the few who seems to maintain a steady and sober detachment. Most other powerful figures have a television persona, often defined by glibness and efforts at cleverness. The public gets a flash of B-roll stock footage of the chairman walking across the street—arriving at an FOMC meeting, he always looks the same—grim, even gloomy, briefcase under his arm, an unrevealing look on his face. Though it isn't, it could be the same suit year after year. It is the same street and the same briefcase.

Although his words are almost unbearably opaque, he appears to be doing something rare—telling the truth. The very act of thinking, the strain in his wrinkled forehead, can be seen in the video footage of him before the microphone. At times it seems painful. But the public has rewarded his caution, reflection and the results with their confidence. That he is the unelected steward of the economy is simply accepted. Yet even with increased public exposure, somehow the mystery deepens.

Straight out of central banker casting, Greenspan is one of the elders who allows the economic party to continue. In *The Wizard of Oz*, when the man behind the curtain emerges, we are let down. With Greenspan, we find comfort. He helps breathe life into the vision of America as strong, the best, invincible. The fascination with Greenspan has become one of the ways in which the country expresses confidence in itself and in its future.

Greenspan also represents something more than the confidence wing of the American personality. He stands at the point where the country's eternal optimism meets up with the country's abiding suspicion that something will go wrong. As citizens get happier about the boom and grow more prosperous, the fear of impending doom seems to grow, though it may often be unstated. Mention the boom, and the words that come to most lips are "When will it end?" Americans always keep one eye cocked at the clock that will run out, or the exit ramp, or circumstances that might bring us down.

That fear also creates a kind of excitement and anticipation. Greenspan stands at the crossroads of optimism and pessimism. Each of us is a character in the nation's great economic soap opera; Greenspan is both director and producer.

Yet his biggest role may lie in the future. No one knows whether the economic expansion will continue for years or whether it is at its summit. But some day, in some form, the economic boom will end. Someone, an authoritative voice, is going to have to tell us when the party is over. Someone with credibility will have to explain and answer questions. What happened? Why? What might it mean? Who is responsible? Someone will have to propose a course of action and outline what has to be done.

AFTERWORD:
AFTER THE BOOM

The HARDBACK edition of *Maestro* was published in November 2000 in the midst of 36 days of uncertainty over the outcome of the Bush-Gore presidential race. The good economic times seemed to be continuing.

By early September 2001, it was apparent that the United States, if not the world, was in a significant and painful economic slowdown. Economic growth in the United States had approached or hovered around zero. The terrorist attacks of September 11 changed the American economy and, at least temporarily, severely damaged it. By any realistic assessment currently available, the economic party, the celebrated boom that improved the economic lives of most Americans, is over.

What happened? What does it mean? And what can be done?

For Greenspan, the slowdown of 2000 was not a surprise; in fact it was what he wanted. The extent of the slowdown and the swiftness with which it occurred was the surprise. As reported earlier in this book, Greenspan shared in the general euphoria in 1999 after the various international crises passed without doing in the U.S. economy, as many, including Greenspan, had feared. Because the economy had weathered these storms, the future seemed bright as far as the eye could see—even to the cautious Greenspan. His analysis of the new technology and the new economy showed that businesses had used only half or less of the high-technology advances currently available to them. That was important good news for future growth. More improvements could be expected in productivity as well as substantial innovations.

He had closely monitored a slowdown in 2000. The weekly

steel capacity utilization rates showed that steel plants in the United States, which had been operating at close to 95 percent capacity in the spring, had slowed to the 70 percent range as the end of 2000 approached. Steel was not the critical economic indicator it had been in decades past, but to Greenspan it was still almost the closest approximation to a durable good. The drop in steel use showed weakening in the heavy-goods industry—still an important part of the American economy.

This downturn was exactly what Greenspan and his colleagues on the FOMC wanted; he even termed it "benevolent." Perhaps the rate increases of 1999 and early 2000 were getting some traction in slowing the economy. The 4 percent plus annual growth of the last several years had not been sustainable. Now the brakes were working, and growth could be brought down to a sustainable rate of, say, 3 percent or 2 percent. This adjustment process in the economy was occurring through the spring and into the summer of 2000 at a fairly rapid pace. That was fine with Greenspan. The economy was possibly coming in for a neat soft landing with no jarring sudden downturn or recession. Just slower, more reasonable, less overheated economic growth. It was the very comfortable Goldilocks economy some were referring to in print—not too hot, not too cold, just right. He didn't want to do anything but practice his notorious hands-off laissez faire.

Then in the first days of December 2000, all of a sudden, the bottom fell out of the American economy. In his dispassionate way, Greenspan found it remarkable. It was as though everybody was waiting for the gun to go off and they would dive together, buy and invest less. It was so quick that there was no cumulative data, no reports assembling weeks or months of information to show a definite trend. But Greenspan was bombarded with letters, calls and various advice. As he traveled the reception, dinner and party circuit, he had a series of what he called "30-second conversations" in which people unloaded their views of economic distress. The Fed staff and district banks conducted surveys, finding very broad anecdotal nationwide information. It was not scientific, but it was good enough to paint a vivid picture, too vivid. Automobile sales, one of Greenspan's favorite indicators, had plummeted. Consumer confidence was down. Many businesses reported shortfalls in sales and earnings. Purchases of computers, software and communications equipment had dropped markedly. At Cisco, the supplier of Internet networking systems and the darling stock of the 1990s, they had been trying to push production to accumulate sufficient inventory—and then, in a matter of weeks, orders and sales dropped at an awesome rate. Poor John Chambers, Greenspan thought, referencing the CEO of Cisco. Other CEOs had similar stories. They had never seen anything like it before. Cash flow dropped and profit margins were crushed.

Greenspan realized that the same new technology that gave businesses almost instant sales, inventory and order information, which in recent years had added substantial efficiencies and increased productivity, was working in reverse. What was true on the way up, he reasoned, was almost certainly true on the way down. The pace was condensed, resulting in a kind of synchronous decision making. In the past, some businesspeople would think things were getting better and others might think they were getting worse. The optimism would often cancel out the pessimism or at least slow the process of reaching a consensus. This time everyone seemed to have reached the same negative conclusion at almost the same time. It was like a thunderclap and everyone jumped on the same pessimistic bandwagon.

The FOMC met on December 19, 2000, just before Christmas, and a week after the Supreme Court ruled in favor of Bush. The committee's directive from the previous meeting was asymmetric, with a bias stating that they thought the greatest risk to the economy was future inflation. Greenspan wanted to change that bias and declare publicly that the risks of economic weakness outweighed the risks of inflation. He considered this a double change, moving from November's stated concern about inflation, through neutral— skipping the symmetric statement—to a declared concern about risks being tilted toward future economic weakness. To also cut rates would in effect be a triple move and too extraordinary, he believed. They had to be careful. Though something dramatic had occurred, the chairman did not want to suggest it was more than what businesses and the public had already detected. The announcement of the change in bias would have some impact in itself and hint that rate cuts were likely coming. He told the committee he contemplated that unless something fairly dramatic happened on the positive side they should lower rates right after the first of the year, or about a month before the next scheduled FOMC meeting. He said he would convene a conference call before acting.

After four and a half hours, the vote was unanimous to change the bias and announce it publicly.

Two weeks later, January 3, 2001, Greenspan convened the FOMC conference call. The news was worse. Manufacturing was especially soft, notably automobile sales. Overall retail sales for the holidays had been below expectations, the worst since the recession of 1990–91. Many businesses and analysts were forecasting declining profits. Greenspan wanted to move immediately, drop the short-term rate ½ percent—double the normal ¼ percentage cut—as the Fed began what would look like a substantial easing cycle. If they acted, they would be in front of a series of negative economic reports that would come out during the month. He didn't want to move on a day in which there were one or two significant statistics publicly released. If they acted on one of those days, people would conclude that was the reason for the move. Greenspan had always argued strenuously that the Fed did not react to a single number, but with so many economic indicators it was becoming increasingly impossible to avoid a coincidence. Better to move sooner rather than later, he reasoned. The ½ percent cut would be forceful, larger than expected in the markets. He received unanimous support, and the announcement was made early that afternoon.

The Nasdaq rose more than 14 percent, or 325 points—the biggest percentage and point gain since the index was created in 1971.

Greenspan does not like to see the stock market jump sharply in either direction. The decline had been sufficiently substantial over the last nine months that a further sharp decline was now unlikely. In a practical sense, a low stock market was more stable.

The real problem in his view was the sudden economic contraction of December. He hoped it was the bottom. It nonetheless was a real turning point. Monetary policy, he knew well, could basically set a platform for stable economic growth, maintain and improve the financial liquidity of the system. But it could not produce economic growth. It is a background force. He looked for an analogy. Monetary policy, the setting of the short-term interest rate, was like the law of contracts. Without a body of contract law that made written agreements within society and the economy enforceable, there would be chaos. Contract law didn't produce anything itself, but it was a structure and foundation that made binding agreements possible. Without them, no business could function; orders and commitments wouldn't be met; consumers wouldn't pay their credit card charges. Monetary policy, by stabilizing the currency and keeping inflation under control, provided the conditions for a growing economy. But businesses were now experiencing severe stress.

• • •

The Senate Budget Committee asked Greenspan to testify later in January and to address the possibility of a federal income tax cut—perhaps the main domestic political issue of the day and central to the new Congress. The federal government was projecting surpluses amounting to trillions of dollars over the next decade. President George W. Bush, the former Republican Texas Governor who had just assumed office, had campaigned hard on the pledge to return a portion of that projected surplus in a tax cut plan then estimated at $1.6 trillion over ten years. Many Democrats had proposed a tax cut of about half that amount.

Greenspan settled in to prepare his testimony and began examining all kinds of economic reports, particularly those on worker productivity—the critical output per hour. The big acceleration in productivity he had detected years earlier was now going to be tested. What would happen in an economic downturn? Indeed, he found that productivity had gone down but not nearly as much as he expected. He reviewed the long-term productivity estimates prepared by the Congressional Budget Office (CBO) and the White House Office of Management and Budget (OMB). They were just too low, he believed. With higher productivity the federal government was going to be collecting more in tax revenue than expected over the next decade. He calculated that at a point in about six years the federal government could have paid off its entire debt of several trillion dollars and accumulated some $500 billion in excess surplus. No one could know where the economy might be in that year, 2006. If that excess was suddenly returned as a tax cut then, it could be disastrously inflationary.

Accordingly, the CBO and OMB had *understated* the available money in surpluses, he believed. Over the years, Greenspan had concluded that if the federal government accumulated surpluses, it was best economically for the money to be used to pay down the government debt. Second best was returning the money as tax cuts. Least desirable was for the government to spend the money in new or expanded federal programs. Since the projections were what Greenspan considered startling, the surplus was going to grow by hundreds of billions of dollars, and, according to his numbers, be more than transitory. One result might be that the federal government could have so much extra money that it might start buying stocks, essentially becoming a large investor on Wall Street. Internal Fed figures showed that the federal government could wind up with a dangerously large portion of private stock holdings in the coming years.

Greenspan was so deeply worried that he told a colleague, "Can you imagine either Lyndon Johnson or Richard Nixon with all of that moola out there, essentially refraining from using it for political purposes?" Then answering his own question, he said, "The chances of that are zero." Such vast sums under the control of the government would create all kinds of potential for mischief, Greenspan felt.

In the first draft of his testimony, he laid out this danger. As he thought more about it and dug deeper into the numbers, he noticed that the CBO showed federal surpluses running well past the year 2030. Though this was admittedly shaky and uncertain, he decided that he needed to speak out.

As he read over the first draft he mused: If this is true, then there is something that has got to be focused on very sharply and stated publicly, because no one had identified the problem. He decided it was time to cut taxes now to forestall the possibility of the government gaining control of so much money by becoming a giant potential investor in the stock market.

The goal, he reasoned, should be near-zero federal debt to be achieved by paying off government bonds and then returning any excess surplus to the taxpayers. This would prevent the government from playing the stock market. As a caveat, he decided to include a suggestion that would limit the tax cut if the projected surpluses did not materialize in future years. When he was done, Greenspan had written that a tax cut was "required"—unusually strong, even unprecedented, language for him. He knew it was a stark conclusion, and he made it clear he was supporting only the principle of a tax cut, not the Bush proposal or the lesser tax cut proposed by various Democrats. Since nearly everyone seemed to be for some kind of tax cut, he was not taking sides or being partisan, he felt.

As he wrote out his thoughts and conclusions, he realized that his formal testimony would be more complex than usual. Greenspan decided it would be unfair to spring it on the Budget Committee cold without giving them advance warning. So he sent copies up to the Hill the day before so the senators and staff could prepare questions.

Senator Kent Conrad, the outspoken senior Democrat on the budget committee, invited Greenspan to his office to discuss his upcoming testimony late on the afternoon of Wednesday, January 24, the day before the chairman was scheduled to appear.

Such an unequivocal conclusion would be a serious mistake, Conrad told him. It might be too subtle for people to understand

and would be interpreted as the chairman of the Fed giving everybody carte blanche to cut taxes. The radical tax cutters, Bush and the Republicans, would use his testimony as support. The declaration that tax cuts were "required" was too strong. Greenspan would be opening a Pandora's box.

Greenspan said he just didn't believe his generalized support for a tax cut would have that much of an impact. He noted that Democrats, including Conrad, were in favor of tax cuts ranging up to $800 billion over the 10 years. It was a matter of degree; he was not supporting either plan, his testimony was not partisan. If you think it's unbalanced, Greenspan replied, do me a favor: During the question and answer period ask me these questions and I will give you the answers I'm giving now.

Conrad said that the forecasts of trillions of dollars of surplus were riddled with uncertainties. You don't bet the farm on a 10-year forecast. CBO was saying that there was only a 10 percent chance that the forecast number would be true. There was a 45 percent chance there would be more money and a 45 percent chance there would be *less* money. Conrad said his worry was that Greenspan's testimony would lead to an abandonment of fiscal discipline and run the serious risk of putting the federal government back into deficits. It is critically important that the floodgates not be opened again, he said. He had spent 15 years trying to help get the federal budget back in order after the disasters of the 1980s and the huge, debilitating deficits. Conrad had been the North Dakota tax commissioner for five years in the 1980s and the danger of debt was forever seared into his head. Please reconsider your testimony, Conrad requested.

I can't fail to tell the truth, Greenspan said. I can't fail to report the numbers.

No one's asking you not to tell the truth or to report the numbers, Conrad said. But it's got to be put into context.

Greenspan promised he would do that.

Conrad also said he thought it was a flawed choice about what to do with the surplus. Greenspan's choices—spend it, return it in the form of tax cuts or the government acquires stocks—were not the only choices. New laws could be passed that would insulate government officials from investment decisions, as has been the case with various government pension plans.

When the Fed chairman left, Conrad called Bob Rubin, the Treasury Secretary who had worked hand in hand with Greenspan during the Clinton years in an unusual alliance that had helped eliminate the annual federal budget deficits.

The senator explained that Greenspan was about to declare that tax cuts were "required," and summarized the rationale about the stock market in the prepared testimony. Call Greenspan, Conrad urged, and try to talk him out of it.

Rubin was somewhat baffled. After all the years they had worked together on fiscal discipline, why would Greenspan shift from urging federal debt repayment to urging tax cuts? He called his friend and tried gently to raise the question of whether this was a good or necessary thing to do.

Greenspan explained that his testimony was carefully balanced and expressed his conclusions from the projected surpluses. "Bob," Greenspan asked at one point, "where in my testimony do you disagree?"

Rubin had not seen the testimony, but he suggested that the surpluses could be given as refundable tax credits when they actually materialized. Since Greenspan was talking years in the future, this did not have to be addressed now. He added that as he understood the testimony Greenspan would be seen as embracing Bush. It's all perception, Rubin said. It did not take much to see how the news media would treat it.

"I can't be in charge of people's perceptions," Greenspan said. "I don't function that way. I can't function that way."

The chairman's testimony leaked. "Greenspan to Back Tax Cuts," blared the large lead headline in *USA Today* the morning of his testimony.

As he testified, Greenspan tried to be careful. He read the last line of his testimony twice, emphasizing the importance of resisting policies that, he said, "could readily resurrect the deficits of the past."

The next morning's near-banner headline in *The Washington Post* said, "Greenspan Supports a Tax Cut." The paper's veteran Greenspan watcher, John M. Berry, wrote that the chairman had "endorsed the idea of a major federal tax cut as not only fiscally prudent but also necessary." A front-page analysis said, "Bush's Hand Greatly Strengthened." It noted that overall the testimony "dispelled the notion that Bush's plan to cut taxes might be reckless, dangerous or even massive"—the central charges that Democrats had made in the presidential campaign against Bush's plan. "You could almost hear the ice cracking across the Capitol."

Republicans, including Bush, immediately embraced Greenspan as an ally. The president said he was "pleased" and Greenspan's words were "measured and just right." Many leading Democrats voiced shock, saying that Greenspan had taken the lid off the punch bowl and would start a stampede. *The Wall Street Journal* called it an "about-face."

Senator Conrad, more influenced by Greenspan than Greenspan by him, said the testimony was "balanced."

Greenspan had also addressed the question of which way the economy might be heading, and he said that the question "is going to be resolved one way or the other in three months or so." He believed they'd know very soon. In business cycles, downturns and upturns are generally clear in a matter of months. The economy does not stay in neutral for prolonged periods of time. That would turn out to be his worst forecast in years.

On January 31, the FOMC announced another ½ percent cut in the rate. Greenspan reasoned that if the economy's adjustment process was accelerated, the FOMC would have to accelerate its monetary policy and cut rates more and faster.

On Sunday, February 11, Greenspan read a long *New York Times* op-ed piece by Bob Rubin, headlined, "A Prosperity Easy to Destroy." It was accompanied by a drawing of two smiling men sawing down a large tree. It did not mention Bush or Greenspan by name, but it wasn't necessary. The article was carefully aimed at the large tax cut and its supporters. "We should avoid committing ourselves to dramatic courses of action that are hard to reverse in the face of the inherent uncertainties of any projections." It was an argument for moderation and prudence—the kind of language normally found in Greenspan's remarks.

On February 14, *The New York Times* hit Greenspan with a Valentine's Day rebuke. In his regular column, Paul Krugman, a Princeton economist respected by Greenspan, excoriated the chairman by reporting a "rumor" that Greenspan "is now engaged in a backdoor campaign to limit the damage" from his assist to those who favor "huge, irresponsible tax cuts.

"If those rumors are true, Mr. Greenspan's performance" in not backing off his tax cut support is "a profile in cowardice." Krugman implied that Greenspan was protecting himself, was not being forthright, did not believe his own argument and had failed "a test of character."

Greenspan realized he was being called a hypocrite. He rarely called a reporter or columnist to protest. On occasion he just took it out on his wife, Andrea. "Is this a colleague of yours?" he once asked her. "He ought to get an education."

Greenspan believed that reporters should normally have two sources for such accusations, and Krugman didn't even seem to have a single source. He was reporting a rumor. Greenspan called him.

"Paul, for God's sakes, you begin your piece by stipulating . . ." the chairman began. To base a column on a rumor! "Lift up the phone, call me and ask me whether it's true," he added. "In fact, it is false. I have never said, nor in fact do I believe, that the tax cut is too high. It's not that large a tax cut, frankly." He noted that he believed in some mechanism or trigger that would limit the tax cuts if the surplus didn't materialize. "You're accusing me of things that you could have found out whether it is true or false by just calling and asking."

"I didn't think you were available," replied Krugman. He was shocked that such a prominent figure as Greenspan would call to complain. Krugman was relatively new to writing a high-profile column for the *Times* and was accustomed to the comparative isolation of academic life.

In a later interview, Krugman accused Greenspan of "violating the trust of his office" by taking a public position on a political issue that was not monetary policy. He said that the chairman of the Federal Reserve "should be scrupulously above politics" and his support of a tax cut was a "colossal misjudgment." Greenspan should have presented a menu of options that were economically acceptable but not endorsed any single one.

It was getting rough out there.

At the Fed, some of Greenspan's colleagues were almost as unhappy as Krugman that Greenspan had endorsed a tax cut—even though he had said, "I speak for myself and not necessarily for the Federal Reserve." How could the Fed chairman be separated from his official role, especially one as powerful and visible as Greenspan? He didn't say. Governor Laurence Meyer had deep reservations about the Fed or its chairman, even under cover of speaking only for himself, taking positions on issues outside the scope of monetary policy. Greenspan had put himself in a position to be used in the political process, Meyer believed, and he put his concerns in writing, though he never circulated it. Greenspan never saw it or heard about it, such was the chairman's isolation from internal criticism.

For his part Greenspan was unrepentant. The concern about the federal government getting into the stock market was real. He alone had identified the problem and blown the whistle. Since everyone was for a tax cut of some sort, all he was doing was agreeing with everyone. As far as the politics were concerned, his assessment was that Congress was going to pass a substantial tax cut no matter what he said.

Greenspan defended his decision privately. To a suggestion that he should have been more cautious, he said, "I would be saying less than I knew, less than I understood, less than I thought was right. And why would I do that?" He said he fudged only when he was worried that his comments might have an impact on the financial markets. "Am I going to fudge because it has political effects? The answer is, I can't do that." He added, "If I had fudged at that particular time, I would have been doing, I think, an injustice to my sworn obligation around here to tell it like it is."

To those who had worked with Greenspan over the years, both inside and outside the Fed, it was obvious that he was aware of the political impact, that he was giving a giant assist to the new Republican president and his friend Vice President Cheney. It was also more than possible that Greenspan had been accommodating to Democrats Clinton and Rubin in order to have smooth relations. With Republicans in control of the White House, he could return to his natural, true beliefs. He liked less government, and to lower taxes when the government was running a surplus made both economic and political sense.

Given that it generally took 6 to 18 months for cuts in the interest rate for short-term fed funds to have their impact on helping the economy, there was widespread understanding within the Federal Reserve that they were really working on next year, 2002, as they were raising rates in 2001. With the suddenness of the steep economic decline, 2001 was pretty much settled.

On March 20, the FOMC again cut the Fed funds rate another ½ percent. Greenspan wanted to communicate to the financial markets a consistent, overall strategy of large, frequent ½ percentage point cuts as the economic news continued to be bad.

On April 2, *The New York Times* front-page headline read: "Once Unthinkable, Criticism Is Raised Against Greenspan." Reporter Richard W. Stevenson wrote, "With the decade-old economic expansion in danger, stock prices tumbling and the Federal Reserve no longer seeming omnipotent or omniscient, Alan Greenspan, who at 75 is in his 14th year as chairman of the central bank, is being second-guessed as never before." He quoted a number of analysts, conservatives and liberals with various critiques. Some said Greenspan had been too bold in raising rates in 2000. Others said he was too timid in cutting rates in the current easing cycle. Greenspan felt they had done it about right and had no second thoughts.

In the late 1990s, Greenspan had been praised. People would come up to him and say, as did one woman, "Oh, thanks for my 401(k)"—referring to the large growth in her pension plan.

He had replied, "Madam, I had nothing to do with your 401(k)."

Now people were blaming him. His conviction was that the economy was at risk in the short term, but in the long run he believed the American economy, even the world economy, was far more dynamic, flexible and capitalistic than it had been 20 or 30 years ago. It now had much more long-term potential. All he could do was proceed with the aggressive rate cutting.

On Monday, April 9, Greenspan sent out the usual 48-hour warning that he would convene a conference call of the FOMC on April 11. He might want to make another move. By the time the committee convened on the phone, circumstances had changed. The markets had been particularly volatile, and a sudden Fed move might be too much of a shock and too much of a risk. They agreed to wait a week.

On April 18, Greenspan got the FOMC members on the phone and won unanimous approval for another ½ percentage point cut— taking the rate down to 4½ percent—the fourth big cut since the beginning of the year. The surprise inter-meeting move sent the Nasdaq up more than 8 percent.

But business investment and profits continued to stay down. The relatively high productivity growth and consumer spending were all that was keeping the economy going. The result was a steady flatness. That was the story, Greenspan realized. His forecast in January that they would know overall where the economy was heading had turned out to be very wrong.

By the end of April, Greenspan felt that the longer term outlook was still positive, putting a floor under the whole economy. But the short-term risk continued. On May 15, the committee lowered rates another ½ percentage point, to 4 percent. The vote was 9 to 1. The lone dissenter, Thomas H. Hoenig, president of the Kansas City bank, wanted only a ¼ percent cut.

In late May, Congress passed President Bush's tax cut, which amounted to $1.35 trillion over ten years. Though there was some short-term stimulus for the economy in the form of immediate rebates of up to $600, most of the cuts were in the later years. On June

27 the FOMC cut only ¼ percentage point. The vote was again 9 to 1. William Poole, the president of the St. Louis bank, wanted them to stop cutting rates. Again, on August 21, the FOMC cut another ¼ point.

Over eight months, a full 3 percentage points had been cut from the fed funds rate, one of the most aggressive series of easing moves in history. The actions had some positive impact on the economy, Greenspan was sure. Mortgage rates had come down, triggering more refinancing. Home sales stayed up, with many homeowners taking substantial amounts of cash out after a sale for consumer spending. The lower short-term rates also made it easier for corporations to reissue bonds. He did not believe monetary policy had failed—to say that, as some had, was to demonstrate a lack of understanding about its limits. But Greenspan realized there might be far larger forces out there that could send the economy down further.

By September, Greenspan was telling people privately, "I cannot say to you that the stock market is undervalued." In other words, further lows were possible. He also reiterated his long-held view: "The business cycle is not dead."

Because of the slowdown, the federal government was collecting less tax revenue and the projected surpluses for the current year and perhaps the next had disappeared. Democrats who had opposed the tax cut were having a field day; it was the Bush economy that was stagnant as hundreds of thousands of people lost their jobs.

The title of this book, *Maestro*, was chosen carefully, and was intended to convey that Greenspan is conducting the orchestra but does not play an instrument. He sets the conditions for the players to play well, if they so choose and if they are capable. His approach is often subtle, never the obvious, baton-waving, savage-faced leader driving the orchestra. He prefers at times to let the orchestra, the players in the economy, set its own tempo. At other times, such as the present, he may have no choice.

As the economy has turned down and criticism of Greenspan increases, he is, to some extent, a victim of his successes. In the old traditional business cycle of every two to three years, it was rational for businesses, investors and consumers to see a high degree of risk in the next six months. An economic downturn was always around the corner, or seemed to be. That made people more cautious. But in the long boom of ten years, it was rational for everyone to think the next six months would be more like the last six months, more of the same continuing growth. Greenspan found that psychologically it was very tough to remember, in an emotional sense, the bad times, which seemed so long ago. The process was, he reasoned, similar to the way that people say they can't remember pain. So the risks seemed less. Capital investment increased and the expansion picked up. But there was a breaking point.

Greenspan realized that the high-technology bubble of wild overexpansion and ridiculously high stock prices had largely caused the economic downturn and dislocation of 2001. He believed he had publicly warned about this. "I kept saying the emperor has no clothes and no one would listen," he said privately. Actually, he had said it forcefully only once, and that was his 1996 "irrational exuberance" comment about the stock market. He had later modified it or so dressed it up with ambiguity that no one knew what he was saying or where he stood. If Greenspan can be faulted, it is his failure to issue clear and repeated but careful warnings about businesses—such as the large Internet companies—with large value that were earning meager profits or none at all. These were not sound investments. Investors put money in stocks instead of more secure bonds, particularly U.S. Treasuries, because they anticipated they would earn more. Greenspan had even joked privately during the high-tech bubble that someone ought to see if activity in the casinos had gone down because the players had moved to the stock market. It was a silly and crazy time. He knew it could not last.

No one knew better or was more aware of the consequences than Greenspan. He believed that he had done all he could. He had spoken in 1996, and all the stock market did was go up. If he had said more, he contended, he might have slowed the exuberance a bit, but in the end it might have made the bubble worse. He would speak out, the markets would slow down for a bit and then take back off, and the economy's aura of invincibility would only increase. That would help create a larger bubble down the road, which would eventually break and have disastrous consequences. All he might have done was postpone the day of reckoning. Why? Because he would be fighting human psychology—the perceived self-interest and greed of investors.

Could Greenspan have raised rates and broken the back of the bubble? Probably yes, he believed, but that would have meant raising the fed funds rate to something like 15 percent—an unimaginably authoritarian and inappropriate action by unelected officials such as himself.

But I think he could have made a greater, more visible and prolonged effort—a careful and repeated warning about exuberance and greed might have tamed the markets. Even if he had failed, it might have been worth trying. In a sense, he held back his greatest asset: his immense knowledge and experience. It could have been his most important forecast.

So in early September, like the rest of the nation and the world, the chairman was waiting to see what might happen next. Would the economy start to recover or tip into recession? At times he thought that after the battering of 2001, the most remarkable fact might be that the economy was still standing. The economic impact of the September 11 terrorist attacks in New York City and Washington is only beginning to be measured as I write this. Dramatic action may be required.

GLOSSARY

Arbitrage The buying of stocks, currency or any security in one market to sell for an expected profit in another market. The strategy is to take advantage of small price differences. Since the differences may be quite small, large volumes must be purchased to make money. It can be risky and expensive if prices move in directions the investor has not anticipated.

Board of Governors The Board of Governors of the Federal Reserve System is made up of seven governors, each of whom is appointed by the president and confirmed by the Senate to a 14-year term. The chairman is a member of the Board of Governors, and his position as head of the Federal Reserve is based on a separate four-year appointment by the president. The board controls the discount rate, and each member of the board is also a voting member of the Federal Open Market Committee. The board also has responsibilities for bank regulation.

Bond A note or obligation requiring the borrower, normally a government or corporation, to pay the lender, normally an individual or institutional investor, the amount of the loan—or face value—at the end of a fixed period of time. That period is normally anywhere from 3 months to 30 years. The borrower must pay the lender a fixed rate of interest—a percentage of the face value—each year until the bond matures. Government and corporate bonds, totaling trillions of dollars of indebtedness, trade in the bond market. Bond prices move in the opposite direction of interest rates.

Central Bank A national bank that operates to control and stabilize the currency and credit conditions in a country's economy, usually through control of interest rates. This is called the nation's money or, more formally, its monetary policy. The Federal Reserve is the central bank of the United States and is assigned by law to pursue specific national economic goals.

Consumer Price Index The consumer price index (CPI) is a measure of the average change over time in the prices paid by urban consumers for certain consumer goods and services. The CPI provides a way to compare what goods and services cost this month with what the same goods and services cost a month or a year ago. The CPI is the most widely used measure of inflation. Many economists, including Alan Greenspan, believe that the CPI overstates inflation by as much as 1 percent, because of the difficulties and errors in measuring prices and weighting them in the overall index.

Discount Rate The rate controlled by the Board of Governors that the 12 Federal Reserve banks charge on daily loans to private commercial banks, savings and loan associations, savings banks and credit unions. In the period roughly from 1987 to 1992, the announcement of changes in the discount rate was the primary means the Fed used to communicate its interest rate policy to the general public.

Ease or Easing To "ease" credit, the Fed pumps money into the nation's banking system through the purchase of U.S. Treasury bonds. This causes the key fed funds interest rate—the rate banks charge each other for overnight loans—to go down, which makes it easier for consumers and businesses to borrow. This normally causes the economy to grow and is a strategy for averting low economic growth and fighting a recession.

Fed Funds Rate The rate controlled by the FOMC that banks charge each other on overnight loans—and, in recent years, the key short-term rate. The rate affects overall credit conditions in the United States and is the Fed's main weapon against both recession and inflation. Since 1994, changes to the fed funds rate have been announced publicly. The markets and bankers realize the power of the Fed to enforce the new rate, so the rate moves to its new level immediately.

Federal Open Market Committee (FOMC) The FOMC consists of the 7 members of the Board of Governors and the presidents of the 12 Federal Reserve Banks. Everybody participates in each meeting, but only 12 people vote: the 7 Fed governors; the president of the New York Fed, who serves as the FOMC's vice chairman and has a permanent voting seat; and 4 of the other 11 bank presidents, who serve one-year terms as voting members on a rotating basis. The committee meets in Washington eight times a year, about once every six weeks, to assess the state of the economy and to decide whether to take any action on the fed funds rate, which the committee controls.

Federal Reserve Act Passed in 1913, the Federal Reserve Act established the Federal Reserve System as an independent government body that had sovereign power over the nation's currency and over a number of regulatory issues concerning the banking system. Since 1913, the act has been modified a number of times—most notably in 1978, with the Full Employment and Balanced Growth Act, which instructed the Federal Reserve to seek stable prices, maximum sustainable growth for the economy and maximum employment consistent with the two other goals.

Federal Reserve System The system includes the Board of Governors in Washington, D.C., and the 12 district Federal Reserve Banks and their outlying branches. The reserve banks are in New York, San Francisco, Boston, Philadelphia, Richmond, Cleveland, Atlanta, Chicago, St. Louis, Minneapolis, Kansas City and Dallas. The Federal Reserve System also processes and clears the great majority of all banks' paper checks, facilitates wire transfers for payments, regulates how much paper currency and coin are in circulation and oversees the entire banking industry.

Gross Domestic Product (GDP) The broadest measure of the output of the U.S. economy, the GDP is the amount of goods and services produced in the United States.

Hedge Fund An investing group that pools large sums of money. The basic strategy is to identify stocks or other investments that will increase in value, but also to identify those that will decline. By short selling those expected to decline, the fund hedges against market downturns and makes more money than it would by investing strictly in securities expected to increase in value.

Inflation A rate of increase in the general price level of *all* goods and services.

Inflation Expectations The rate of increase in the general price level anticipated by the public in the period ahead, which affects purchasing decisions, business expansion or contraction and investment decisions.

Long-term Interest Rates Interest rates on loan contracts—or debts such as Treasury bonds or corporate bonds—having maturities greater than one year.

Monetary Policy A central bank's actions to influence short-term interest rates and the supply of money and credit in accordance with national goals. The main tool of U.S. monetary policy is open market operations, the buying or selling of U.S. Treasury bonds, to control the fed funds rate.

Money Supply Technically, the amount of money in the economy—including currency, bank deposits and money market accounts. As people moved large amounts of money into mutual funds in the early 1990s, the money supply became almost impossible to measure.

NAIRU The non-accelerating inflation rate of unemployment is an economic concept that holds that there is a certain rate of unemployment that the economy can sustain without severe inflation. Economists who believe in the NAIRU think that if the unemployment rate dips below the NAIRU, the workforce will insist on wage increases and trigger inflation.

Open Market Operations Purchases and sales of government and other securities in the open market through the Domestic Trading Desk at the Federal Reserve Bank of New York, as directed by the FOMC. Open market operations effectively set short-term interest rates. Purchases inject money into the banking system and stimulate growth of money and credit, while sales contract credit.

Productivity Output per worker per hour.

Short Selling A technique used to take advantage of an anticipated decline in the price of a stock or other security by borrowing stock from a broker and selling it immediately. If the investor is right and the price of the stock declines, the borrowed shares can be replaced by buying them at the cheaper price from the market. The profit is the difference between the price at which the investor sells the shares and the price at which the investor buys them later on. If the price of the shares rises, however, the investor will lose money when the shares have to be replaced.

Stocks Certificates representing partial ownership in a corporation and a claim on the firm's earnings and assets. Stocks of profitable corporations normally yield periodic payments of dividends. The value of a stock often rises or falls in the market as a company meets, or fails to meet, earnings expectations.

Tighten or Tightening To "tighten" credit, the Fed sells U.S. Treasury bonds, which withdraws money from the banking system. With the supply of money decreased, banks become less willing to lend—which causes the fed funds and other short-term interest rates to rise. This makes borrowing more difficult and usually causes the economy's growth to slow. Tightening is the Fed's main weapon against inflation.

NOTES

Most of the information in this book comes from extensive interviews with those who made, participated in or witnessed the decisions recounted here. Since the story is about politics, money and Washington, nearly all of the sources declined to allow me to identify them by name or position. In addition to these sources, I and my assistant, Jeff Himmelman, have been able to use some of the extensive documentary records kept by the Federal Reserve. Most important have been the verbatim transcripts made from tape recordings of the FOMC meetings. These transcripts, available only for the period 1987 to 1994, amount to hundreds of pages for each year—providing an unusual, intimate and real-time record of the discussion about decisions on key interest rates and other matters.

Prologue

Most of the information in this chapter comes from the author's interviews with four primary knowledgeable sources, who provided specific recollections based on an agreement that their identity would not be revealed. The first source provided specific information during three interviews; the second source was interviewed on June 2, 2000; the third source was interviewed on three occasions; and the fourth source was interviewed on four occasions. In addition, former Reagan White House Chief of Staff Howard Baker was interviewed in detail about these incidents on the record on May 15, 2000. President Reagan, who is seriously ill, could not be interviewed.

16   Reagan, who saw virtue in Volcker's anti-inflation campaign: For more information on Reagan's relationship with Volcker, see Lou Cannon's comprehensive biography, *President Reagan: The Role of a Lifetime* (2000 edn.), 227–239.

16   Baker had no illusions that a Fed chairman: The Federal Reserve System is independent only in the sense that nobody within government—the

president, the Congress, the courts—can reverse its decisions. Congress does have oversight over the system, because the Constitution gives Congress the power to coin money and set its value—a power that, in the Federal Reserve Act, Congress delegated to the Federal Reserve. The Fed must work within the framework of the overall objectives established by the government, so the Fed describes itself as "independent within government" instead of independent of it. For more information on the basics of the Federal Reserve System, see also "The Board of Governors of the Federal Reserve System," *The Federal Reserve System: Purposes and Functions* (1994), 1–15. The publication can be ordered from the Federal Reserve or found on-line at www.federalreserve.gov/pf/pf.htm.

17   Board members are appointed to 14-year terms: the 14-year terms are essentially rolling. If a governor is appointed to a 14-year term but leaves after 6 years, the next governor to fill that slot signs on for the remaining 8 years and then has to be reappointed to another 14-year term.

18   On February 24, 1986: For another account of this event, see also William Greider's thorough account of the Volcker Fed, *Secrets of the Temple* (1987), 698–701.

24   Baker left unsure: In his interview with the author on May 15, 2000, Howard Baker said that his meeting with Volcker at the Federal Reserve was an effort to try to find out whether Volcker wanted to be reappointed, not an effort to convince him to stay. A June 3, 1987, story in *The Wall Street Journal* reported that Volcker declined renomination during the meeting, and that Baker then asked Volcker to reconsider. According to one of Baker's top aides quoted in the *Journal* story, Baker told Volcker, "Paul, I hope you will think about this while you're fishing this weekend because I can tell you the president will want to talk to you about staying." According to the *Journal*, Baker "continued to hope that Mr. Volcker would reconsider," but Baker was not interviewed for the *Journal* story. In his interview with the author, Howard Baker said this was the first time he was giving the complete version of what really happened. See Gerald F. Seib and Ellen Hume, "Change at the Fed: Volcker's Decision to Quit Fed Was Sealed at Gathering in Reagan's Living Quarters," *The Wall Street Journal*, June 3, 1987, A20.

24   Yes, he said in milliseconds: Greenspan quoted from "Change at the Fed," cited above.

CHAPTER 1

Most of the information in this chapter comes from the author's interviews with three primary knowledgeable sources. The first source was interviewed about the matters covered in this chapter five times between 1992 and 2000. The second source was interviewed eight times over that same period, and the third source was interviewed four times.

28   "We spent all morning": Transcript, Federal Open Market Committee Meeting, August 18, 1987, 24. All quotations from FOMC meetings and conference calls from the period 1987–94 come directly from transcripts released

by the Federal Reserve. Historically, the Fed had never made transcripts public, but in 1993 Greenspan publicly acknowledged that the FOMC tape-recorded its meetings for certain in-house purposes. A number of public officials in turn demanded that the Fed release transcripts to the public, and after a long back-and-forth, the Fed agreed to release "lightly edited" transcripts of its meetings, with a five-year lag. As of the writing of this book, only the transcripts through 1994 were publicly available. Specific mentions of confidential information—the names of specific companies that have privately shared information, for example—are at times deleted. Knowledgeable sources say that no substantive changes are made and that the edits are solely for grammar and clarity.

29   starting to go straight up: Lead times are the amount of time that it takes for a factory or warehouse to deliver an item after the initial order for that item has been placed. Rising lead times means that it is taking longer and longer for people to get what they've ordered. The scarcity often leads to rising prices.

31   The staff report: In the weeks before each FOMC meeting, the Fed staff prepares a report, known at the Fed as the Greenbook, which includes a description of the present state of the economy and a forecast of what the economy will look like over the next year. Until 1995, the staff built a specific monetary policy into its forecast, specifying anticipated interest rate increases or decreases. The members of the FOMC could then either agree or disagree with it. Beginning in 1995, at the urging of Governors Alan Blinder and Janet Yellen, the Greenbook began to incorporate some alternatives. Regardless of whether everybody agrees with its outlook, the Greenbook is the basis from which discussion of the economy during FOMC meetings begins.

31   "While the staff ": Dialogue through "the real world" taken from Transcript, Federal Open Market Committee Meeting, August 18, 1987, 25.

31   "The risk of snuffing out": Transcript, Federal Open Market Committee Meeting, August 18, 1987, 33.

32   It was the first increase: The Fed had last raised the discount rate in April of 1984, when the rate went up from 8½ percent to 9 percent; since then, the Fed had lowered the rate to 5½ percent.

34   In 1968: Greenspan met Nixon after running into Leonard Garment, a Nixon law partner who had played in the Henry Jerome Band with Greenspan during the 1940s. Garment was advising Nixon and brought Greenspan to meet him.

35   In the summer of 1974: Nixon had asked Greenspan to come to the Council of Economic Advisers twice before, but Greenspan had refused him both times. Arthur Burns, Greenspan's mentor at Columbia and chairman of the Federal Reserve from 1970 to 1978, pushed Greenspan hard to take the CEA job in 1974, saying that Greenspan was badly needed in the post.

35   "There is always something": Dialogue through "evidence of actual inflation" taken from Transcript, Federal Open Market Committee Meeting, September 22, 1987, 34–35.

36   "The actions we are taking": Greenspan quoted from Transcript, Federal Open Market Committee Meeting, September 22, 1987, 42.

37   Johnson took out a one-inch-thick binder: The staff at the New York
Federal Reserve Bank had prepared a confidential document called "Summary
Papers on Risks in the U.S. Financial System," begun while Volcker was chairman. The document sketches out a variety of potential catastrophes and possible responses to them and contains a seven-page section on the stock market
that was finalized on September 25, 1987.

40   "The Federal Reserve": Federal Reserve statement quoted from "After
the Crash—On the Spot: Stock Market's Frenzy Puts Fed's Greenspan in a
Crucial Position," *The Wall Street Journal*, October 21, 1987, A1.

43   By about 11:30 a.m.: The account of the events of Tuesday, October
20, contains information from a number of the author's interviews; this section
also uses information from *The Wall Street Journal*'s series on the crash: James
B. Stewart and Daniel Hertzberg, "Terrible Tuesday," November 20, 1987,
A1; James B. Stewart and Daniel Hertzberg, "The Crash of '87—Before the
Fall," December 11, 1987, A1; Randall Smith, Steve Swartz and George An-
ders, "The Crash of '87—Black Monday," December 16, 1987, A1; and Steve
Swartz and Bryan Burrough, "The Crash of '87—The Aftermath," December
29, 1987, A1.

43   "very temporary": Ruder quoted from "The Crash of '87—Black Monday," *The Wall Street Journal*, December 16, 1987, A1.

44   The specialists on the stock exchange floor: Specialists are small but
powerful firms required by the New York Stock Exchange to buy and sell assigned stocks during volatile times to keep prices as orderly as possible. Otherwise known as "market makers," the specialists are supposed to be an investor's
last resort; in normal times, they are the reason an investor can buy or sell
a stock when no other investors are in the market. If they invest wisely, specialists can make quite a bit of money—but they got hammered during the
1987 crash. Without any other buyers, some specialist firms were forced to
buy huge quantities of stock out of their own capital in order to comply with
what was required of them. Most specialist firms keep something in the neigh-
borhood of $60 million on hand, which was nothing next to the billions of dol-
lars in sell orders that came through. See the series in *The Wall Street Journal*,
cited above.

CHAPTER 2

Most of the information contained in this chapter comes from three primary
knowledgeable sources. The first source was interviewed four times, the second source was interviewed five times and the third source was interviewed
seven times.

48   "Passing a Test": See Alan Murray, "Passing a Test: Fed's New Chairman Wins a Lot of Praise on Handling the Crash," *The Wall Street Journal*,
November 25, 1987, A1.

48   "The financial system came close to gridlock": The Brady Report
quoted from James B. Stewart and Daniel Hertzberg, "The Brady Report—

Market Medicine: Brady Panel Proposals Underscore Worries '87 Crash Could Recur," *The Wall Street Journal*, January 11, 1988, A1.

49   "One thing about this meeting": Greenspan quoted, through "break the stock market," from Transcript, Federal Open Market Committee Meeting, February 9–10, 1988, 44–45.

50   "My congratulations": Boehne-Greenspan dialogue quoted from Transcript, Federal Open Market Committee Meeting, February 9–10, 1988, 76.

50   "use a sledgehammer": Greenspan quoted from Transcript, Federal Open Market Committee Meeting, February 9–10, 1988, 52.

50   "we will feel the necessity": Greenspan quoted from Rose Gutfelt, "Greenspan Criticizes Top Treasury Aide for Attempting to Influence Fed's Policy," *The Wall Street Journal*, February 25, 1988, A3.

50   The next day's headline: See John M. Berry, "Greenspan Tells Administration to Stop Pressure," *The Washington Post*, February 25, 1988, B1. For another description of the political pressure and Greenspan's reaction to it, see Steven Beckner's book about Greenspan's early tenure as Fed chairman, *Back from the Brink: The Greenspan Years* (1996), 76–80.

51   "If the inflation rate": Corrigan quoted from Transcript, Federal Open Market Committee Meeting, June 29–30, 1988, 16.

52   On Tuesday, August 9: For a full explanation of the Greenspan-Seger scene and the preparations for the August 1988 rate increase, see Louis Uchitelle, "Alan Greenspan; Caution at the Fed," *The New York Times Magazine*, January 15, 1989, 18.

54   "a sound reason": Fitzwater quoted from Robert D. Hershey Jr., "Federal Reserve Steps Up Interest to Slow Inflation," *The New York Times*, August 10, 1988, A1.

54   Greenspan had learned to adapt early on: Most of the biographical information about Greenspan comes from the author's own interviews and research, but a few articles were particularly helpful for background. See Joseph Vitale, "Alan Greenspan," *NYU Business*, 1983, 28–33; John Cassidy, "The Fountainhead," *The New Yorker*, April 24 and May 1, 2000, 162–175.

55   In 1935, when Greenspan was eight: Herbert Greenspan episode is recounted, and quoted, from Louis Uchitelle, "Alan Greenspan; Caution at the Fed," *The New York Times Magazine*, January 15, 1989.

56   Branden wrote in his memoir: See Nathaniel Branden, *Judgment Day: My Years with Ayn Rand* (1989), 131–133, 241.

57   "He was almost too good a loser": Kavesh quoted from an interview on February 16, 1993, conducted by David Greenberg, the author's assistant at that time.

CHAPTER 3

Most of the information in this chapter comes from five knowledgeable sources. The first four sources were interviewed numerous times over a period of eight years. The fifth source was Robert Parker, who was interviewed on the record on August 3, 2000.

59   "I frankly don't recall": Greenspan quoted from Transcript, Federal Open Market Committee Meeting, February 7–8, 1989, 47.

59   "I think it is very important": Greenspan quoted, through "said my piece," from Transcript, Federal Open Market Committee Meeting, February 7–8, 1989, 50.

60   Greenspan issued a blunt warning: Greenspan quoted from John Berry and Paul Blustein, "Price Rise Is Fastest Since 1987; Fed Chief Finds Data 'Disturbing,' " *The Washington Post*, February 23, 1989, A1.

61   "If we had complete capability": Greenspan quoted from Transcript, Federal Open Market Committee Conference Call, June 5, 1989, 4.

61   "I'm concerned": Greenspan quoted from Transcript, Federal Open Market Committee Meeting, July 5–6, 1989, 49–50.

62   who had been described by *Newsweek*: See Thomas M. DeFrank and Ann McDaniel, "Say Hello to Charmin' Darman," *Newsweek*, June 5, 1989, 24.

62   Nine months earlier: See Richard Darman, *Who's in Control?* (1996), 201–2.

62   Darman said he feared: Darman quoted from Transcript, NBC's *Meet the Press*, Sunday, August 13, 1989, 11.

64   Sunday's papers: See Paul Blustein, "Fed Ready with Cash to Cool Market Fears," *The Washington Post*, October 15, 1989, A1; Clyde H. Farnsworth, "Federal Reserve Moves to Provide Cash to Markets," *The New York Times*, October 15, 1989, A1. *The Wall Street Journal* did not run a similar story because the *Journal* appears only on weekdays.

64   Corrigan blasted: Corrigan quoted from Transcript, Federal Open Market Committee Conference Call, October 16, 1989, 2.

64   "I think any official policy position": Greenspan quoted from Transcript, Federal Open Market Committee Conference Call, October 16, 1989, 5.

65   Savings and loans (S&Ls), known as "thrifts": Much of the history of the S&L industry provided here is taken from a section called "A Short History of S&L's" in Kitty Calavita, Henry N. Pontell and Robert H. Tillman's book about the S&L scandal, *Big Money Crime: Fraud and Politics in the Savings and Loan Crisis* (1997), 8–16.

65   William Seidman, the man who chaired: Seidman quoted from *Big Money Crime: Fraud and Politics in the Savings and Loan Crisis* (1997), 15.

65   Greenspan had written a seven-page letter: Greenspan letter quoted from *Big Money Crime: Fraud and Politics in the Savings and Loan Crisis* (1997), 107.

66   "Of course I'm embarrassed": Greenspan quoted, through "doesn't make sense," from Nathaniel Nash, "Greenspan's Lincoln Savings Regret," *The New York Times*, November 20, 1989, D1.

CHAPTER 4

Most of the information in this chapter comes from the author's interviews with five knowledgeable sources, each of whom was interviewed on numerous occasions.

68   On August 2: See also Bob Woodward, *The Commanders* (1991), 218–261.

68   "The odds of an actual war": Greenspan quoted, through "providing a degree of stability," from Transcript, Federal Open Market Committee Meeting, August 21, 1990, 36–38.

69   The committee members voiced: See Transcript, Federal Open Market Committee Meeting, August 21, 1990, 38–44.

69   "I don't think I have asked": Greenspan quoted, through "substantial consensus," from Transcript, Federal Open Market Committee Meeting, August 21, 1990, 45.

69   "There is a lot of 'real stuff' ": Greenspan quoted, through "not responding to a real budget agreement," from Transcript, Federal Open Market Committee Meeting, August 21, 1990, 42–48.

70   "we go down ¼ percent": What Greenspan actually said was "we go down 25 basis points," but the author has changed it to ¼ percent, here and elsewhere in the book. Economists divide each 1 percent into 100 basis points. If the rate goes from 5½ percent to 6 percent, the rate has gone up 50 basis points in the jargon of the Fed and Wall Street. For consistency and ease of reading throughout the narrative, the author has changed the form of those references into fractions, which are used in most news accounts.

70   "reward to the boys on the Hill": Seger quoted from Transcript, Federal Open Market Committee Meeting, August 21, 1990, 55.

70   "It is not a good precedent": Angell quoted from Transcript, Federal Open Market Committee Meeting, August 21, 1990, 54.

70   Greenspan held his ground: Greenspan quoted from Transcript, Federal Open Market Committee Meeting, August 21, 1990, 58.

70   Corrigan cautioned the chairman: Corrigan-Greenspan dialogue quoted from Transcript, Federal Open Market Committee Meeting, August 21, 1990, 59.

71   A furious debate: See also the author's four-part series, "Making Choices: Bush's Economic Record," *The Washington Post*, October 4–7, 1992.

72   "Slowing inflation": Greenspan quoted, through "too dangerous," from Transcript, Federal Open Market Committee Meeting, November 13, 1990, 42.

72   Citibank, which six years earlier: For more information on Citibank in particular and the crisis of the banks during this period in general, see Richard B. Miller, *Citicorp: The Story of a Bank in Crisis* (1993).

74   "But recessions always end": Greenspan quoted, through "overdo it," from Transcript, Federal Open Market Committee Meeting, December 18, 1990, 35.

CHAPTER 5

The bulk of the information in this chapter comes from the author's interviews with seven knowledgeable sources. The first six were each interviewed on numerous occasions on background, and the seventh, Fed Governor Wayne Angell, was interviewed on the record about these events three times: September 18, 1992; November 30, 1992; and December 17, 1992.

75   "We're in a slowdown": Bush quoted from Mark Memmott, "White House Concedes USA Is in Recession," *USA Today*, January 3, 1991, 3B.

75   he laid down almost a challenge: All quotations from this scene taken from Transcript, Federal Open Market Committee Conference Call, February 1, 1991, 2–3.

76   "I don't know whether you consider this": Melzer quoted from Transcript, Federal Open Market Committee Conference Call, February 1, 1991, 2.

76   A story had run: See Louis Uchitelle, "Federal Reserve Acts Warily in Combating This Recession," *The New York Times*, January 11, 1991, A1.

76   Greenspan appointed a number of Fed economists: See Transcript, Federal Open Market Committee Meeting, February 5–6, 1991, 1.

77   the task force presented: For the full task force presentation and discussion, see Transcript, Federal Open Market Committee Meeting, March 26, 1991, 1–7.

77   Johnson wrote in his newsletter: All quotations taken from "Fed Confrontations Create Gridlock," *A Johnson Smick International Report*, April 2, 1991, 1–2.

77   *The Wall Street Journal* ran a short article: See Alan Murray, "Dispute Flares Up at Fed Over Greenspan's Authority," *The Wall Street Journal*, April 4, 1991, A3.

77   the *Journal* ran its long front-page article: See Alan Murray, "The New Fed: Democracy Comes to the Central Bank, Curbing Chief's Power," *The Wall Street Journal*, April 5, 1991, A1.

78   More stories appeared: See John Berry, "Greenspan's Sway Over Rates Topic of Internal Fed Debate," *The Washington Post*, April 5, 1991, F1; Louis Uchitelle, "Greenspan's Authority Curtailed on Interest Rates, Officials Say," *The New York Times*, April 8, 1991, A1.

78   On April 10: See David Wessel, "Greenspan Is Doing 'Fine Job' at Fed, Says White House—Money Managers Endorse Chief's Reappointment as His Term Nears End," *The Wall Street Journal*, April 10, 1991, A2.

78   Greenspan convened an early conference call: All quotations from this conversation taken from Transcript, Federal Open Market Committee Conference Call, April 12, 1991, 1–8.

80   William Greider's 1987 best-selling book: Greider's book about the Fed under Volcker provides a comprehensive description of how the Fed makes monetary policy. The book also makes the somewhat controversial point that inflation is better for the underclass than prolonged periods of stable prices. The fundamental argument is that inflation reduces debt burden, because mortgages and other personal debts can be paid off in inflated dollars. Though wages rise, so do the prices of everything else—and most economists now believe inflation kills off jobs and that unemployment rises in times of high inflation.

81   On April 18: See John Berry, "Did Greenspan Face Fed Revolt? Reports of Internal Challenge," *The Washington Post*, April 18, 1991, A1.

81   "In my judgment": Greenspan quoted from Transcript, Federal Open Market Committee Meeting, April 30, 1991, 1.

81   "Look, we've got to decide on Greenspan": See also the author's series

"Making Choices: Bush's Economic Record," *The Washington Post*, October 4–7, 1992.

83   "Just to top the day": Greenspan-Bush dialogue quoted from *Weekly Compilation of Presidential Documents*, volume 27, number 28, Monday, July 15, 1991, 934–938.

84   Two days later: See "A Stiffer Spine for Mr. Greenspan," *The New York Times*, July 12, 1991, A28.

84   "At this stage": Greenspan's testimony and the analysis of his comments quoted from David E. Rosenbaum, "Greenspan Optimistic on Economic Outlook," *The New York Times*, July 17, 1991, D1.

85   On October 28: Greenspan's speech quoted from John Berry, "Greenspan Notes Weak Recovery; Prospect Is Raised for Interest Rate Cut," *The Washington Post*, October 29, 1991, D1.

86   On December 19, 1991: See Board of Governors of the Federal Reserve System, *78th Annual Report to Congress*, April 15, 1992, 96. The Federal Reserve's annual report covers the overall economic situation in a given year, and it also lists the specific actions—and reasons for those actions—of the Board of Governors and the FOMC. The report records all votes and briefly explains the rationale both for the votes and for any dissents from those votes. The FOMC section includes minutes for each meeting; in the absence of transcripts, those minutes are useful for an understanding of the period 1995–99.

86   "It's sort of Merry Christmas": See John M. Berry, "Fed Lowers Key Rate to 3.5 Percent," *The Washington Post*, December 21, 1991, A1.

87   *The Wall Street Journal* published a long front-page story: See Alan Murray and David Wessel, "Giant Step: Changing Its Course, The Fed Boldly Tries to Bolster Economy . . . How Greenspan Turned the Tide," *The Wall Street Journal*, December 23, 1991, A1.

Chapter 6

Most of the information in this chapter comes from the author's interviews with six knowledgeable sources.

88   Greenspan hoped: For more information on the Greenspan-Darman-Brady relationship, see the author's series "Making Choices: The Bush Economic Record," *The Washington Post*, October 4–7, 1992.

91   On June 23: See Steven Greenhouse, "Bush Calls on Fed for Another Drop in Interest Rates," *The New York Times*, June 24, 1992, A1.

91   Lawrence Lindsey: See Transcript, Federal Open Market Committee Meeting, June 30–July 1, 1992, 32.

91   Greenspan didn't say anything: Greenspan quoted, through "where I come out," from Transcript, Federal Open Market Committee Meeting, June 30–July 1, 1992, 66–67.

92   The Board of Governors immediately voted: See Board of Governors of the Federal Reserve System, *79th Annual Report to Congress*, April 16, 1993, 107–108.

92   Greenspan convened: See Transcript, Federal Open Market Committee Conference Call, July 2, 1992, 1–2.

92   On September 4: See Board of Governors of the Federal Reserve System, 79th *Annual Report to Congress*, April 16, 1992, 161.

92   On October 6: See David Wessel, "Pushing Policy: Fed's Vice Chairman, Seeking Lower Rates, Furthers a Bush Goal . . . Has Shown He Can Sway Greenspan," *The Wall Street Journal*, October 6, 1992, A1.

92   "We likely will be confronted": Mullins quoted from Transcript, Federal Open Market Committee Meeting, October 6, 1992, 34.

92   "This has to be": Greenspan's interaction with the FOMC quoted from Transcript, Federal Open Market Committee Meeting, October 6, 1992, 41–52.

94   "This would be an irresponsible action": Greenspan quoted from "Fed Chief Affirms Its Independence," Associated Press, as it appeared in *The New York Times*, October 11, 1992, A32.

94   Clinton had promised presidential action: "The economy, stupid," or "It's the economy, stupid," was one of the main slogans of Clinton's campaign for the presidency. Initially placed on the wall of the Clinton campaign headquarters in Little Rock—known as the War Room—by James Carville, the slogan and its folksy focus on the country's economic woes became a centerpiece of the Clinton campaign and became Clinton's first order of business after his election.

95   When President-elect Clinton invited Greenspan: For the first published detailed account of this meeting, see Bob Woodward, *The Agenda* (1994), 65–69.

CHAPTER 7

Most of the information in this chapter comes from the author's interviews with three knowledgeable sources.

98   Greenspan's real connection: For more on the relationship among Greenspan, Bentsen and the Clinton administration's deficit targets, see also Bob Woodward, *The Agenda* (1994), 112–162.

101   On February 19: Greenspan quoted from Steven Greenhouse, "Clinton's Program Gets Endorsement of Fed's Chairman," *The New York Times*, February 20, 1993, A1. See also Eric Pianin, "Clinton Plan Gains Greenspan Praise," *The Washington Post*, February 20, 1993, A1; John Berry, "Greenspan Vows to Help Clinton," *The Washington Post*, February 20, 1993, C1.

101   "Just yesterday": Clinton quoted from Transcript, Remarks by the President to the U.S. Chamber of Commerce, Constitution Hall, Washington, D.C., February 23, 1993, 11:15 a.m.

103   "Regrettably": Greenspan quoted from Alan Greenspan, "Remarks to the Economic Club of New York," April 19, 1993, 12.

103   On May 13: See Lucinda Harper, "Consumer Prices Jumped 0.4%

During April—Uptick Contradicts Pace of Recovery, Possibly Posing Problem for Fed," *The Wall Street Journal*, May 14, 1993, A2.

105   "I think you are all aware": Greenspan quoted, through "meeting came out," from Transcript, Federal Open Market Committee Meeting, May 18, 1993, 1.

105   He summarized: See Transcript, Federal Open Market Committee Meeting, May 18, 1993, 6.

105   Turning to the perplexing inflation: Greenspan quoted, through "really doing," from Transcript, Federal Open Market Committee Meeting, May 18, 1993, 9–10.

106   One bank president suggested: For the FOMC's general discussion, see Transcript, Federal Open Market Committee Meeting, May 18, 1993, 12–32.

106   "The longer we go": Angell quoted, through "strong about it," from Transcript, Federal Open Market Committee Meeting, May 18, 1993, 33.

106   David Mullins argued: See Transcript, Federal Open Market Committee Meeting, May 18, 1993, 35–37.

106   After a coffee break: Greenspan, Corrigan and Mullins quoted from Transcript, Federal Open Market Committee Meeting, May 18, 1993, 38–52.

107   Greenspan reminded them again: Greenspan quoted, through "three times out of four," from Transcript, Federal Open Market Committee Meeting, May 18, 1993, 53–54.

108   Six days later: See David Wessel, "Fed Vote Shows Growing Worry About Inflation," *The Wall Street Journal*, May 24, 1993, A2.

108   *The New York Times* wrote: See Steven Greenhouse, "The Federal Reserve Prepares for a Rate War," *The New York Times*, June 1, 1993, D1.

108   "Obviously, it's good news": Myers quoted from Transcript, White House Press Briefing by Dee Dee Myers, June 11, 1993, 8.

109   Moynihan had written a long: See Daniel Patrick Moynihan, "Don't Blame Democracy," *The Washington Post*, June 6, 1993, C7.

110   Greenspan noted: Greenspan quoted, through "quite dramatically," from Transcript, Federal Open Market Committee Meeting, July 6–7, 1993, 73–74.

110   "Just remember": Greenspan quoted from Transcript, Federal Open Market Committee Meeting, July 6–7, 1993, 87.

110   "If you appear to be backing off ": Greenspan quoted from John Berry, "Greenspan Urges Congress to Cut Deficit $500 Billion," *The Washington Post*, July 21, 1993, F1.

110   In August: For a more detailed account of the passage of Clinton's economic plan, see also Bob Woodward, *The Agenda* (1994), 280–367.

110   He settled into the newest: See U.S. Department of Commerce, Economics and Statistics Administration, "Current Industrial Reports: Manufacturers' Shipments, Inventories, and Orders," September 2, 1993.

111   He examined the Labor Department unemployment statistics: See U.S. Department of Labor, Bureau of Labor Statistics, "The Employment Situation: August 1993," September 3, 1993.

111   Next he examined: See U.S. Department of Labor, Bureau of Labor Statistics, "Productivity and Costs: Second Quarter 1993," September 9, 1993.

112   "There is something wrong": Greenspan quoted, through "just don't square," from Transcript, Federal Open Market Committee Meeting, September 23, 1993, 35–36.

112   The "Survey of Current Business": See U.S. Department of Commerce, Bureau of Economic Analysis, "Survey of Current Business: The Business Situation," October 1993.

112   At the November 16 FOMC meeting: Greenspan quoted from Transcript, Federal Open Market Committee Meeting, November 16, 1993, 87.

113   "In short," he said: Mullins quoted from Transcript, Federal Open Market Committee Meeting, December 21, 1993, 25.

113   Greenspan remarked: Greenspan quoted, through "begin today," from Transcript, Federal Open Market Committee Meeting, December 21, 1993, 31–32.

113   "We have one additional item": Greenspan and discussion of taping quoted from Transcript, Federal Open Market Committee Meeting, December 21, 1993, 40–52.

CHAPTER 8

Most of the information in this chapter comes from the author's interviews with five knowledgeable sources.

116   On January 21, 1994: See also Bob Woodward, *The Agenda* (1994), 377–379.

118   He testified: Greenspan quoted from Paulette Thomas, "Higher Rates Are Expected by Greenspan," *The Wall Street Journal*, February 1, 1994, A2; see also Thomas D. Lauricella and Lauren Young, "Greenspan's Comments on Interest Rates Appear to Have Little Impact as Most Bond Prices Fall," *The Wall Street Journal*, February 1, 1994, C23.

119   "We are at the point": Greenspan quoted, through "running away," from Transcript, Federal Open Market Committee Meeting, February 3–4, 1994, 45–47.

119   "Well," Greenspan responded: Greenspan quoted, through "measure we know of," from Transcript, Federal Open Market Committee Meeting, February 3–4, 1994, 53.

120   "You know," Greenspan finally said: Greenspan-Lindsey-McDonough-FOMC exchange quoted from Transcript, Federal Open Market Committee Meeting, February 3–4, 1994, 55–58.

122   Greenspan expressed pride: Greenspan quoted from Transcript, Federal Open Market Committee Conference Call, February 28, 1994, 3.

122   On March 22: For the FOMC's rationale for the March and April increases, see Board of Governors of the Federal Reserve System, *81st Annual Report to Congress*, May 25, 1995, 139–151.

122   At the May 17 committee meeting: Greenspan quoted from Transcript, Federal Open Market Committee Meeting, May 17, 1994, 32–33.

123　　Mortimer B. Zuckerman: See Mortimer B. Zuckerman, "Is the Fed Paying Attention?" *U.S. News & World Report*, July 12, 1993, 95; Mortimer B. Zuckerman, "It's the Global Economy, Stupid," *U.S. News & World Report*, August 9, 1993, 99; Mortimer B. Zuckerman, "Greenspan Goofs Again," *U.S. News & World Report*, February 14, 1994, 62; Mortimer B. Zuckerman, "Amending John Maynard Keynes," *U.S. News & World Report*, April 18, 1994, 80; Mortimer B. Zuckerman, "It's Still the Economy," *U.S. News & World Report*, October 24, 1994, 92. After 1995, Zuckerman thought Greenspan managed interest rate policy brilliantly. Mortimer B. Zuckerman, "The Fed Taps the Brakes," *U.S. News & World Report*, May 29, 2000, 68.

CHAPTER 9

Most of the information in this chapter comes from the author's interviews with five knowledgeable sources.

125　　In a lecture loaded with charts: See Bob Woodward, *The Agenda* (1994), 82–86.

127　　Though a piece in *The New York Times:* See Keith Bradsher, "2 Economists Nominated to Fed," *The New York Times*, April 22, 1994, A39.

127　　the Associated Press piece: See "Senate Confirms Clinton Pick for Federal Reserve Board," Associated Press, June 24, 1994, Business News.

127　　Other stories: See Steve H. Hanke and Sir Alan Walters, "Glitter in Gilts," *Forbes*, June 20, 1994, 268; Virginia Postrel, "Fed Up: The Problems of the Federal Reserve," *Reason* 26, 3 (July 1994), 4.

127　　one story in *Investor's Business Daily:* See "The Economy; Blinder, Yellen Named," *Investor's Business Daily*, April 25, 1994, B1.

129　　"I'd just like to say": Blinder quoted from Transcript, Federal Reserve Open Market Committee Meeting, August 16, 1994, 24.

129　　Yellen said she agreed: Yellen quoted from Transcript, Federal Reserve Open Market Committee Meeting, August 16, 1994, 28.

129　　"Let me get started": Greenspan-Blinder scene quoted from Transcript, Federal Open Market Committee Meeting, August 16, 1994, 30–35.

131　　Nearly all of the coverage: See Keith Bradsher, "Federal Reserve Raises Key Rates to Cool Economy," *The New York Times*, August 17, 1994, A1; Paulette Thomas, "Fed Lifts Short-Term Rates by Half a Percentage Point," *The Wall Street Journal*, August 17, 1994, A2; Clay Chandler, "Fed Raises Short-Term Rates Again," *The Washington Post*, August 17, 1994, A1.

131　　"It is quite clear": Blinder's speech quoted from Paul Starobin, "Blindsided," *National Journal*, October 8, 1994.

132　　Blinder was dismayed to read: See Keith Bradsher, "Fed Official Disapproves of Rate Policy," *The New York Times*, August 28, 1994, A6.

132　　On Monday: See Keith Bradsher, "A Split Over Fed's Role; Clashes Seen After Vice Chairman Says Job Creation Should Also Be a Policy Goal," *The New York Times*, August 29, 1994, D1. Bradsher was relatively new to the Fed beat, and a number of people who attended Blinder's speech maintain that Bradsher made too much of the matter. Blinder's comments—though perhaps a bit testy and provocative—were generally in line with the Federal Reserve Act. See John Berry, "The Fed's Storm That Wasn't; Alan Blinder Finds a Short Talk Can Make One Monetary Policy Look Like Two," *The Washington Post*, September 8, 1994, B11; Hobart Rowen's op-ed, "Frankness and the Fed," *The Washington Post*, September 15, 1994, A17.

132   A *New York Times* story disagreed: See Keith Bradsher, "Tough-Decision Time for the Federal Reserve; New Vice Chairman Stirs the Board's Pot," *The New York Times*, September 26, 1994, D1.

132   *Newsweek* columnist Robert J. Samuelson declared: See Robert J. Samuelson, "Economic Amnesia," *Newsweek*, September 13, 1994, 52.

133   The next day: See Keith Bradsher, "Fed Deputy Denies Rift with Chief," *The New York Times*, September 9, 1994, D1.

133   He talked to *The Wall Street Journal*: Blinder quoted from David Wessel, "Blinder Denies There's a Rift with Fed Chief," *The Wall Street Journal*, September 9, 1994, A2.

135   "Now, what concerns me most": Yellen and Blinder quoted from Transcript, Federal Open Market Committee Meeting, November 15, 1994, 30–33.

136   "I must say": Greenspan quoted from Transcript, Federal Open Market Committee Meeting, November 15, 1994, 34–36.

136   "I fear that doing": Blinder-Greenspan exchange quoted from Transcript, Federal Open Market Committee Meeting, November 15, 1994, 42–43.

CHAPTER 10

Most of the information in this chapter comes from the author's interviews with nine knowledgeable sources. Eight were interviewed on numerous occasions on background. Senator Robert Bennett was interviewed on the record on July 19, 2000.

144   Treasury eventually loaned: For more on Greenspan's, Rubin's and Summers's rationale for intervention in Mexico, see U.S. Government Printing Office, Hearings Before the Committee on Banking, Housing, and Urban Affairs, "The Mexican Peso Crisis," Friday, March 10, 1995, 353–365.

145   In the February 1, 1995, meeting: For more information about the discussion at the meeting, see Board of Governors of the Federal Reserve System, *82nd Annual Report to Congress*, May 6, 1996, 110–126.

146   Greenspan noted: Greenspan quoted from U.S. Government Printing Office, Hearing Before the Committee On Banking, Housing, and Urban Affairs, United States Senate, "Federal Reserve's First Monetary Policy Report For 1995," 14.

147   On the good news front: Greenspan quoted from Keith Bradsher, "Greenspan Sees Chance of Recession," *The New York Times*, June 8, 1995, D1.

147   contradictory headlines: See Keith Bradsher, "Greenspan Sees Chance of Recession," *The New York Times*, June 8, 1995, D1; John M. Berry,

"Recession Is Unlikely, Greenspan Concludes," *The Washington Post*, June 8, 1995.

147   "Well," Panetta said: Panetta quoted from Keith Bradsher, "A Rare Nudge for a Drop in Rates," *The New York Times*, June 12, 1995, D2.

148   Rubin said in a public statement: Rubin quoted from Clay Chandler, "Panetta Urges Fed to Cut Short-Term Interest Rates," *The Washington Post*, June 12, 1995, A6; Dean Foust, "In a Fix at the Fed," *BusinessWeek*, June 26, 1995, 34.

148   Greenspan again left contradictory impressions: See Keith Bradsher, "Doubts Voiced by Greenspan on a Rate Cut," *The New York Times*, June 21, 1995, A1; John M. Berry, "Greenspan Hints Fed May Cut Interest Rates," *The Washington Post*, June 21, 1995, F1.

149   On Thursday, July 6: For more information about the FOMC's discussion, see Board of Governors of the Federal Reserve System, *82nd Annual Report to Congress*, May 6, 1996, 149–161.

150   He had written articles: See Felix G. Rohatyn, "The Budget: Whom Can You Believe?" *New York Review of Books*, August 10, 1995, 48–49; Felix G. Rohatyn, "Getting Past the Gamesmanship," *U.S. News & World Report*, August 28, 1995, 102.

151   On November 30: See Felix G. Rohatyn, "Cut and Be Prosperous," *The Wall Street Journal*, November 30, 1995, A20.

153   The FOMC met December 19, 1995: For more information about the FOMC's discussion, see Board of Governors of the Federal Reserve System, *82nd Annual Report to Congress*, May 6, 1996, 188–197.

CHAPTER 11

Most of the information in this chapter comes from the author's interviews with 14 knowledgeable sources. Twelve were interviewed on numerous occasions on background; Robert Bennett was interviewed on the record on July 19, 2000, and Robert Parker was interviewed on the record on August 3, 2000.

154   The news of his departure: See David Wessel, "Blinder Will Leave Fed at End of Term Later This Month," *The Wall Street Journal*, January 17, 1996, A4.

157   On January 19, 1996: See David Wessel, "Rohatyn Considered for No. 2 Fed Post," *The Wall Street Journal*, January 19, 1996, A2.

160   at the January 31, 1996, FOMC meeting: For more information about the FOMC's discussion, see Board of Governors of the Federal Reserve System, *83rd Annual Report to Congress*, May 28, 1997, 106–123.

162   *The Washington Post* ran a front-page story: See John M. Berry, "Rhetoric Aside, Spurring Economic Growth Unlikely," *The Washington Post*, January 29, 1996, A1.

162   Paul R. Krugman weighed in: See Paul R. Krugman, "Stay on Their Backs," *The New York Times Magazine*, February 4, 1996, 36.

165   "An example of what should not be done": Clinton quoted from the White House, Office of the Press Secretary, "Remarks by the President at Presidential Gala," February 15, 1996.

165   "Today I am pleased": Clinton scene quoted from the White House, Office of the Press Secretary, "Remarks by the President in Announcement of Federal Reserve Vacancies," February 22, 1996.

166   Tyson held a press conference: Tyson scene quoted from the White House, Office of the Press Secretary, "Press Briefing by Dr. Laura Tyson," February 22, 1996.

167   "What are corporations doing": See Richard Pucci, "Comments on the Comments," *I/B/E/S Inc.*, September 1995, 4–7.

170   During the FOMC's two-day meeting: For further information about the FOMC's discussion, see Board of Governors of the Federal Reserve System, *83rd Annual Report to Congress*, May 28, 1997, 140–151.

171   "Look at these numbers": *The Wall Street Journal* would later report that nearly everybody in the room wanted to raise rates in August. See David Wessel, "In Setting Fed's Policy, Chairman Bets Heavily on His Own Judgment; Greenspan Loves Statistics but Uses Them in Ways That Puzzle Even Friends—Some Forecasts Go Awry," *The Wall Street Journal*, January 27, 1997, A1.

174   *BusinessWeek* magazine: The "Tug-of-War" story was particularly strong, citing a "division inside the Fed's hallways" and saying that "a new showdown will occur on Sept. 24." See Dean Foust, "Tug-of-War Inside the Fed," *BusinessWeek*, September 24, 1996, 46; Dean Foust, "Political Hardball Inside the Fed: Using the Press, Regional Banks May Force Greenspan's Hand," *BusinessWeek*, September 30, 1996, 38.

174   As the FOMC gathered: For a description of the FOMC's discussion, see Board of Governors of the Federal Reserve System, *83rd Annual Report to Congress*, May 28, 1997, 159–168.

174   He quoted from the Slifman and Corrado study: The Slifman and Corrado Study, called "Decomposition of Productivity and Unit Costs," was published on November 18, 1996. At the bottom of that draft, in fine print, is a list of people to thank—which includes Greenspan. When Slifman and Corrado refined some of their data and republished it in May 1999 under the same title, they included a list of "other contributors to this report." Buried in the middle of that list is Alan Greenspan.

175   the consumer price index was overstating inflation: That the CPI overstated inflation was widely accepted by 1996. The largest problem with the CPI was that it tracked the same goods over time—and, as a result, failed to capture dramatic improvements in existing products or consumer shifts to lower-price substitutes. Michael Boskin, former chairman of Bush's Council of Economic Advisers, headed a Bush administration task force that explored this issue in the period 1989–90, then later headed another commission on the same subject in 1995. See John M. Berry, "Bush Seeks More Money for Economic Statistics," *The Washington Post*, January 26, 1990, F3; Martin Crutsinger, "Economists Question Accuracy and Value of U.S. Statistics," Associated Press, as it appeared in *The Washington Post*, July 5, 1990, D1; Daniel Patrick Moynihan, "The CPI: An Easy Fix . . . ," *The Washington Post*, September 26, 1995, A19. The Bureau of Labor Statistics eventually decided to change the way they measured the CPI in March 1996, but many—including Greenspan—remained unconvinced.

177   "Fed Avoids Rate Hike": See John M. Berry, "Fed Avoids Rate Hike, Sensing Slower Growth," *The Washington Post*, September 25, 1996, A1; David E. Sanger, "Federal Reserve Makes No Change in Interest Rates," *The New York Times*, September 25, 1996, A1.

179   She walked next door: See also Jacob M. Schlesinger, "Change Agent: How Alan Greenspan Finally Came to Terms with the Stock Market," *The Wall Street Journal*, May 8, 2000, A1.

180   *The Washington Post* had published: See John M. Berry, "U.S. Sails on Tranquil Economic Seas; Recessions No Longer Seem Inevitable," *The Washington Post*, December 2, 1996, A1.

CHAPTER 12

Most of the information in this chapter comes from the author's interviews with nine knowledgeable sources.

182   On February 26, he testified: Greenspan quoted from John M. Berry, "Greenspan Escalates Warning on Stock Risks," *The Washington Post*, February 27, 1997.

182   "That's not what I was intending to do": Greenspan quoted from Jackie Calmes, "Greenspan Defends Remarks on Market," *The Wall Street Journal*, March 5, 1997, A2.

184   At the FOMC meeting on Tuesday: For more information on the FOMC's discussion, see Board of Governors of the Federal Reserve System, *84th Annual Report to Congress*, May 28, 1998, 114–123.

184   *The Wall Street Journal* said: See David Wessel, "Fed Lifts Key Short-Term Interest Rate Amid Speculation More Rises Are Likely," *The Wall Street Journal*, March 26, 1997, A2.

184   *The Washington Post* said: See John M. Berry, "Fed Boost Benchmark Interest Rate; Inflation Risk Cited," *The Washington Post*, March 26, 1997, A1.

184   Meyer had agreed to give a speech: For much of the information about Meyer's speech on April 24, including the wire service headlines, see David Wessel, "When Fed Governor Talks, People Listen; But Do They Hear?—How Hard Mr. Meyer Tries Not to Move the Markets; Why He Failed Yesterday," *The Wall Street Journal*, April 25, 1997, A1; see also "Fed's Meyer Says Solid Growth Requires Pre-Emptive Stance," Dow Jones Online News, April 24, 1997.

185   The next morning Meyer read: See David Wessel, "When Fed Governor Talks, People Listen; But Do They Hear?—How Hard Mr. Meyer Tries Not to Move the Markets; Why He Failed Yesterday," *The Wall Street Journal*, April 25, 1997, A1.

186   "The Meyer Fed?": See "The Meyer Fed?," *The Wall Street Journal* (editorial), May 20, 1997, A18.

187   After a long discussion of the economy: For more information on the FOMC's discussion, see Board of Governors of the Federal Reserve System, *84th Annual Report to Congress*, May 28, 1998, 123–132.

188   "We have as close to stable prices": Greenspan quoted from John M. Berry, "Greenspan Expects Strong Economy Through 1998," *The Washington Post*, July 23, 1997, A1.

189   On October 8: Greenspan quoted from Christopher Georges, "Greenspan Raises Prospect of Rate Rise," *The Wall Street Journal*, October 9, 1997, A2; Clay Chandler, "Greenspan Warning on Economy, Stocks Again Roils Markets," *The Washington Post*, October 9, 1997, A1.

189   This sent Rubin out: Rubin quoted from Adam Zagorin, "Greenspan and His Friends: How the Fed Chairman, Treasury Secretary Rubin and Their Crash Team Navigated a Scary Week," *Time*, November 19, 1997, 46.

190   Greenspan understood that new technology: Greenspan's views are taken in part from his testimony before the House Banking and Financial Services Committee. See U.S. Government Printing Office, Hearings Before the Committee on Banking and Financial Services, U.S. House of Representatives, "East Asian Economic Conditions—Part 2," January 30, 1998, 209–221.

CHAPTER 13

Most of the information in this chapter comes from the author's interviews with 15 knowledgeable sources.

193   On Friday, January 30, 1998: Hearing scene quoted from U.S. Government Printing Office, Hearings Before the Committee on Banking and Financial Services, U.S. House of Representatives, "East Asian Economic Conditions—Part 2," January 30, 1998, 10–67.

193   who as CEA chairman in 1974: See Stuart Auerbach, "Brokers Hit Worst, Ford Aide Tells Poor," *The Washington Post*, September 20, 1974, A1; James Risen, "Greenspan: Supreme Survivor," *Los Angeles Times*, May 30, 1991, A1.

196   In a rare television interview: Bush quoted from "Bush Pins the Blame for '92 Election Loss on Alan Greenspan," *The Wall Street Journal* (Politics and Policy), August 25, 1998, A16.

198   Speaking obliquely: Greenspan quoted from "Excerpts from Fed Chairman's Speech," *The New York Times*, September 5, 1998, C2.

199   Front-page news stories: See David E. Sanger, "Greenspan Hints That a Rate Cut Isn't Unthinkable," *The New York Times*, September 5, 1998, A1; John M. Berry, "Fed Chief Hints at Possible Rate Cut," *The Washington Post*, September 5, 1998, A1.

199   As an example: See Michael Siconolfi, Anita Raghavan and Mitchell Pacelle, "All Bets Are Off: How the Salesmanship and Brainpower Failed at Long-Term Capital," *The Wall Street Journal*, November 16, 1998, A1.

205   Around the table: For a comprehensive description of LTCM's unwinding, including a seating chart for the September 23 meeting at the Fed in New York, see Michael Siconolfi, Anita Raghavan and Mitchell Pacelle, "All Bets Are Off: How the Salesmanship and Brainpower Failed at Long-Term Capital," *The Wall Street Journal*, November 16, 1998, A1.

206   On Tuesday, September 29: For more information on the FOMC's

discussion, see Board of Governors of the Federal Reserve System, *85th Annual Report to Congress*, May 1999, 174–184.

208   The session began: Hearing scene quoted from U.S. Government Printing Office, Hearing Before the Committee on Banking and Financial Services, U.S. House of Representatives, "Hedge Fund Operations," October 1, 1998, 1–72.

211   On October 15: See Board of Governors of the Federal Reserve System, *85th Annual Report to Congress*, May 1999, 184.

212   The bond market soared: For more information on the markets' reaction to the September rate cut, and on the Fed's rationale for cutting rates again in October, see David Wessel, "Credit Record: How the Fed Fumbled, and Then Recovered, in Making Policy Shift," *The Wall Street Journal*, November 17, 1998, A1.

212   On Tuesday, November 17: For more information about the FOMC's discussion, see Board of Governors of the Federal Reserve System, *85th Annual Report to Congress*, May 1999, 184–197.

CHAPTER 14

Most of the information in this chapter comes from the author's interviews with seven knowledgeable sources.

213   On January 14, 1999: See Michael J. Prell, "Remarks at the Charlotte Economics Club," January 14, 1999, available at www.federalreserve.gov/boarddocs/speeches/1999/19990114.htm.

213   articles praising the chairman: See Rob Norton, "In Greenspan We Trust," *Fortune*, March 18, 1996, 38; Dean Foust, "Alan Greenspan's Brave New World," *BusinessWeek*, July 14, 1997, 44.

214   In early February 1999: See Joshua Cooper Ramo, "The Three Marketeers," *Time*, February 15, 1999, 34.

214   On March 4: See "Who Needs Gold When We Have Greenspan," *The New York Times* (editorial), May 4, 1999, A30.

215   At the May 18 FOMC meeting: For more information on the FOMC's discussion, see Board of Governors of the Federal Reserve System, *86th Annual Report to Congress*, May 2000, 224–232.

215   "Fed Won't Hike Rates": See John M. Berry, "Fed Won't Hike Rates—For Now," *The Washington Post*, May 19, 1999, A1.

215   At the June 30 FOMC meeting: For more information on the FOMC's discussion, see Board of Governors of the Federal Reserve System, *86th Annual Report to Congress*, May 2000, 232–244.

216   "The Fed smiled": See E. S. Browning, " 'Friendly' Fed Move Lifts Indexes to New Highs," *The Wall Street Journal*, July 1, 1999, C1.

216   In a commencement speech: Greenspan quoted from Pamela Ferdinand and Michael Grunwald, "At Two Commencements, Perspective Is the Reality," *The Washington Post*, June 11, 1999, A3.

218   In a speech on August 27: See Louis Uchitelle, "Greenspan Ties Debate on Rates to the Markets," *The New York Times*, August 28, 1999, A1.

Chapter 15

Most of the information in this chapter comes from the author's interviews with four knowledgeable sources.

221   The White House press office: See "Greenspan Stopped Split Stories," *Washingtonian*, February 2000, 10.
223   In the Oval Office: Reappointment scene quoted from *Weekly Compilation of Presidential Documents* 36, 1 (Monday, January 10, 2000), 13–16.

ACKNOWLEDGMENTS

Simon & Schuster and *The Washington Post* once again have backed me completely on this project, giving me the necessary time and independence to pursue it.

Alice Mayhew, who has been my editor at Simon & Schuster for the past 28 years, provided the idea for this book. We first considered a book about the leading figures in the American economic boom, their minds and the way their thinking drove the expansion. Though I pursued this broader project initially, she instantly saw that the central figure was Greenspan. She was right. And, as always, she was willing to devote her considerable energy and keen eye to conceiving the book and then improving three full drafts of the manuscript.

Leonard Downie Jr., *The Washington Post*'s executive editor, and Steve Coll, the *Post*'s managing editor, have yet again allowed me to wander on what is perhaps the longest leash in American journalism. This enables me to pursue book-length, in-depth projects. Along with them, I also want to thank the *Post*'s owners, Katharine Graham and Don Graham. The support of these four makes my work possible.

I once again thank Jennifer Belton, director of news research, and her staff for her numerous assists.

Olwen Price transcribed interviews, often under serious time pressure. She always found a way to meet my requests.

Joe Elbert and his photo staff at the *Post*, the best in the business, provided most of the pictures in this book.

At Simon & Schuster, a special effort was made by Carolyn K. Reidy, the president and publisher, to once again put this book on the fast track so it would be in the bookstores soon after completion. I also thank Jonathan Newcomb, the chairman; Jack Romanos, the president and chief operating officer; David Rosenthal, the publisher, who is always full of creative ideas; Anja Schmidt, the associate editor, who suggested numerous improvements; Elisa Rivlin, the general counsel; Victoria Meyer, the director of publicity; Aileen Boyle, the associate director of publicity; Jackie Seow, the art director and jacket designer; Deirdre Amthor, the associate design director; Brooke Koven, the designer; George Turianski, the production manager; and K. C. Trommer, the assistant to Alice Mayhew.

A special thanks to Stephen Messina, the copy supervisor, for his care and expertise with all details—small, medium and large.

Sona Vogel came to Washington and spent a week copyediting the manuscript. I thank her very much for her steady, precise work and her acceptance of a less formal style.

I thank Kelly Farley for her painstaking attention to typesetting details.

The core of this book comes from more than 100 sources who agreed to provide information as long as their identities would not be revealed. Some were official and some unofficial; some might not mind having their names mentioned, others would. Exercising maximum care, I will thank none by name. To all those unnamed I offer my thanks and gratitude. Many spent hours, and some spent dozens of hours, with me engaging the subject. What is presented is not the way any single person would do it himself or herself. Despite its shortcomings, all should recognize this book as a scrupulous and careful effort to find what was for me the best obtainable version of the truth.

The Wall Street Journal, which provides the most comprehensive financial and economic coverage, and *The Washington Post*, particularly its veteran Fed reporter John Berry, were invaluable for this project. Their reporting and analysis are the starting point and the foundation for a book attempting to cover 13 years. My assistant Jeff Himmelman and I relied on their work, both directly and indirectly. We also relied heavily on *The New York Times*, *BusinessWeek*, *Newsweek*, *Time*, *U.S. News & World Report*, the *Los Angeles Times*, *The New Yorker*, *National Journal* and the Associated Press.

A number of books offered important background. They are William Greider's *Secrets of the Temple*, Stephen K. Beckner's *Back from the Brink*, David M. Jones's *The Politics of Money*, and Steven Solomon's *The Confidence Game*. These books assisted us in our understanding of the Volcker and early Greenspan years at the Fed.

Alan Blinder's *Central Banking in Theory and Practice* and Lawrence Lindsey's *Economic Puppetmasters* provided useful information about the Fed's decisions and responsibilities. *Kiplinger's Practical Guide to Investing* and the Fed's publication *Purposes and Functions* were of great help in creating our own glossary.

Lou Cannon's *President Reagan: The Role of a Lifetime*, the definitive book on Reagan, was also a great help.

Robert B. Barnett, my agent and attorney, again provided the soundest advice and guidance—counselor in the sense of friend, almost an extra brother.

Jim Wooten of ABC assisted me at a critical point in the writing.

Thanks again to Rosa Criollo, Norma Gianelloni and Jackie Crowe.

Tali Woodward, my older daughter and a reporter for the *San Francisco Bay Guardian*, took a week to read the manuscript and offered many wise and penetrating suggestions.

Elsa Walsh, my wife and true confidant, has established a loving house and life for all of us. Her editing, suggestions and questions helped immeasurably. She is a woman and writer of both tenacity and conscience. For me, she has done nearly everything but invent the Internet.

INDEX

PHOTO CREDITS

GRAPHS CREDIT

ABOUT THE AUTHOR

Bob Woodward, an assistant managing editor of *The Washington Post*, has been a newspaper reporter and editor for 30 years. He has authored or coauthored eight number one national nonfiction bestsellers. They include four books on the presidency—*All the President's Men* (1974), *The Final Days* (1976), *The Agenda* (1994) and *Shadow* (1999)—and books on the Supreme Court (*The Brethren*, 1979), the Hollywood drug culture (*Wired*, 1984), CIA (*Veil*, 1987) and the Pentagon (*The Commanders*, 1991). He has two daughters, Tali and Diana, and lives in Washington, D.C., with his wife, Elsa Walsh, a writer for *The New Yorker*.